Publishing Director: Sarah Lavelle
Copy-editor: Eve Marleau
Art Direction and Design: Nicola Ellis
Photographer: Mowie Kay
Food Stylist: Marina Filippelli
Prop Stylist: Louie Waller
Production Director: Vincent Smith
Production Controller: Katie Jarvis

Published in 2019 by Quadrille,
an imprint of Hardie Grant Publishing

Quadrille
52–54 Southwark Street
London SE1 1UN
quadrille.com

Cataloguing in Publication Data:
a catalogue record for this book
is available from the British Library.

Text © Catherine Phipps 2019
Photography © Mowie Kay 2019
Design © Quadrille 2019

ISBN 978 1 78713 240 5

Printed in China

Oven temperatures are conventional throughout.

LEAF

LETTUCE, GREENS, HERBS, WEEDS
OVER 120 RECIPES THAT CELEBRATE
VARIED, VERSATILE LEAVES

CATHERINE PHIPPS

Photography by Mowie Kay

Hardie Grant

QUADRILLE

For my parents

contents

Introduction

The kernel of the idea for this book started with a childhood obsession of mine – the popular fairy tale *Rapunzel*. I was fascinated by Rapunzel's poor pregnant mother, who was so desperate with need and desire for the greens in the witch's walled garden that she (or her husband) bargained her daughter's life away for them. We so often hear of forbidden or longed-for fruits having a profound impact on a story, but rarely forbidden greens. I had a Ladybird version of the book that gave me a very clear picture of the garden – the neat rows of vegetables with those much-desired greens cheek-by-jowl with grids of fat cabbages, danger hinted at by the large patch of foxgloves (perfect for a witch's garden). I remember the thatched cottage with the hint of a forest of trees in the background. I imagined the garden at night, glimpsed over the high, vine-covered wall and pale in the moonlight. It probably – along with Mary Lennox – kick-started my enduring love of walled gardens. There is something so thrillingly secretive, self-contained and possessed about a walled garden, but when it is functional and productive too it is alive with possibility and gives a certain kind of security – the same feeling of well-being you get from a well-stocked larder or still room. I would also imagine the kitchen within, when I expected that not only would the witch (like every storybook old lady who lives close to the wood) eat and cook and infuse and preserve everything she grew in the garden, but everything she could take from the woods beyond, where all the wild leaves grew.

I have read numerous versions of *Rapunzel* over the years, and I am always drawn to those greens. I used to be reminded of them in the days when I had only myself to feed and was in the habit of walking through my own garden, picking a variety of leaves for a quick vegetarian salad or sauté. The thought of a large bowl of wilted leaves, intensely savoury, earthy yet refreshing, slightly bitter and metallic, with a succulent, salty tang appealed to me. This is how they tasted in my imagination – complex and obviously good for you; very satisfying. I used to wonder what kind of greens they were – imagining a chard or a fatter, more substantial spinach, or the mixture of wild greens collectively known as *horta* in Greece, which I gorge on every time I am there. The clue was in the name. Rapunzel is the German name given to rampion, *campanula rapunculus* in fact, a type of campanula with a pretty, star-shaped bell flower and greens that are, thank heavens, spinach-like (and often used as a substitute), but more succulent with a little nutty bite. It is a lovely thing to grow; messy-looking clumps spill out from a central point for the first year before it shoots up and flowers. It's useful and happy in dappled shade and if you decide to do so, you can eat it cooked or raw just like spinach. Rapunzel is also *feldsalat*, which we know as corn salad, or mache, or lamb's lettuce – another useful salad green, but not quite in the same class as the succulent greens I imagined.

The appeal of that bowl of greens has never left me, and it is part – but not all – of what I want to showcase in this book. I hope that *Leaf* is a celebration of edible and aromatic leaves, and all they can offer us. It has been a slightly daunting task, as the scope is so broad, but an absolute joy at the same time, as I have focussed primarily on foods that I love. They are a disparate lot, leaves; just in terms of flavour, the choice is immense, something to suit every mood or craving. Consider the bitterness of endives and wild dandelion; the pungency of wild garlic, mustard and curry leaf; icy, spicy menthol from mint and shiso; citrus from verbena and French sorrel, resinous astringency of pine and rosemary, mellow nuttiness of butterhead lettuces and sprout tops,

deeply savoury, saltiness of seaweeds and agretti and the
succulent, thirst-quenching coolness of iceberg, purslane
and borage. I could go on and on, and this is before I even
start thinking about how much we can change and layer
all these flavours, through cooking, fermenting and pairing.

Visually and texturally, leaves are a riot – the palest
shades of white and yellow; every possible shade of green;
from early season fluorescence via bright pea green and
cobwebby silver to deep, almost black forest; they can
be burnished browns, purples, reds, dainty rose pinks,
variegated in numerous combinations. They can be crisp
and tightly furled torpedoes or bullets (think endives and
Brussels sprouts), floppy with a peony blowsiness about
them (sprout tops, oak leaf lettuce and certain types

of chicory), spiky (pandan, puntarelle, pine, rosemary, wild garlic, agretti), crinkly and curly (kale, cavolo nero, savoy cabbage), delicate and feathery (dill, chervil, fennel, carrot tops). They range from the tiniest of microherbs – those two leaves poking out of the soil to show that germination has been successful, as small as a baby's fingernail, to huge elephant ears, a meal in a leaf. They can be dull, or with a rich, glossy sheen, diaphanous or thick, protected by hair or thorns. It is no wonder that they all cook very differently too – stiff and robust leaves that keep their shape and some of their texture, others that wilt down to almost nothing, and those that do not yield or soften at all. They offer every texture from a crunch, to a scratchiness if not carefully prepared, or can collapse into something as smooth as silk.

The uses of leaves are myriad. We are most used to eating them as side dishes, within salads and soups, or as a flourish of green to add to stews, potages and curries. But there is so much value in making them the main part of the meal – roasted or grilled heads of leaves can be as satisfying as a steak, in part because they still have a tough resistance at their core. I don't mean that we should all immediately become vegetarian or vegan – this is definitely not the book for that – but what I do like doing is using meat, fish and dairy as a flavour accent to the vegetables rather than the other way round. I feel the same way about herbs. Of course,

I use herbs for flavour – in a sauce, as a garnish, added at various points to a dish, fresh and dried, but I also emulate clever cuisines that treat them as the main event. What I like to do most of all is layer everything up together – dried or woody herbs or stems, loose or bouquet garni'ed at the beginning of the cooking time, greens as part of the main bulk, and more herbs for those fresh hits of flavour at the end.

A further use for leaves is all about flavour and how we infuse it. At a basic level, the most used leaf in infusions has to be tea leaves, but think also of the different herbal infusions – lemon verbena or mint, and those in alcohol (for example, zubrowka, a vodka infused with buffalo leaf) or vinegar (primarily herbs). Leaves we don't normally eat are frequently used to infuse syrups, dairy products or chocolate – bay, kaffir lime, fig leaves, blackcurrant and berry leaves, scented pelargoniums or geraniums. Infusions do not always need liquid – and we also use leaves as flavour for smoking food, particularly types of tea and some of the resinous herbs. We infuse some leaves that we would not eat, and there is an important reason for this – when we infuse, the aroma and associated flavour is absorbed, but not necessarily the taste. Take a bay leaf as an example. If you smell it, you remember that its flavour is the same, but chew on the leaf, and it will taste unpleasantly bitter.

Sourcing Leaves

The focus of this book has very much been about the ingredients I can easily get my hands on. There are a few with very short seasons that are not available all year round (I treasure these), and a very few – wild garlic and three-cornered leeks, nettles and dandelions, seaweed when I am on the coast – that are foraged. I'm not sure anyone needs help finding nettles or dandelions, even in the most urban of areas, but any local internet group will likely point you in the direction of a patch of wild garlic. There are also leaves – just a few – that aren't easy to buy or forage. Some of the leaves that fall into this category are mainly from plants and trees that we grow for culinary reasons, just not usually for their leaves. For example, citrus trees, peach trees, fig trees, grape vines, blackcurrant bushes provide us with fruit (or not), Szechuan peppercorns provide us with the berries we dry for their mouth-tingling heat – but in all these cases, the leaves can also be used. Some have hard-hitting flavours – think of the kaffir lime, coconutty fig, and a Szechuan pepper leaf, which packs as much punch as the berry. But with other leaves, the value is in their subtlety. I have never loved blackcurrants as I find them too astringent, but I'm taken with their milder leaves. Tomatoes, too – when I have had yet another crop fail on me because of blight, I can at least take solace in the leaves. I don't eat them, but will use them to infuse – they will punch that intensely stuffy, yet fruity vine-ripened aroma into your tomato sauce or soups – freeze a few to use in the middle of winter.

Other leaves that I hope are becoming easier to source are the by-crops of other vegetables. Some plants have always been valued for their ability to provide more than one food stuff – think beetroots (beets) and their leaves, Brussels sprouts and their tops, further afield dasheen and taro roots and their elephant-ear leaves. Pea shoots are very popular now, and are often grown as a salad crop and harvested before they have a chance to flower and throw out pods of peas. Looking at the plant as a whole has much to do with our desire to reduce food waste, and even the supermarkets are catching on. For a long time, only a decent greengrocer or farmers' market would sell carrots, radishes and celery in all their leafy glory, and these are places I still prefer to go for freshness and lack of plastic packaging. Many more leaves fall into this category but are scarcely eaten in the UK; they do, however, feature heavily in other cuisines. For example, a group of leaves that I love includes squash, pumpkin, courgette (zucchini) and sweet potato – these are eaten all over Africa and Mediterranean Europe. I hope that, one day, they will become more mainstream.

Using farmers' markets – and, in fact, exploring markets wherever you go – is a really good way to understand the local seasons and what ingredients might be cooked together. There is a practice, which occurs all over the world, of bunching ingredients together for sale, assuming the locals would not dream of buying one without the other. We see this emulated in our supermarkets – packets of aromatics for a Thai, Caribbean or Indian curry, vegetables for stir frying, roots for a winter casserole. In Caribbean markets, brush-like woody bunches of thyme are sold with cieve – the local variety of spring onion, the green tied back and longer than your arm. In Greece I see bunches of horta – amaranth and chicory – or perhaps courgette leaves, flowers and fruit bunched up together. In Germany every spring, the ingredients of Frankfurt grüne soße are sold together – bunches of cress, borage, chervil, parsley, salad burnet, sorrel and chives.

Where to get some of the harder-to-find leaves? I grow some of them in my garden; the rest I beg and barter. When I realised quite how good some of the leaves could taste, the frustration of trying to grow decent Mediterranean and tropical fruits in a temperate-zone garden was massively alleviated. If you can't grow them yourself, you can do one of two things. First, use your eyes. It is amazing what you can see when walking round an urban landscape, on the way to work or on the school run. Fig leaves spilling over a garden wall, vine leaves running along a fence and olive trees, bay and rosemary growing into magnificent specimens in front gardens in my neighbourhood of London, England. Sometimes trees crop up in the most unlikely places. I recently saw a small but vigorous fig tree that had grown, I am sure accidentally, through a crack in the pavement at the base of a fire escape on an industrial estate. I doubt anyone would mind your taking a few leaves from anything that spills out of gardens onto the road or pavement, but I always seek permission. Second, ask around. Most people will know someone with a garden or an allotment who grows the leaves you are after. And while there are few people who would happily give up the precious fruit of their labours, especially in the UK when crops are not always what you would wish for, the chances are they will let you have as many leaves as you need. I have found fig and vine leaves from friends, allotmenteers and neighbours, and vegetable leaves too. Every gardener knows that the tips of broad (fava) beans need pinching out to help prevent an infestation of black fly, but most gardeners won't know the value in those tips and may consign them to the compost heap if you don't get your request in first (in early spring). Others might spend months nurturing two or three pumpkins or squashes on a single

vine and might be happy to give you some of the leaves – they are very prolific and can dominate in no time if not culled. It is a huge investment of space to grow any kind of gourd as the vines grow all season long and throw out leaves late into autumn – it is a boon to know that the leaves aren't only edible, but actually taste really good.

Growing Your Own

This is a very subjective list of the things that I like to grow, and they are pretty much based on the leaves I would hate to be without. Unless you live somewhere very metropolitan, buying anything tropical such as laksa leaf or shiso, and even kaffir lime is difficult and/or prohibitively expensive online, but you can often buy a small plant much more cheaply than the exorbitant price of a bunch of leaves and, even if you live in a hardy area, keep them going all winter long if you leave them on a sunny windowsill or wrap them in fleece. This applies to lemon verbena, too – it is very rare to find it sold fresh, and when it is, it is incredibly expensive. It is available dried, but with some honourable exceptions (Postcard Teas is just about the only one I've found), anything you buy will have lost its bright, sherberty citrus flavour and will take on murky, spice rack tones. I use these fresh from the garden until the first frost is forecast, then cut them back, fleece wrap and dry the leaves with great success (see page 17). The other thing I would recommend everyone go out and buy at once is ginger rosemary. I can usually take or leave hybrid varieties of herbs (by which I mean herbs that have been crossed with other plants to change the flavour profile, such as pineapple sage or cinnamon basil), but this one is special. I now use it interchangeably

with the regular kind of rosemary, so bear that in mind whenever you see rosemary used in a recipe.

If you are very short on space for growing, consider two things – what do you really love the flavour of but is hard or expensive to source? And what gives you the most value in terms of space/flavour ratio? As well as the leaves mentioned above, I always come back to herbs. I grow as many as I can, as well as hard-to-find greens. The value in growing herbs isn't always about having a constant supply; while I can grow enough of the woodier herbs, which are generally grown in smaller quantities, I could never grow enough parsley or coriander (cilantro) for my culinary needs. What I love about growing some of these softer herbs is how it gives you an appreciation for the way in which their flavours can change and develop over the growing season. Micro-herbs often have concentrated bursts of flavour – the most successful I find are basil, coriander and fenugreek – and then they will grow into the flavours you know and expect. But then, if you let them keep growing to the point of flowering and setting seed, quite radical transformations can take place. This is probably quite an obvious thing to gardeners, but I only noticed it a few years ago when I was trying to figure out what the herbs were in the pot of beans I was eating – the chef insisted it was just parsley, but it didn't taste like any parsley I had ever eaten. When I tried to question her (she was Greek, with no English, and I have no Greek) she pulled a large bunch out of her fridge to show me. It was parsley, but it was parsley that had started bolting – the leaf

structure had changed from a filigree round to an elongated, delicate frond, and the flavour had changed to something much less grassy, more towards tarragon; it's a unique taste that I find very appealing. The same thing happens with coriander – the flavour becomes sweeter, closer to cinnamon, the soapy, citrusy flavour muted. I deliberately let these herbs grow to this stage and always look for fronds when buying large bunches of both from my local grocers – sometimes I am lucky. Of course, the reverse can happen with this. I cannot bear the smell of basil when it flowers, and lemon balm also changes to something quite unpleasantly musky, but it is always interesting to make these discoveries, and I love the fact that even with ingredients we are used to using all year round, there can still be these seasonal differentiations to look forward to.

I also like to sow fast-growing leaves that can be cut at any stage. Thin out a line of salad leaves – there are many mixes available, or you can make up your own – for bursts of micro-leaf flavour, then treat them as a cut-and-come again crop. Do this also with roots such as beetroot, radish and turnip and harvest the leaves while you wait for the bulbs to appear. Cut-and-come-again is a cheap way to try lots of Chinese and Japanese greens, such as mustard greens, mizuna, mibuna and baby bok choy, many of which are very expensive. For some things, you might find one sowing is all you need. I sowed borage a few years ago and it has self-seeded every year since. Some perennials, such as French sorrel, grow fast then just keep going year after year.

There are other crops I grow because they fill the hunger gap – they keep going all through winter and are abundant in late winter/early spring before everything else has had a chance to get going. Chard grows like a weed in my garden, and so do various types of kale and collard greens. These might get eaten almost to death by caterpillars in the summer months, but they will recover and keep growing so you have a healthy crop of leaves just when you need them.

This is a cookery book and not a book on growing your own, so I will stop here, but please think about growing a couple of your favourite things, even if it just a case of keeping something going on a windowsill, or investing a couple of weeks in nurturing a few cress-like microherbs on some cotton wool. I promise your taste buds will thank you.

LEAF ECONOMY AND PRESERVING

How to Store Leaves

There are few things more disheartening then reaching for a bunch of leaves, once a promising and healthy green, stiff-stemmed and peaky-leaved, only to realise that they have yellowed, desiccated, or even worse, turned to an olive brown sludge at the bottom of the salad drawer in the fridge. It has happened to us all. Every time it happens to me, I resolve to do better, but sometimes, life really does get in the way. You buy a bunch of fresh herbs with a specific dish in mind, your plans change, you are too tired to cook, you stick them in the fridge without care or thought (or even, and I hesitate to admit this, leave them in a tote bag on the kitchen floor) and forget all about them. It is easy to lose things in today's cavernous yet over-packed fridges: out of sight, out of mind. How to avoid this?

First, a buying strategy. Make sure the produce you are buying is in good condition – it will always last longer if it is fresher when you buy it. Try to avoid bagged leaves, and go for those with the stems intact. This is hard to do if you are dependent on the supermarket and want to buy rocket or any kind of baby leaf or spinach, but if you have a choice, go for bunches – don't buy, for example, bags of shredded kale that start drying on the stems as soon as it has been cut, as by the time it reaches your kitchen, the kale is already past its prime. Learn to recognise when leaves are fresh – prise bunches apart so you can check the centre. If you absolutely have to buy bagged leaves and want to keep them for more than a day or two, try not to leave them in the bag. And especially try to avoid opening a bag, using a few leaves and leaving the rest in the bag – they will wilt or go slimy even more quickly. It is laborious, but the best thing to do is to wash and dry the leaves, wrap in kitchen towel and put into a container – this will keep them air-tight, the paper will help absorb excess moisture, and because you have put them in

something sturdy, they won't get bashed about and bruised. You can prolong shelf life by over a week this way.

Get into the habit of storing leaves properly as soon as you get them home. Do not leave them out unless you are certain you are going to use them that day as they will start going yellow very quickly. Do not throw them into a fridge, loose and uncovered, unless you are absolutely positive you are going to use them in the next few hours. Robust greens should be fine with the stems wrapped in moist kitchen towel and put in a large plastic bag or tub; everything here on refers mainly to herbs. If you have space, keeping them upright on a tall shelf in the door of the fridge will keep them fresh for 3–4 days. Trim the ends of the stems if they are dry, put some water in a jar, add the herbs so the tips of the stems sit in the water. Cover with a plastic bag, seal with an elastic band around the jar to keep a snug environment, and leave. Keep an eye on them and keep the water fresh. If keeping them upright is not possible, soak a piece of kitchen towel in water, wrap around the stems and store flat in a bag or preferably an airtight container.

If it is likely that using the herbs as a whole bunch isn't on the cards, the best way to store them is by separating leaves from stems. Pinch out the very soft tender sprigs and leaves from thicker stems. This can take some time, especially with large bunches of coriander or parsley, but I put a podcast on to listen to and the time passes quite happily. Then bunch the stems together and either wrap in damp kitchen towel for storing in the fridge, or straight into a box in the freezer. If you leave them long like this, they are brilliant for adding to any stocks or bouquet garnis you might be making. Alternatively – and this I do especially with coriander and parsley – chop the stems as finely as you can and store in a tub in the freezer. They will not lose any flavour at all, and they are perfect for adding to all kinds of things. I use them daily, especially first thing in the morning when I am assembling lunch dishes for children's Thermos flasks – a few beans, a couple of frozen blocks of spinach, some finely chopped herb stems for flavour and you almost have a meal. I hate being without them. As for the leaves and tender tips, these I will carefully wash and dry and store in an airtight container in the fridge – I have found that they can last for up to 2 weeks stored this way, if they were very fresh when you bought or picked them. Alternatively, finely chop, pack into ice cube trays and top with water, olive oil or melted butter for freezing – you can then turn them out into a bag or box for easy storage. You can also mix with softened butter and roll into logs (see page 20).

It's worth adding a few notes on freezing here. Individual leaves respond very differently to freezing. I find that greens that tend to keep their shape when cooked do not do so well if frozen raw – the texture deteriorates, and you lose the crunch. A way around this is to salt them first as if you were making Sauerkraut (see page 24). Greens you expect to wilt down when cooked, such as spinach, wild garlic, chard, are useful things to keep in the freezer. Pack them into bags or tubs, or blanch first, for literally seconds, then plunge into iced water, drain and pack into small freezer-proof containers.

Some of the harder leaves you would expect to use whole from the freezer do very well, including kaffir lime leaves and other citrus leaves, curry leaves and pandan (screwpine). The exception seems to be laksa leaf, which strangely dries out. The flavour is still there – just – but I have found it doesn't rehydrate so well. So I treat laksa like a soft herb and push it into ice cube trays to be covered in oil or water.

The freezer can also be used to tenderise. This works particularly well with vine leaves, and is useful if you want to preserve your harvest without resorting to curing or even blanching. Wash or wipe clean, and store flat in bags – they will tenderise within a couple of months. Alternatively, if you think you will want to use them sooner, blanch the leaves for 2 minutes, then plunge into iced water so they retain their colour, then drain and dry.

If you want to prolong life for larger amounts – for example, if you have a glut to deal with or are cutting back before leaves turn yellow in autumn – there are other ways you can preserve them over the next few pages.

How to Dry Herbs

I am quite picky about dried herbs. I feel quite strongly that most soft herbs, such as basil, tarragon, chervil, coriander, do not dry well at all. If you do them yourself, you will get a better result than anything you can buy – they will be fresher after all – but they will still seem a bit dusty and without the same intensity of flavour of their fresher counterparts. The exceptions to my soft-herb rule are mint, lemon verbena and shiso, which keep their flavour very well.

Many of the woody herbs are brilliant dried, but as they are also all quite hardy I don't normally feel the need to dry them, unless I am making up flavoured salts (see page 18). However, to do so is simple – I just tie them in bundles and hang them upside down for a few days. You can then leave them be or strip the leaves from the stems and store in jars. Alternatively, you can lay them out on a wire rack somewhere cool and dark for a few days, turning regularly, or use a dehydrator on a low setting.

The dried herbs I would not do without are very limited, as there is usually a better way of storing them. I always, always dry as many lemon verbena leaves as I can in the autumn so I have a supply of leaves for tea throughout the winter. Likewise, mint – some of these manage to last through the winter, but as I usually feel like mint tea after dinner whatever the season, it is more convenient to keep some dried. I buy dried Mediterranean herbs when I know they are very good quality – large bagfuls of oregano from Greece, dried thyme (often flowers and leaves) and rubbed sage. Virtually all other herbs are better either fresh or frozen – forget about laksa, curry leaves, kaffir lime leaves – even bought and freeze-dried, they keep their flavours much better frozen or preserved in oil or vinegar.

I do, however, dry non-herbal leaves. Fig leaves keep their flavour – and aroma – amazingly well. As I write this, I can smell some dried fig leaves that are dangling above my kitchen counter – they were dried in a bunch last autumn, and are still throwing out their scent. Wild garlic responds very well to most methods of preserving (I freeze it, lacto ferment it, add it to butters and vinegars), but one of my favourite seasonings comes from drying it. I use a dehydrator. Wash the wild garlic leaves thoroughly then dry on a tea towel. Set your dehydrator to its lowest setting and lay the leaves out over the mesh trays. Alternatively, arrange over wire racks and put in a very low oven with the door open. The leaves will only take around 4 hours to dry – you will know they are ready because they will feel brittle and crumble very easily. Crumble up into a powder and store in an airtight jar. This will work for kale and rocket, too.

Drying is also one of the best ways to preserve seaweed. The time this takes depends on the variety – thick, leathery kelp will take much longer than sea lettuce, for example. Long pieces can be draped over a clothes airer or pasta drying rack and just left somewhere warm, or you can cut them to size and put them in a very low oven or in a dehydrator. There are various options as to how you store seaweed. I crumble up or grind some as above, to be sprinkled as a seasoning over food, with or without salt, or added to miso paste for instant seaweed flavour that doesn't need infusing. You can store larger pieces for making stocks.

Flavoured Salts

Many dried herbs and leaves combine very well with salt, even some of the sweeter ones. I make small amounts of salts at a time – just 50g (1¾oz) of sea salt with around 1 tablespoon of dried leaves or herbs, and any other aromatics I like. They can all be blitzed together to a fine powder so the salt has a slightly grittier texture than icing (confectioners') sugar, or bashed together using a pestle and mortar for a coarser texture. I love wild garlic or seaweed with salt, or a combination of the woodier Mediterranean herbs – try a mix of oregano, bay and thyme with 1 teaspoon of crumbled fig leaf and dried lemon zest. Or mix mint, lemon verbena and lemon thyme for a fresh rub for fish.

Some salts can use dried leaves, which I wouldn't usually dry for use on their own. For example, this method works for curry leaves, laksa leaves and lime leaves (you can try mixing the three together, too). Take a handful of leaves and add them to a dry pan. Stir over a medium-high heat until the leaves are looking crisp and brittle – they should crumble easily. Don't worry if they brown. Grind to a powder and mix with salt. This works well with other aromatics – try mustard seeds, peppercorns or chilli flakes.

Furikake

For the powder

2 nori sheets, or 2 tbsp dried crumbled seaweed or shiso leaves

2 tbsp sesame seeds

½ tsp caster (superfine) sugar

½ tsp sea salt

A pinch of MSG (optional)

1 tbsp dried shrimp or anchovies, finely chopped (optional)

Furikake is a seasoning that includes both sugar and salt. I use it mainly to pep up leftover noodles in an instant miso broth, but see page 100 for a more involved soup. You can make a very different version of this by using dried shiso leaves in place of the seaweed – or use both.

Break up the nori sheets, if using, and toast the leaves and half the sesame seeds in a dry pan over a medium heat. When they are lightly toasted, remove from the heat. Blitz the remaining sesame seeds with the sugar and salt until you have a coarse powder. Mix with the toasted sesame seeds and seaweed, along with the MSG and dried shrimp or anchovies, if using.

If making a seaweed broth, you can also reuse kombu to make the above furikake. Sprinkle a piece of it with 1 teaspoon each of soy sauce and mirin and the sugar. Toast until completely dry and add half the sesame seeds. Proceed as above.

How to Make Herb Oils

I don't make large quantities of herb oils because they do not keep particularly well, and making an instant one by blitzing together oil and herbs is such a simple thing to do. This works particularly well with soft herbs, and any leftovers can be poured into ice cube trays and frozen. In fact, the best way to have a supply of herb-flavoured oil to hand is to freeze it. Finely chop any type of herb, pack loosely into ice cube trays and cover with oil. Freeze then decant into a bag or airtight container.

There are many methods of making a bottled herb oil. This is a method that works best with soft herbs, but be warned, it is relatively time-consuming. It is still worth it, though, because it will keep well. You need roughly half the amount of herbs to oil – use a light olive oil without too much flavour. Bring a saucepan of water to the boil and blanch the herbs for a scant 10 seconds. Transfer immediately to a bowl filled with iced water, then drain and pat dry. Blitz with the olive oil to a purée, then strain through a jelly bag, coffee filter, or sieve lined with a double layer of scalded muslin. Leave it to drip overnight – when the pulp left behind looks dry and you have a decent amount of oil, decant into sterilised bottles. This is best kept in the fridge.

This method takes less time, and the fusion is faster, which is ideal for woodier herbs, such as rosemary and thyme. Take several sprigs of your chosen herb and make sure they are very fresh and bone dry – this means if you need to wash them, give them a decent amount of time to dry out before using. Bruise very lightly and put in a bowl. Heat your oil in a small saucepan over a low heat until just warm, then pour over the herbs. Leave to cool. Strain as above – this will be a much faster process as the herbs aren't puréed – and transfer to a sterilised bottle. If you have any dried herbs, you can put these in the bottle, but this will adversely affect the shelf life of the oil.

You can of course add different aromatics to any of these oils as well to make compound oils, but I tend not to as it is much harder to distinguish the flavours in these.

How to Make Herb Butters

These are all made in virtually the same way – soften the butter, finely chop the herbs and other aromatics, season with salt, then either mix together by hand or whizz in a small food processor for a more homogeneous look. I prefer them to look flecked, though, not smooth.

To store, simply pile onto a piece of plastic wrap, shape into a log, roll up tightly, store in the freezer and cut slices as necessary.

All of these work with 100g (3½oz) butter.

Shiso butter
10g (⅓oz) red shiso leaves, finely chopped
½ tsp sea salt
1 piece of sushi ginger, finely chopped
1 tsp tamari (optional, but it makes it
 a lovely colour)

Wild garlic and tarragon butter (my favourite)
20g (⅔oz) wild garlic or fermented wild garlic
 (see page 27)
10g (⅓oz) tarragon
½ tsp sea salt

Seaweed butter
2 nori sheets or equivalent dried seaweed,
 ground to a powder
½ tsp salt or 1 tsp seaweed-flavoured salt
 (see page 18)

Classic parsley and garlic
25g (¾oz) parsley
3 garlic cloves
1 tsp lemon zest
½ tsp salt
Black pepper

Thyme and smoked chilli flakes
Leaves from a large sprig of thyme
1 tsp smoked chilli flakes

Dill and lemon
15g (½oz) dill fronds
Zest of ½ lemon
2 tsp aquavit or anise-flavoured spirit

Coriander and lime
15g (½oz) coriander (cilantro)
Zest of ½ lime
1 garlic clove

One for robust fish or grilled lamb
A few sprigs of rosemary
A few sprigs of thyme
1 shallot, finely chopped
1 garlic clove, crushed

Summer herb
1 tbsp each of tarragon, basil, parsley,
 chives, chervil

Kimchi
3 tbsp kimchi, sieved to remove as much
 liquid as possible and finely chopped

Curry leaf and mustard seed
Slightly more complicated; pour 1 tablespoon olive oil into a small pan over a medium heat, add mustard seeds and finely chopped curry leaves and fry until popping. When cool, mix with butter and a pinch of salt.

Salt Preserving

One of the most fascinating topics I researched while writing this book was preserving with salt, and the various ways in which different cuisines use remarkably similar processes. For example, the process of mixing salt with herbs and other aromatics is found all over Eastern Europe, and in terms of method is very similar to that of Japanese *yuzu kosho*, which I explored in my previous book, *Citrus*. This is when a strict ratio of salt to chilli and citrus zest is used to create a wet paste. The paste can be used immediately, but is markedly better after a week's slow fermentation. There are several herbal versions of this. For example, *adjika* is a Georgian paste of mint, chilli and garlic, made popular by Olia Hercules in her book *Kaukasis*. In Romania, I have seen the same process with lovage; skip over the Atlantic, and the French Canadians have *herbes salées*, which is a mixture of any garden herbs, including parsley, chives, savoury, thyme, rosemary, celery leaf, sorrel, chard and wild garlic, which is then mixed with leeks or spring onions (scallions) and, usually, diced carrot. Incidentally, most of the French Canadians ended up in Louisiana; I looked and looked for a Cajun version of *herbes salées* and failed miserably. I can only think that as the Louisianan growing season is all year round, there wasn't the need to preserve herbs in the same way.

To make this salty, fermented herb paste, the method is simple. You need four parts herbs (and any other ingredients you might want to add) to one part salt. Finely chop everything, process with the salt and transfer to a sterilised jar. Store in the fridge. You can use immediately or leave for several days, but preferably a week. You will find the flavour has developed – you will not lose the fresh flavour of the herbs, but it will be altogether more rounded.

Herbes salées has a slightly different method, but the same four to one ratio. To make this, finely chop your chosen herbs and vegetables, then layer up with salt: 2cm (¾in) of the herb mix followed by a sprinkling of the salt. Cover and leave in the fridge for a couple of weeks, then strain off the liquid, which will have been drawn out of the vegetables by the salt. Pack into sterilised jars and keep in the fridge – this will keep indefinitely.

The layering can also be done with whole leaves – for example, shiso leaves are often preserved this way. In this instance, layer them with salt, weigh down, and leave in the fridge for a few days. These are excellent chopped into Larb (see page 72) or used as wraps.

You can experiment with all kinds of combinations. These are very salty preparations, and are best used at the beginning and end of cooking. At the beginning, they work in marinades, either mixed with oil or yogurt, and give a bit of depth when added to sauces, especially green ones. Soups and stews both benefit from these additions towards the end of cooking.

If you think you are getting close to the end of a shelf life with any of these pastes, you can prolong it by mixing them with oil or melted butter and freezing in ice cube trays as on page 19 for a more complex herb oil.

Cured Vine Leaves

This is a wet cure, as opposed to all the dry salting described opposite. I have come to really appreciate the flavour of cured vine leaves; although I can buy them very easily (my local Turkish shop has around 20 brands to choose from), I like to make them myself. They tend to have a fresher flavour (sometimes the bought ones have a bit of a whiff of silage), and they will also be more tender.

First of all, the best time of year to pick vine leaves is in early summer, when the leaves are a bright green and still very flexible – you don't want them any older or tougher. Pick medium-sized leaves for wrapping and smaller ones for anything else, keeping a short piece of the stem intact on all of them (this helps prevent the leaves from tearing). Make sure the leaves are clean, and if necessary, wash them and pat dry. Take 8–10 leaves at a time and roll them up. Put the rolls upright into sterilised preserving jars, packing quite tightly so they don't unravel. Traditionally, you need to make a brine that is salty enough to make an uncooked egg float – this is usually around 10 per cent salt. So 100g (3½oz) salt to 1 litre (34fl oz/4 cups) of preferably spring or filtered water. Bring the salt and water to the boil and simmer until the salt has dissolved. Test with an egg if you like, then pour the hot brine over the rolls of leaves, checking to make sure they are completely covered. Seal the jars and leave to cure. You can use them after a couple of weeks, and they will keep for a year.

If you want to use vine leaves immediately, however, you can simply blanch the leaves in the brine. They can take anything from 30 seconds to upwards to soften, but I usually find that 2 minutes is enough. Once blanched, immediately refresh in iced water then use in your recipe.

This method also works with other greens, such as amaranth or mustard greens.

Sauerkrauts

My first encounter with a recipe for sauerkraut was daunting. It was in Robin Howe's *German Cooking* from 1953, and the quantities are huge – 23kg (50lb) at a time in a large wooden tub or 'there would be no point in bothering at all'.

You may not be surprised when I say that this put me off. I also thought it was nonsense. Admittedly, in the UK we don't eat sauerkraut in anything like the same volume as they do in Germany and Poland, but this book – written in English – was presumably aimed at British, not German, housewives. Regardless, I am a great believer in making small batches of things. There are a few reasons for this, but it is mainly because I like to vary flavour, and I don't want to risk losing ingredients – even cheap-as-chips cabbage – in case something goes wrong, or I just don't like the taste.

Sauerkraut is simply the German name for cabbage that is lacto fermented. The process is very easy – you massage shredded cabbage with salt, weigh it down for a while (this can be as little as 5 minutes), massage it again just so you can see enough liquid is collecting at the bottom of the bowl, and then pack into sterilised jars. Over the course of days and weeks the cabbage will ferment, leaving you with slightly tangy cabbage that can be used in so many ways.

The traditional cabbage to use for a sauerkraut is the ubiquitous white – firm, tightly furled, size-wise anything from a large clenched fist to bigger than the average head. It makes sense – if you are going to shred a lot of cabbage, this is the one to use, mainly because it is firm enough to glide its way through a mandolin without tearing. A pointed cabbage and anything with looser leaves will be tricky to shred very finely, but doable if you roll the leaves up very tightly and shred them by hand.

I rarely limit myself to white cabbage, however. The reason for this is that I live in an area that has a large Polish community and I can buy excellent, plain, multipurpose sauerkraut just about everywhere. So I will usually either add different flavours to white cabbage, or use entirely different ingredients. I give a few of my most successful combinations below, but my advice would be to experiment to your heart's content. The important thing is the method.

In terms of quantities, I usually use 1 medium white cabbage, around 700g (1lb 3¾oz), or the equivalent. This will fill two large jars, with enough headspace for a weight. I also make smaller quantites as necessary. For example, one of my favourite ways of preserving wild garlic is to lacto ferment it, but it wilts down like spinach, so you need a huge amount to fill just one small jar. And just in case you are wondering – the wilting down does not mean that you end up with a mound of offputtingly slimy pulp – no, the salting and fermentation process means that they will retain some bite and definition. This means you can also get away with fermenting lettuces and soft greens, such as mustard greens, if you wish.

The Basic Method

Shred 700g (1lb 3¾oz) greens of your choice as finely as you can and put into a large, deep bowl – try one with a larger capacity than you think necessary, as the shreds do have a tendency to escape as you massage – then sprinkle with a heaped tablespoon of sea salt. Massage this into the greens – I start by scrunching up together, then using a kneading motion, turning it all over and pressing it down into the bowl. You should immediately start to see moisture forming – it

may not look as distinct as a droplet, but will definitely catch your eye. Keep massaging until the greens look more uniformly wet. Now you have a choice. You can keep going, massaging, and squeezing, until you can see that when you squeeze, a fair amount of water collects at the bottom of the bowl, or you can simply weigh down to help it along, then have another quick massage to check it.

At this point, you can add in any aromatics you like, before pressing into crocks or jars. A traditional German flavouring might be caraway seed – I use this, dill seed and/or weed, juniper, grated apple or quince. But I also like acknowledging that white cabbage is ubiquitous – it grows everywhere. It is also one of my favourite things to stir fry. So I might add some cumin or nigella seed and some turmeric, to add to a cabbage and potato stir fry, or perhaps coriander and/or laksa leaf with a splash of fish sauce and lime leaf to use as condiment. I might sprinkle in a tablespoon or two of dried seaweed, or rehydrate strips of seaweed and add that too. You can do pretty much anything you like here. I will often buy two medium white cabbages and make four types of sauerkraut at the same time, which means you only have to do one lot of prep before dividing it up and adding whatever flavours you like to the individual jars. And it keeps indefinitely, so as long as you have storage and/or fridge space, it is a good use of time.

When you have packed the cabbage into jars, divide the liquid between them and press down – you need to make sure it is free of air bubbles. Then top with a weight. As I use them all the time, I invested in some glass rounds which fit neatly into my jars, but you could use instead the base of the stem of the cabbage, or as a last resort (I don't like the use of plastic here) a plastic bag filled with water. What is important is that the cabbage is completely submerged. If, when you have pressed it down as much as you can and the liquid still doesn't quite cover the cabbage, add a little spring water – not tap water, you don't want to chlorinate your cabbage. Seal down and leave somewhere dark for a few days. You can get special lids for lacto fermentation that let the gas out – they are rubber or silicone with a little teat. If you don't have these, it is best to use a screw-top lid and loosen it once a day just to prevent the gas building up inside the jar. Don't forget to do this! After a few days taste the sauerkraut – it should taste pleasantly sour. When you are satisfied with the taste you can slow the fermentation process by putting in the fridge. At this point you can replace the lid and screw down properly.

A Few Uses

I've got into the habit of putting lacto-fermented greens on the table at mealtimes as a condiment, but they can be used in all kinds of ways. Sauerkrauts are very good braised with other greens and in particular with pork dishes – see the sausage dish on page 175, for example. I often add a spoonful or two to cabbage stir fries. They will also add depth to virtually any of the green sauces you will find in this book, including the pestos. If you are making, for example, a wild garlic pesto, think about adding some lacto fermented wild garlic too – it will add depth to the flavour.

A Few Ideas

A red cabbage makes an excellent kraut, especially with a balance of sweet and bitter notes. For one large jar, take 300g (10½oz) red cabbage and 100g (3½oz) red radicchio. Add 2 Granny Smith apples, peeled and grated, some dill fronds and a teaspoon of juniper berries.

Wild garlic kraut is something I use endlessly – possibly my favourite way of all is chopped into a toasted cheese sandwich – but I also use it with other greens. Take around 500g (1lb 1½oz) wild garlic or a combination of wild garlic and other greens, but don't bother shredding the wild garlic.

You can add anything else you like; one of my most successful combinations included 1 tablespoon grated ginger, 1 teaspoon grated or powdered turmeric, 2 shredded lime leaves, a few laksa leaves, a small bunch of coriander leaves, 1 teaspoon fish sauce and 1 teaspoon sugar.

You can use any greens available in late spring for a very green ferment – I use a base of spring greens and include carrot tops (in moderation), young nettle tips, dandelion leaves and some lemony sorrel leaves. Add a mixture of herbs – fennel fronds, tarragon, parsley, all in moderation and perhaps some lemon zest. I was warned that fennel and other aniseedy flavours can veer too much towards salted liquorice when fermented, but I have found I really like it if it is added in very small quantities.

CABBAGE IS KING

I grew up in cabbage country. Lincolnshire, an area in the English Midlands, is a county that has vast expanses of flatlands devoted to all kinds of brassica. Driving along military-straight Roman roads that cut through hedgeless fields of cabbages, Brussels sprouts, kale and oil seed rape, the smell creeps up on you long before you reach them and lingers long after you have left them behind. That smell is not particularly pleasant – the whiff of sulphur is reminiscent of overcooked cabbage, especially when the outer leaves of the plants have begun to yellow and wilt.

Sadly, this overcooking of brassicas pretty much epitomises what, for a very long time, was wrong with British cooking. I generalise, of course (I need to say this, as there was never a soggy Brussels sprout in my mother's kitchen), but it's a pretty familiar image: cabbage or Brussels sprouts boiled to oblivion by an indifferent cook, sitting in a pool of water, bland but still odiferous, part of a classic meat-and-two-veg dinner. I hope this is a thing of the past, that we have more care and love for our vegetables today, but it is probably fair to say that for a long time, brassicas were reviled. Instead of inspiring a term of endearment, as with the French 'mon petit chou' (little cabbage, my sweetheart), they have spawned an insult – 'cabbage eater', someone of little intellect or sensibility. Why? Why were brassicas derided as poor man's food, while they were celebrated as part of a peasant cuisine elsewhere? Here, they were second only to gruel in workhouses and prisons, used endlessly in fiction as markers of poverty – those poor Buckets, cursed with an unremitting diet of cabbage soup, double on Sundays.

We knew they were good for us (eat your greens!), and even if we didn't associate them with Vitamin C, the Navy did, barrelling them up to ward off scurvy (if no cabbage was available, they used the also reviled sea kale, now seen as a delicacy and crazily expensive). As for kale, it went under the radar, as it was traditionally seen as fit for nothing but animal

fodder. Even Jane Grigson is dismissive, calling
it and other loose-leaved brassicas the 'nastier aspects of
the cabbage clan', only useful if you need to 'work off your
sadistic impulses'.

The rest of the world has not treated cabbage and kale quite
so badly. We think of brassicas as cold-climate plants, but they
aren't particularly – I have seen white cabbages bigger than
my own head do just as well on a hillside in the tropics as
they do on a muddy field in the north of England. They crop
up – literally – everywhere, with remarkably similar processes
too. Think of German sauerkraut and Korean kimchi, both so
much better than in-your-face pickled red cabbage.

I love them all. I look forward to the *cime di rapa* (broccoli
rabe) and sprout-top seasons more than wild garlic and
asparagus. I take pleasure in the preparation – cutting into a
sprout top, or a cabbage, revealing the heart in a cross section
which is remarkably beautiful with its halo-esque upward
swoop of the stems. And as a cook, I sometimes feel as though
I am only just getting to grips with all the varieties of kale –
mainly Italian – that have become available in recent years. It
isn't that long ago that I had never heard of buttonhole kale
(furled silver-green leaves, pink-veined), or minestra nera
(spiky, visually a cross between puntarella and cavolo nero), or
even kalettes, the sprout of the kale world and just as versatile.

The best thing to come out of the upsurge in vegetarianism
and veganism in recent years is that producers, costermongers
and chefs are all looking for different varieties of greens
and interesting things to do with them. We can turn to other
cuisines for inspiration – I do frequently, especially to France
and Italy – but also applying traditionally meaty processes to
vegetables can pay dividends. I would never have thought ten
years ago that eating a thick slab of grilled or roasted cabbage,
charred and papery on the outer edges, sweet and tender
within, could please me as much as a steak, and now I almost
prefer it. That in itself is revelatory.

Kimchi

Makes 1 x 900g (2lb) jar

1 Chinese cabbage (Napa cabbage)

20g (⅔oz) sea salt

Spring or filtered water

For the paste

1½ tsp sugar

4 garlic cloves, grated

10g (⅓oz) ginger, peeled and grated

2 tbsp fish sauce or shrimp paste or jarred salted shrimp

Up to 3 tbsp Korean chilli powder or 1 tbsp Kashmiri chilli powder and 2 tbsp sweet paprika (according to taste)

Optional extras

1 carrot, peeled and julienned

½ daikon (mooli) or any type of radish, julienned

2 turnips, peeled and julienned

4 spring onions (scallions), cut into rounds

Large handful of herbs such as coriander (cilantro), laksa, thyme, wild garlic, shiso

The process of making kimchi is slightly different from sauerkraut, but essentially the same type of fermentation is taking place, and you can make it in exactly the same way if you prefer. Both methods produce a fair amount of liquid. I like this, as the sweet, briny liquid is great as a condiment in its own right, and can be added to all sorts of things, from soups to salad dressings. Again, I am keeping the quantities fairly small – increase as you like. And as with sauerkraut, you can use different kinds of leaves for this. I usually stick with Chinese cabbage, but have used all kinds of quite robust greens. I find I prefer using kale in kimchi to sauerkraut – the flavours round it off better.

First, prepare the cabbage. Cut into quarters lengthwise, then cut into thick strips. Traditionally, the cabbage would be cut through and left intact at the stem end, but I find this harder to use as you need to cut it off as you need it, rather than just spoon a few pieces out.

Put the cabbage into a large bowl with the salt. Rub the salt into the cabbage and continue to massage it until you can feel it starting to release liquid. Press the cabbage down with your hands then add just enough water to cover it. Weigh it down – a plate with a couple of tin cans on top should do it – and leave to stand for a couple of hours, then drain. Rinse thoroughly, then taste to see how salty it is – if it is unpleasantly so, rinse again.

Make the paste by mixing together all the ingredients – it is up to you how spicy you want to make it. Combine with any of the optional extras. Mix with the cabbage and pack into a large sterilised jar, pressing down to remove any air pockets. Seal the lid and leave to stand at room temperature, somewhere dark, for 24 hours. Open and press the cabbage down again and leave for another 24 hours. At this point, the kimchi should start to smell slightly sour. Transfer to the fridge. You can start eating it now, but it will continue to improve in flavour over the next week or so as it ferments at a slower rate.

Vinegars

Vinegars are an excellent flavour receptacle. Again, I make small batches of different types, rather than a large batch of any single herb, but having said that, there are some I will make more of – tarragon vinegar, for example, is a vinegar I will use all year round.

The method is the same for all of them and is very simple. Take plenty of your chosen herb and gently bruise it – the easiest way is to bash using a pestle and mortar. Pack loosely into a sterilised jar and cover with your choice of vinegar (just make sure it is at least five per cent acidity). Make sure the herbs are completely submerged, then seal down. It is important that the vinegar does not come into contact with anything metal, so use a lid that is either non-metallic or has a non-metallic lining. I use rubber-sealed Kilner jars, then leave it somewhere cool and dark for between one month and six weeks. Strain into a bottle, preferably through a double layer of muslin (cheesecloth) that has had boiling water poured over it or a coffee filter. It will store indefinitely.

There is also an 'emergency' method for making herb vinegar, which I have taken from Jekka McVicar's *Herb Cookbook*. Put the chopped herbs in a bowl and cover with vinegar. Set over a saucepan of cold water, making sure the bowl does not touch the water, then bring the water to the boil. Remove the bowl from the pan and leave to cool and infuse for 2 hours. You can use the vinegar at this point – strain and bottle as before.

The type of vinegar used is up to you, but I prefer to use a good-quality one – usually a raw cider vinegar or white wine vinegar, and red wine vinegar for robust flavours.

Here are just a few favourites, but you should experiment with your own favourite herbs and other aromatics:

Tarragon vinegar is something I use more than any other. The flavour is outstanding, and I use it year-round in everything from salad dressings to flavouring big pots of beans (see page 222). I usually make it pure, but it does partner very well with garlic, so I might add a few wild garlic leaves in late spring. Use white wine or cider vinegar.

Wild garlic makes a fine vinegar on its own too, which I much prefer to a regular garlic vinegar.

Curry leaf vinegar is not something to which I have ever seen many other references, so I thought it might not work, but I tried it and – wow. The flavour really comes out. What hits you initially with curry leaf is the low notes – the dark, smoky, pungency of it, but muddle them a bit and the top citrusy notes come through. Cover the leaves with vinegar – coconut, or as suggested by Angela Clutton, author of *The Vinegar Cupboard*, rice vinegar – and the two meld and turn into something quite wonderful. I found the flavour very pronounced after a few hours and this did intensify for a few days. This is best used within a few days and not weeks, so do it in small quantities. Try it with the lentil soup on page 93, use it in the salad dressing on page 140, or drizzle at the end of curries where you would normally add lemon or lime.

Rosemary or ginger rosemary again work brilliantly in dressings for robust salads or with beans. I will use fresh rosemary on its own, or perhaps char one sprig too (in a hot oven for 5 minutes, no oil). You can safely use red wine vinegar with this one.

Oregano and bay with a few pieces of pared lemon zest make a well-balanced dressing using white wine vinegar – the flavours of the Med really sing out and I will use it in marinades for chicken, or in a salad dressing, probably using some dried oregano too, just to help create that Mediterranean dustiness.

Dill on its own or with a twist of lemon or orange or some crushed juniper or allspice. This is quite a potent one. I like a few drops in a mustardy potato salad or in place of malt vinegar for Scandinavian fish and chips.

Fruit-flavoured herbs –think pineapple or blackcurrant sage, lemon or orange thyme, lime basil – or fruit leaves, such as fig, lime, blackcurrant – can make sweet, distinctive vinegars that are very good for dressings or for combining with a little sugar syrup or honey to drizzle over fruit salads, or have as a drink. Use a good apple cider vinegar.

Pine needle vinegar gives a good, citrusy, slightly resinous, lift to all kinds of things. We associate evergreens very much with winter, but the best time to harvest is in spring, as the flavour is in the soft, new growth. See page 212 for more details on this, and try it with the mushrooms on page 214.

A Few Useful – and Versatile – Sauces

There are salsas and pestos and pastes and all sorts littered throughout this book, but the reality of what happens at home is that they frequently get mixed up together. What I mean by this is that a method for one sauce might be applied to the ingredients of another, or that leftovers and fridge pickings will combine together with fresh ingredients to make something completely different. There are times when I have mixed the last spoonful of a bought tapenade into some leftover salsa verde, or jazzed up a sauce vierge with some leftover harissa. What I have come to learn during the writing of this book is how much I value all the fermented foods in my fridge. I love marrying the fresh – herbs just bought or picked from the garden, citrus zest and juice – with fermented or salted foods. Anything fermented adds depth, complexity and a degree of sourness that I always find irresistible. The dregs of a jar of kimchi or kraut – sometimes even just the liquid, mixed with some fresh herbs and a couple of chopped tomatoes. Fermented wild garlic stirred into a green pesto with lots of fresh mint and tarragon. Sauerkraut chopped finely into relishes and coleslaws. There are endless possibilities. Here are a few of the sauces that I often have in the fridge or freezer.

Zhoug

Makes 1 x 200g (7oz) jar

1 tsp coriander seeds

1 tsp black peppercorns

½ tsp caraway seeds

Seeds from 1 tsp cardamom pods

1 tbsp dried mint

1 large bunch of coriander (cilantro)

1 small bunch of parsley

2 mild green chillies

3 garlic cloves

Juice of 1 lemon

4 tbsp olive oil

Sea salt

This is originally from Yemen, but is found all over the Middle East and North Africa. It is wonderful as a spicy dip, especially with meatballs or falafel, or whisked into dressings or soups and stews last minute in place of herbs and citrus juice. Try it with flatbreads (see page 61).

This keeps quite well in the fridge, but I do sometimes help it along a bit. For example, if I have any of the salted herbs on page 22, or leftover liquid from a jar of anything lacto fermented, I might stir these in to improve flavour and add shelf life. And while this is very Middle Eastern, I can't help but use it as a base to explore other flavours. I have replaced the parsley with laksa leaf and a little Thai basil, and the lemon juice with lime to make a sauce I would toss with noodles or stir into warmed coconut milk for a quick soup.

Toast the spices in a dry frying pan over a medium heat until they are aromatic, then cool and grind to a powder. Put in a food processor with all the remaining ingredients and plenty of salt and blitz until you have a green-flecked paste. Use immediately, or store in a jar in the fridge, covered with a layer of olive oil to protect it.

Green Harissa

This is another one useful for jazzing up soups – it's also good used as a marinade with more olive oil for fish or chicken, or for stirring through yogurt as a condiment. Try it tossed through beans, vegetables, giant couscous – it will freshen everything up.

Makes 1 x 450g (1lb) jar

1 tsp cumin seeds

1 tsp coriander seeds

2cm (¾in) piece cinnamon stick

2 cloves

1 garlic clove, finely chopped

1 green chilli, deseeded if you like, chopped

½ large bunch of parsley, roughly chopped

½ large bunch of coriander (cilantro), roughly chopped

1 small bunch of lemon verbena, roughly chopped

100ml (scant ½ cup) olive oil

Juice of 1 lemon

Toast the spices lightly, then leave to cool and add to a small food processor or grinder. Add all the other ingredients and blitz until you have a green-flecked paste, pushing down from the sides at intervals as necessary. Transfer to a sterilised jar, cover with a little more olive oil to protect the colour, then store in the fridge for up to a week. Alternatively, spoon into ice cube trays and decant into a bag or box when they are frozen.

Chimichurri

Chimichurri is an Argentinian green sauce. Food and wine writer Fiona Beckett pointed me in the direction of Francis Mallmann and his method of making a saltwater solution (*salumera*), which acts as both a flavour enhancer and preservative. This means it keeps for weeks in the fridge. A chimichurri is always better the day after it is made, but the salt water ensures that it will continue to improve. There is an adapted version of this recipe on page 124.

Makes 1 x 450g (1lb) jar

For the salt water (salumera)

250ml (1 cup) spring or filtered water

1 tbsp sea salt

For the chimichurri

1 large bunch of parsley or coriander (cilantro), finely chopped

Leaves from 1 large sprig of fresh oregano, finely chopped

Leaves from 1 large sprig of thyme, finely chopped

Leaves from 1 sprig of rosemary (optional, use with parsley, not with coriander), finely chopped

4 spring onions (scallions), finely chopped

2 garlic cloves, finely chopped

1 green chilli, such as jalapeño, very finely chopped

4 tbsp olive oil

2 tbsp red wine vinegar

First prepare the salumera. Put the water in a saucepan and bring to the boil. Add the salt and reduce the heat. Stir until the salt has completely dissolved into the water. Leave to cool.

To make the chimichurri, mix together all of the ingredients, including the salt water. Transfer to a sterilised jar and store in the fridge. Wait for at least a day before using, preferably two.

Coriander and Mint Chutney

Makes 1 x 450g (1lb) jar

1 large bunch of coriander (cilantro),
   roughly chopped

1 small bunch of mint, leaves only, roughly
   chopped

50g (1¾oz) cashew nuts, lightly toasted

Juice of 1 lime (or half a lemon)

1 tbsp jaggery or light soft brown sugar

A pinch of ground turmeric

1–2 green chillies (optional), deseeded if you like

Sea salt

Roughly chop the coriander and mint, and
put in a food processor or blender with all the
remaining ingredients and 1 teaspooon salt.
Pulse, pushing down until all the leaves are
well combined with everything else, then start
drizzling in 75–100ml (¼–scant ½ cup) until
you have a smooth, slightly runny, very bright
green paste. Taste and adjust as necessary – you
might want more salt, sugar, chilli, citrus. Store
in a jar in the fridge for up to a week, or freeze
in ice cube trays – a cube or two of this paste is
an excellent way to freshen up any soup.

Mint Sauce

**An English classic. No matter how I dress it
up, or what other flavours I put with lamb, I
always return to this eventually.**

Makes 8–10 servings

Take a bunch of mint and pick off all the leaves.
Finely chop – as fine as you possibly can –
then put in a bowl with a tablespoon of caster
(superfine) sugar. Pour over 75ml (⅓ cup) freshly
boiled water and stir to dissolve the sugar.
Season with salt, and add 1 tablespoon cider
vinegar. Taste and add more vinegar 1 teaspoon
at a time until you are happy you have the
balance right. Leave to infuse. There is enough
for at least one roast here, but it will keep in
a jar in the fridge for any leftover lamb, or the
next weekend.

Serves 4–6

2 tbsp white wine vinegar

1 tbsp oil, such as walnut, sunflower or mild olive

1 tbsp mustard

A pinch of caster (superfine) sugar

3 eggs, hard-boiled

250g (1 cup) sour cream or crème fraîche

50g (scant ¼ cup) yogurt

2 shallots, finely chopped

250g (8¾oz) herbs, such as sorrel, chervil, chives, parsley, salad burnet, land cress, borage, washed, dried and finely chopped

Sea salt and freshly ground black pepper

Grüne Soße of Sorts

Several people told me about this particular version of green sauce, but food writer Christie Dietz gave me the low-down. The herbs themselves are collectively known and sold as Frankfurter Grüne Soße and thanks to EU geographical protection, have to be grown within the city's environs to make a true Grüne Soße. I hope this isn't as confusing as it sounds. Clearly we can't all get to Frankfurt, so this is my German-inspired green sauce. Coincidentally all the herbs in the true version grow well in my garden, so I've stuck with tradition.

The quantities of individual herbs are likely to be different every time you make this, depending what is available and of course you can make substitutions – watercress for land cress, for example, but just make sure the overall quantity is around 250g (8¾oz).

Whisk together the vinegar, oil, mustard and sugar and season with salt and pepper. Separate the eggs and mash the yolks into the mixture until smooth, then finely chop the whites and stir these in with the sour cream or crème fraîche, yogurt and shallots. Stir in the herbs. Using a hand-held blender, blitz a couple of times until you have a finely flecked sauce, then taste for seasoning. Add more salt, vinegar or sugar if you need to.

How to Make Herb Jellies

These are the sort of jellies that are used to enhance savoury dishes. You can go very retro and serve them with baked cheeses, or use them to add sweetness and flavour to gravies and sauces, or simply serve them on the side as you would a mint, redcurrant or cranberry.

The ones I find I make the most often are rosemary, thyme and mint; I'm afraid that, out of nostalgia (my granny's roast dinner), I will add a drop of green colouring to the mint jelly.

You don't have to stick to apple here. I usually use Bramleys or crab apples as a base, but I might add blackberries too. You can also replace 1–2 tablespoons of the apple cider vinegar with any herb vinegars you might have made.

Makes 3–4 x 225g (8oz) jars

1.5kg (3lb 5oz) Bramley apples or equivalent, roughly chopped, bruised parts discarded

1 handful of fresh herbs, stems and leaves separated, plus extra sprigs for the jars

Granulated sugar (see method)

100ml (scant ½ cup) apple cider vinegar

A few drops of green food colouring (optional)

Put the apples into a lidded large saucepan. Add 1 litre (4 cups) water, then bring to the boil. Turn down the heat and cover. Simmer for around 20–25 minutes, until the apples are well on their way to breaking down, then add the herb stems. Simmer for another 5 minutes.

Scald a jelly bag or a muslin-lined sieve with boiling water, then set over a large bowl. Ladle in the apples, then cover. Leave to stand for several hours – preferably at least 12 – until the apple pulp looks very dry. Make sure you don't help it along by pushing down on the pulp as it will affect the clarity of your jelly.

When you are ready to make the jelly, put a couple of saucers into your freezer to chill, and make sure your jars are sterilised (put through a hot wash on your dishwasher, or wash thoroughly and leave to dry out in a low oven). Finely chop your herbs.

Weigh the apple juice. For each 600ml (2½ cups) of juice, add 450g (2¼ cups) sugar. Put in a large saucepan or preserving pan along with the vinegar and stir over a very gentle heat until the sugar has dissolved. When you are confident the sugar has dissolved, bring the liquid up to the boil and keep at a rolling boil until it reaches setting point. Start testing after 5 minutes. Drop a small amount onto one of the chilled saucers and leave it to cool for a minute. Gently prod it with your finger – if it wrinkles up on the surface, it is ready. If it isn't yet set, boil for another couple of minutes and try again.

When your jelly has set, remove from the heat and stir vigorously to disperse any scum – skim off any that remains. Stir in the herb leaves and leave to cool for 5 minutes – this will help stop the herbs from rising to the top of the jelly when you decant it.

Ladle the jellies into the jars. Scald the herb sprigs with boiling water and push under the surface of the jelly, one per jar. Leave to cool before tightening the lids.

BRUNCH DISHES

Spiced Creamed Spinach with Eggs and Cheese

Serves 2

1 tbsp olive oil

1 tbsp butter

1 onion, sliced

4 eggs

1 tbsp medium curry powder or 1 tbsp Spice Mix (see below)

4 garlic cloves, very finely chopped

15g (½oz) piece ginger, peeled and grated

1kg (2lb 3oz) frozen chopped spinach, defrosted

A bunch of fenugreek (methi) leaves only, finely chopped (optional)

A small bunch of coriander (cilantro), finely chopped (optional)

2 medium tomatoes, peeled, deseeded and coarsely chopped

200g (¾ cup) double (heavy) cream or crème fraîche

200g (7oz) melting cheese – Ogleshield is best, but Cheddar or Gruyère are also great

Flatbreads or hot buttered sourdough toast, to serve

For the spice mix

1 tsp ground turmeric

1 tsp ground coriander

½ tsp cinnamon

½ tsp cardamom

Pinch of ground cloves

Pinch of cayenne pepper

Pinch of white pepper

Pakistani comfort food, courtesy of my mother-in-law. Sadly she no longer cooks, but I have made sure I have learned some of the family favourites over the years. I add a fraction of the cream she did, but it's still quite rich. This is one of those dishes that will scoop up any other vegetables you might need to use up – I have added mushrooms and cooked potatoes before.

First heat the olive oil and butter in a wide, straight-sided frying pan. Add the onion and cook over a medium heat until softened to a golden brown-tinged translucency, about 10 minutes.

While the onions are cooking, boil the eggs. They need to be just set – so a deep orange yolk, the soft side of fudgy. Bring a saucepan of water to the boil. Lower the eggs in, one at a time on a spoon, then time to boil for 7 minutes. Transfer immediately to an ice bath or run under cold water to cool, then peel. Cut in half and set aside.

When the onions have softened, add the curry powder, garlic and ginger and cook for 2–3 minutes. Add the spinach – don't worry about squeezing out too much of the moisture from it – and the fenugreek and coriander, if using, to the pan. Stir to combine with the contents of the pan, then leave to simmer until the mixture is quite dry. Mix in the tomatoes and double cream or crème fraîche.

Push in the eggs, cut-side up, covering with spinach to prevent the yolk from cooking much more. Sprinkle with the cheese, then grill until melted and browned in patches. Eat with flatbreads or piled on top of sourdough toast.

Variations

Cook to the stage before you add the eggs and cheese, then serve as a side dish.

Add the cheese without the eggs as a side or a main dish.

Treat like shakshouka – make wells in the mixture, break in raw eggs, top with cheese, cover and cook until the eggs are set and the cheese has melted.

Use any type of wilting green – chard, curly kale or nettles.

Bubble and Squeak Waffles

Makes around 16

50g (3½ tbsp) butter, melted

60ml (¼ cup) buttermilk

2 large eggs, separated

1 tbsp wholegrain mustard

500g (1lb 1½oz) mashed potato

500g (1lb 1½oz) cooked greens –
anything robust (I like sprout tops,
shredded sprouts, chard, kale)

100g (3½oz) Cheddar cheese, grated
(optional)

85g (⅔ cup) plain (all-purpose) flour

½ tsp baking powder

¼ tsp bicarbonate of soda (baking soda)

Sea salt and freshly ground black
pepper

A very good cook I know called Jeni Hewlett told me about how she made savoury waffles using any typical bubble and squeak ingredients, so I tried them and was hooked. They offer a more robust density than a regular waffle, but are still lighter than bubble and squeak, so no stodge. And while they are more time-consuming to cook, the process is easier as you aren't fiddling around with shallow frying.

You can use any kind of greens for this, and you don't have to limit it to fresh greens either – substitute a small amount of it for any kind of sauerkraut or kimchi and you will give extra complexity to the flavour.

Heat your waffle maker to medium.

Mix together the butter, buttermilk, egg yolks and wholegrain mustard, then stir in the mashed potatoes, greens and cheese, if using. Whisk the flour, baking powder and bicarbonate of soda with a generous amount of salt and pepper. Fold this through the batter, making sure you keep the mixing to a minimum. Whisk the egg whites to stiff peaks, then fold a tablespoon into the batter, just to loosen it slightly. Add the rest, again, folding in as gently as possible and keeping the mixing to the absolute minimum.

Spread some of the mixture over your waffle iron, making sure you don't over-fill it – it should just barely cover the tips of the indentations. Cook until set and turning a rich brown on the ridges – often up to around 10 minutes, depending on your waffle iron. Keep the cooked waffles warm in a low oven while you make the rest.

Serve with anything you like – I spread them with butter and/or top with bacon and maple syrup.

Variation

You can of course just make bubble and squeak. Just mix the potato and greens together along with any additions you like, including the cheese. To cook, I often leave in one large round and cook it in a cast iron pan, flipping over onto a plate and sliding back into the pan when I am absolutely sure I have left it long enough to form a decent crust. I will usually fry in a little lard or olive oil.

Kimchi Omelette Sandwich

Serves 1

2 eggs

25g (¾oz) green, white or Napa
  cabbage, finely shredded

½ small carrot, finely shredded

1 spring onion (scallion), shredded

1–2 tbsp Kimchi (see page 30)

A knob of butter

2 slices of bread (traditionally white,
  but anything goes)

25g (¾oz) hard cheese, such as Cheddar,
  grated (optional)

Sriracha, gochujang or ketchup
  (optional)

Mayonnaise (optional)

Sea salt and freshly ground black
  pepper

This is based on Korean 'street toast', a concept I first read about not in a Korean recipe book or blog, but in Genevieve Taylor's book *A Good Egg*. It captured my imagination then and for years it has been a favourite solo brunch. I vary it a lot; the only constants are the cabbage omelette and chilli sauce. Sometimes I make it into a sandwich. I will also add kimchi, or any other ferments I have to hand (sauerkraut, fermented wild garlic, even achar pickle) and often I will add cheese. Adding cheese so it turns into a proper melt makes it slightly more complicated to make, but it is definitely worth it – it will be one of the best cheese toasties you've ever eaten.

Break the eggs into a bowl and whisk until broken up. Add the cabbage, carrot and spring onion, then season with salt and pepper.

Stir in the kimchi if you like at this stage so it is distributed through the whole omelette – or wait until later to keep it more discrete. Melt half of the butter in a small frying pan. Add the egg mixture and cook over a medium heat until the base is crisp and brown. While the omelette is setting it is possible to shape into the same shape and size of your bread – but this is not essential. You can add the kimchi at this stage if you've held back until now, either swirled through the eggs or just dotted about. When the omelette easily comes away from the pan, ease it onto a spatula and flip over. Cook until the reverse side has set and very lightly browned, then remove from the pan and keep warm.

Add a little more butter to the pan. Place one of the slices of bread into it. If using the cheese, add it now and cover the pan for a minute or two to let the cheese melt. Otherwise, just fry the bread on one side. Remove from the pan and fry the other slice on one side too.

To assemble, put the omelette on top of one of the slices of bread (cheese-coated or un-fried side up) and top with a chilli sauce, or ketchup, or both. Add mayonnaise if you like and perhaps a little more kimchi. Top with the remaining slice of bread and eat immediately.

Herb Omelette

Serves 1

3 eggs

2 sprigs each of tarragon, parsley, lemon thyme, chives, chervil, dill or fennel, finely chopped

A large knob of butter

4 handfuls of baby salad leaves, such as baby leaf lettuces, spinach, rocket (arugula), pea shoots, sorrel, borage, beetroot (beets), mitsuba (also called honeywort or Japanese wild parsley), amaranth or new-growth chamomile fronds

A few small borage leaves and flowers, to serve

Sea salt and freshly ground black pepper

This isn't a *fines herbes*, folded omelette – more of a loosely set frittata. It is very free-form, made with whatever you might need to use up or have growing in the garden. The greens are added in three stages. First, herbs are whisked into the omelette mixture; next, salad leaves are wilted in the pan just before the eggs go in, and finally more herbs are stirred through just before serving.

You could add any kind of cheese to this too, or a handful of cherry tomatoes.

Break the eggs into a bowl and season with salt and pepper. Stir in half of the finely chopped herbs.

Melt the butter in a small frying pan. When it starts to foam, add half the baby salad leaves. Stir around the pan until they have wilted, then pour in the egg mixture. Stir the omelette in from the sides to the centre, allowing the runny eggs to fill the exposed pan until it is almost set, then add the remaining salad leaves. Leave until just set.

Sprinkle on the reserved herbs along with the borage leaves and flowers just before serving, then carefully slide onto a plate.

CHOOSING GREENS

While writing this book, I made it my business to try as many greens as I possibly could – not just to work out what they were, which isn't always as easy as you might think, but also to whittle out those I didn't like, felt indifferent to, or thought just weren't worth the money. I wasn't so concerned with the ones with which I was already familiar – I know, for example, that I prefer cavolo nero to curly kale, and that I will always choose chard over spinach. I ate my way through every kind of endive and chicory (love them all), the wild broccolis and turnip tops and mustard greens – and especially the numerous types of kale (Red Russian, buttonhole, redbor, kalettes) during a season when it felt like I was discovering new ones almost weekly.

Every time I visited Chinatown I looked for different greens to try, and this was where it grew more interesting. The herbs were relatively straightforward. I knew that I would always want to buy laksa leaf, Thai basil and Chinese chives. Then I bought a large bag of sawtooth coriander (also known as culantro, long-leaved coriander, Mexican coriander or in the Caribbean, chadon beni). I had used it fresh in the Caribbean and knew it had pretty much the same flavour as regular coriander, but was much, much stronger. But this batch wasn't. In fact, it was like a pale imitation of coriander, and several times the price. I bought another bag, had the same result, and have had to reluctantly come to the conclusion that it isn't worth the money. I intend to try growing it instead.

I also worked my way through all the leafy greens. I loved the distinctive flavour of cha plu/lolot pepper and the pleasant, nutty flavour of sweet potato leaves. I used all the more succulent greens interchangeably – bok choy (pak choi or pok choi), choy sum, gai lan (a leafy Chinese broccoli), Chinese spinach – and will always buy them, especially in the Chinatown markets where they are sold in bulk at a fraction of the price of the supermarkets. I came unstuck with two types of green – the first was chrysanthemum leaves.

Those I could buy were not tender enough to eat raw, and when cooked, the flavour was much milder than I was expecting. I wanted a slight bitterness, but they were grassier and slightly on the unpleasant side of that hothouse mustiness. It reminded me of my grandmother's greenhouse where she grew chrysanthemums and sickly, metallic carnations for her church buttonhole. Not what I want to eat. They were also crazily expensive. The other green was acacia leaf, or *cha-om*. As far as I am concerned, acacia leaf smells as bad as durian. I swear people were moving away from me on the tube home, and within moments of getting in the door, the whole house reeked of it. So I thought it best to deal with it immediately. An important thing to note is that you don't actually get much edible leaf from a large bag of acacia. The leaves are delicate – they look a bit like floppy grass-heads and have to be stripped from the thorny stems. This is easy to do: you just hold each stem upside down, run your fingers along it, and the leaves will drop off. Then wash thoroughly. The most common way to cook it is in an omelette, so I did just that. The smell dissipated, thank goodness, and I was left with a mild and pleasant-tasting green, which was – I hate to say this – quite bland. I didn't dislike it, I just did not think it was worth the smell, the waste and, most of all, the cost, because one bag gave me just enough for one omelette and, again, was very expensive.

I confirmed to myself something I've always known – if I'm buying anything that isn't local or reasonably priced, there has to be a good reason for it. It has to offer something different in terms of taste and texture. If I lived somewhere where acacia leaf was as cheap to buy as many of the greens I take for granted, I'm sure it would become part of my repertoire, smell or not. But I don't, and it isn't.

Shakshouka

Serves 2

3 tbsp olive oil

2 red onions, peeled and sliced

2 green peppers, cut into long slices

A large bunch of chard, leaves and stems separated, shredded

4 garlic cloves, finely chopped

½ tsp ground turmeric

½ tsp cumin seeds

½ tsp caraway seeds

½ tsp ground cardamom

½ tsp cayenne pepper

4 ripe tomatoes, peeled, deseeded and chopped

A squeeze of lemon juice

A small bunch of coriander (cilantro), roughly chopped

A small bunch of parsley, roughly chopped

4 large eggs

4 tbsp thick yogurt or labneh

Sea salt and freshly ground black pepper

Chickpea and Mint Pancakes, to serve (see page 210)

A *shakshouka* is literally a mixture of ingredients, and so is by its very nature infinitely adaptable. This is a greener version than the more usual red. I love the earthy tones of chard with warm spices, but you can use pretty much anything, as long as it is the sort of green that wilts down and softens.

I prefer meals that include eggs for breakfast or brunch, but of course this is a very quick supper, too. All you need to serve is some bread, but I do like serving it with the Chickpea and Mint Pancakes on page 210 – they are based on *socca*, from the South of France, a place where chard is also plentiful.

If you feel like eating meat, sliced merguez sausages could be added along with the onions.

Heat the olive oil in a large, lidded frying pan. Add the onions, peppers and chard stems and season with salt and pepper. Cook over a medium heat until starting to soften but still al dente, around 10 minutes – don't let the onions and peppers collapse down.

Add the garlic and spices and cook for a further 2 minutes, then add the tomatoes, the shredded chard leaves and 100ml (scant ½ cup) water.

Cover and simmer until the chard has wilted down – around 10 minutes. The mixture should be quite dry. Taste for seasoning and add a squeeze of lemon juice and more salt and pepper as necessary.

Reserve a couple of tablespoons of the coriander and parsley, then stir the rest into the pan. Make four little holes in the mixture, well spaced out. Break the eggs and carefully pour them into the holes, then dollop the yogurt or labneh onto the yolk of each egg – this will help prevent it setting too quickly while the whites cook. Cover again and cook for a few more minutes, until the egg whites are set but still a little wobbly, and the yolks are still runny.

Serve sprinkled with the remaining herbs and with Chickpea and Mint Pancakes for scooping, if you like.

Herb Custards

Serves 2

3 eggs, cracked into a bowl and weighed

Butter, for greasing

250ml (1 cup) milk

1 small garlic clove, halved

1 large sprig of tarragon, parsley or chervil, bashed

Up to 150ml (⅔ cup) single (light) cream

50g (1¾oz) hard cheese, such as Cheddar, grated

1 tbsp chopped herbs, such as tarragon, chervil or parsley

To top

1 tbsp snipped chives

2 tbsp hard cheese, finely grated

These custards are soft, soothing, uncomplicated – the perfect way to ease yourself into the day when you don't want or need a punchier start.

You can serve these on their own with just some toast soldiers, but they are also good with greens underneath or on the side. You can put anything in the base – try wilting some greens (spinach, chard, wild garlic, nettle) in a splash of water, squeezed of excess liquid.

First, make a note of the weight of the eggs once you have cracked the shells – you will need double the amount of liquid. Grease two medium-sized ramekins with butter.

Put the milk in a small saucepan and add the garlic clove and herb sprig. Slowly bring the milk to the boil, then remove from the heat and leave to infuse until cool. When cool, strain and measure your amount of milk. Add enough cream to the milk to make double the weight of the eggs – for example, if your eggs weigh 150g (5¼oz) collectively and your milk has reduced to 200ml (¾ cup), you will need 100ml (scant ½ cup) cream. Melt the cheese into the milk mixture over a gentle heat, then cool to blood temperature.

Beat the eggs until combined but without whisking air into them – you do not want froth and bubbles – then stir into the milk mixture. Strain through a sieve into a jug then stir in the herbs. Divide between the ramekins, then sprinkle with the chives and remaining cheese.

There are various options when it comes to cooking these, involving either a bain marie or a steamer basket. If you make these in a traditional bamboo steamer basket, you will not need to cover them with plastic wrap as enough steam escapes to stop condensation forming. Otherwise, cover the ramekins with plastic wrap.

Put the ramekins in your steamer, or if using the bain marie method, put a cloth in the base of a large saucepan and place the ramekins on top of that. Pour boiling water in the base of your steamer or carefully pour around the ramekins so the water comes halfway up the sides. Cover and simmer for 15–18 minutes until just set – they should still wobble in the centre. Serve immediately.

Wild Garlic Potato Cakes

Makes 8

600g (1lb 5oz) potatoes, peeled and diced

50ml (¼ cup) milk

25g (1½ tbsp) butter

50g (1¾oz) fresh wild garlic leaves, finely shredded

50g (1¾oz) fermented wild garlic, finely shredded (page 27; optional)

100g (3½oz) good melting cheese, such as Ogleshield

50g (1¾oz) plain (all-purpose) flour

1 egg, beaten

75g (scant ½ cup) fine breadcrumbs

Olive oil, for frying

Sea salt and freshly ground black pepper

For the salsa

300g (10½oz) tomatoes, cored and finely diced

A small bunch of tarragon, finely chopped

1 tbsp sherry vinegar (or tarragon vinegar if you have it)

Zest of ½ lemon

2 tbsp olive oil

To serve

A few baby spinach or other salad leaves

A few basil microleaves

4 eggs, poached (optional)

The winning combination of wild garlic and cheese is given a funkier complexity here, with the addition of some lacto fermented wild garlic, the recipe for which can be found on page 27. If you don't have any, you could substitute with another kind of sauerkraut, or just double the amount of fresh wild garlic you use.

These cakes can be enhanced by any soft herbs or leaves, but this is my favourite, especially paired with the salsa, which is also good with the Herb Custards (page 49).

Put the potatoes in a saucepan and cover with water. Add salt, then bring to the boil. Simmer until the potatoes are tender, around 10 minutes. Drain thoroughly, then add the milk and butter. Mash! Stir in the fresh and fermented garlic leaves along with the cheese and check for seasoning. Add salt and copious amounts of freshly ground black pepper.

Put the flour, egg and breadcrumbs on separate plates or in shallow bowls. Divide the potato mixture into 8 flattish cakes – they will be around 100g (3½oz) each – then dip each one in the flour. Dust off any excess, dip in the egg and then coat thoroughly in the breadcrumbs. It is a good idea to chill them at this stage, while you make the salsa.

Next, make the salsa by mixing all the ingredients together and season with salt and pepper.

To cook the patties, pour a thin layer of olive oil into a frying pan and set over a medium high heat. Fry the potato cakes for 3–4 minutes on each side until crisp and brown. Do not crowd the pan – fry in two batches if necessary. Some cheese may escape the confines of the crust; if so, scoop it up as a chef's perk, or allow it to spread and brown like a Parmesan crisp, rather than removing it.

Arrange the cakes over the leaves and sprinkle with the basil. Serve with the salsa and a poached egg, if you like.

Variation

I love the flavour of laverbread but (and I am flying in the face of my Welsh heritage here) I don't love it mixed into oatmeal. Instead I like it mixed into these potato cakes in place of the garlic, and served with cockles and bacon.

Fenugreek Pancakes with Curry Leaf and Coconut Yogurt

Serves 4

125g (1 cup) plain (all-purpose), spelt or wholemeal (wholewheat) flour

1 tsp ground coriander

¼ tsp ground turmeric

¼ tsp ground cinnamon

1 tbsp light soft brown sugar

1 egg

300ml (1¼ cups) whole (full-fat) milk

50g (1¾oz) fenugreek (methi) leaves, washed, dried and finely chopped

3cm (1¼in) piece ginger, peeled and grated

1 green chilli, finely chopped (optional)

Oil or ghee, for frying

Sea salt

For the yogurt

A small bunch of coriander (cilantro), very finely chopped

2 green chillies, deseeded and finely chopped (more or less according to taste)

2 tbsp ghee or oil

25g (¼ cup) desiccated coconut

1 tsp mustard seeds

1 tsp jaggery or light soft brown sugar

250g (1 cup) thick yogurt

20 curry leaves

Sea salt

I really love the combination of these pancakes with the yogurt. I made them to offer an alternative to the sort of pancake my son smothers in maple syrup but actually, you can dress these in maple syrup too. And for a really fusion breakfast, try with some grilled chorizo or bacon rashers – both work harmoniously with the smokiness of the curry leaves and fenugreek.

Fenugreek leaves are sold in Indian markets under the name *methi*. They are succulent with a hint of smoky bitterness. The yogurt is also a great all-rounder; I like it with barbecued chicken and plenty of lime juice.

Make the yogurt first – you can do this well ahead of time, even the night before. Put the coriander and chillies into a mini food processor and add a tablespoon of water. Blitz until you have a rich green paste. Set aside.

Heat half the oil or ghee in a small frying pan. Add the coconut and stir over a medium heat until it has started to turn golden brown. Add the mustard seeds and jaggery or sugar and stir again for a couple of minutes, or until it smells toasted. Remove from the heat and leave to cool.

Put the yogurt in a bowl with a pinch of salt. Stir in the coriander mix and the coconut mix. Wipe out your frying pan and add the remaining oil or ghee. Fry the curry leaves for around 30 seconds until they are crisp. Use to garnish the yogurt just before serving. If making ahead, keep in the fridge and remove 30 minutes before you are going to eat.

To make the pancakes, put the dry ingredients into a large bowl and add a generous pinch of salt. Add the egg and start working it into the flour, trying to keep the mixture as smooth as possible, then gradually add the milk until you have a batter the consistency of single (light) cream. Stir the fenugreek leaves into the batter with the ginger and chilli, if using. Leave to stand for half an hour.

Melt a little oil or ghee in a crêpe or frying pan and add a ladleful of the batter – just enough to thinly coat the base. Swirl it round, then leave to set. When you can see that the underside has set, gently flip with palette knife to cook the other side. Keep warm on a tea towel-lined plate while you make the rest. Serve the pancakes with the yogurt.

Sweet Cicely-Cured Fish

Serves 4

Approximately 1.2–1.5kg (2lb 10oz–3lb 5oz) salmon or sea trout in two equal fillets, skin on

75ml (⅓ cup) vodka or aquavit

100g (6 tablespoons) flaky sea salt

125g (⅔ cup) granulated sugar

1 tsp black peppercorns, coarsely crushed

A bunch of sweet cicely (or alternative), finely chopped

Zest of 1 lemon (optional)

Sweet cicely gives a subtle, sweet aniseed flavour to the fish that I love – it can be replaced with other aniseed-flavoured herbs if you can't find it. Anise hyssop's flavour is slightly less sweet and more herbal and, of course, fennel is a good alternative, and I don't think I need to describe that flavour – use either bronze fennel or the fronds found attached to fennel bulbs. For sweetness, you can also use dulse seaweed here, soaked and finely chopped.

You can scale down this recipe significantly to use smaller pieces of fish, but what is important is to have two pieces of a similar size, as they are placed on top of each other.

Take a rectangular earthenware dish. Place one of the fillets in the dish, skin-side down, and drizzle with half the vodka. Mix the salt, sugar, peppercorns, sweet cicely and lemon zest, if using, together and spread over the fish. Drizzle the rest of the vodka over the flesh side of the other piece of fish, and place this, flesh-side down, on top of the first fillet.

Cover with a piece of plastic wrap or foil and weigh down – I use some weights from some old scales, but you can use tins or jars. Leave to cure in the fridge for 2 days. Turn the fillets over every 12 hours, straining off any accumulated liquid at the same time.

When the fish is ready, it will be much denser and drier-looking. Scrape off any excess cure (although the herbs will be perfectly edible) and slice as you would smoked salmon, making sure you discard the skin.

I eat this with scrambled eggs, or with dollops of sour cream, caviar if I'm feeling extravagant, and the Blinis on page 211.

Pinto Beans and Greens with Coriander Tortillas and Tomatillo Salsa

Serves 4

For the beans and greens

2 tbsp olive oil

2 red onions, thinly sliced

2 garlic cloves, finely chopped

1 tsp cumin seeds

A pinch of ground cinnamon

400g (14oz) spring greens, kale or chard, or a combination, shredded

250g (8¾oz) cooked Pinto Beans (see page 220, or from a tin)

2 ripe tomatoes, finely chopped

Sea salt

For the salsa

300g (10½oz) tomatillos, dehusked

2 green chillies (preferably jalapeño)

2 garlic cloves

4 spring onions (scallions), trimmed

Juice of 1 lime

A few coriander (coriander) leaves, roughly chopped

A few mint leaves, roughly torn

To serve

Blue Corn Coriander Tortillas (see page 221)

There are lots of elements to this recipe, but much of it can be prepared ahead, so do not be put off – you can assemble it very easily in no time at all. This is a vegan dish if you use vegetable shortening when you make the tortillas, but there are plenty of optional extras you could add, including melting cheese over the beans, or fried eggs. You can simplify it further – the salsa is a roasted one, but the same ingredients could just be finely chopped and mixed together for a quicker, fresher version.

A note on mint – it is always best to add it at the last minute to anything fresh if you are going to cut or tear into the leaves, as it goes black quite quickly.

First make the salsa. Put the tomatillos, chillies, garlic and spring onions in a frying pan – preferably a cast-iron skillet. Cook over a medium-high heat for around 15 minutes, shaking the pan, until everything is lightly charred. The tomatillos will probably take longer than everything else – keep a close eye and remove the chillies and garlic when they blacken.

Remove from the heat. When cool either chop finely (you can deseed the chillies if you like) or put in a food processor and pulse to a chunky-textured purée. Add plenty of salt and the lime juice, then stir through the coriander. Set aside.

To make the beans and greens, heat the oil in a large lidded frying pan or casserole dish (Dutch oven). Add the red onions and cook over a medium-high heat until softened and slightly charred. Add the garlic, cumin seeds and cinnamon, and cook for a couple more minutes. Add the greens to the pan along with 100ml (scant ½ cup) water. Press down into the pan (they will be voluminous) then cover. Cook until the greens have just wilted down – I keep them quite al dente, so cook for only 5 minutes, but you can cook them for up to 10 minutes for a softer texture. Stir in the beans and tomatoes and cook just long enough for everything to be piping hot.

Check for seasoning and adjust accordingly. Stir the mint leaves through the salsa and serve together with the tortillas.

STARTERS AND LIGHT MEALS

Crab, Little Gem and Chervil Fritters

Serves 4

3 eggs

60g (2oz) plain (all-purpose) flour

2 little gems, shredded

A large bunch of chervil, finely chopped

A small pot of crab meat (around 100g (3½oz), mixture of white and brown meat)

1 tsp lime juice

Nutmeg, for grating

Olive oil, for frying

Sea salt

For the béarnaise

1 tbsp white wine vinegar

1 shallot, very finely chopped

1 egg yolk

50g (3½ tbsp) butter, well chilled and cubed

A small bunch of chervil

For the cucumber pickle (optional)

½ cucumber, peeled, deseeded and diced

½ tsp caster (superfine) sugar

½ tsp sea salt, plus extra to taste

2 tsp white wine vinegar

White pepper

A discussion with seafood expert Mike Warner resulted in my pairing crab and chervil together, and he is absolutely right – their delicate flavours really do complement each other. I add the cucumber because this is a rich dish and I like to have something cutting through it. It is not essential, however.

First, if using, make the cucumber pickle. Put the cucumber in a colander and sprinkle with the salt. Leave for half an hour, then transfer to a bowl. Add the sugar and white wine vinegar and leave to stand. Taste for seasoning and add (preferably white) pepper and more salt, if necessary.

Next make the béarnaise. Put the vinegar and shallot into a double boiler or, if you are very confident, a small saucepan. Boil until the vinegar has reduced by half, then turn the heat down as low as possible. Add the egg yolk with 1 tablespoon of water. Whisk to combine, then start adding the butter, a cube at a time, whisking as it melts. You are after an emulsion here – if at any point it looks as though the mixture is splitting, because it looks curdled or because there is a resistant layer of melted butter on the surface, remove from the heat, whisk in a tablespoon of cold water, and continue. When you have whisked in all the butter you should have a light, airy sauce. Check for seasoning and stir in the chervil. Keep covered while you make the fritters.

Finally, make the fritters. Break the eggs into a bowl and whisk to break up. Add the flour with a generous pinch of salt. When you have a smooth batter, stir in the little gems, chervil, crab meat and lime juice. Finely grate in a little nutmeg.

Coat the base of a frying pan with olive oil. Add heaped tablespoons of the batter mixture, making sure they are well spaced out, then cook for a couple of minutes on each side until crisp and brown. You will probably have to do this in more than one batch.

Serve the crab cakes with the béarnaise and the cucumber pickle.

Coriander Lamb Kebabs
with Borage Leaf Raita

Serves 4

500g (1lb 1½oz) lamb mince

1 small onion, finely chopped

1 medium tomato, finely chopped

1–2 green chillies, deseeded and finely chopped

4 garlic cloves, crushed

5cm (2in) piece ginger peeled and grated

50g (1¾oz) coriander (cilantro), finely chopped, plus leaves to serve

25g (¾oz) fresh mint leaves, finely chopped

1 tbsp dried pomegranate seeds, crushed (optional)

1 tsp ground cumin

1 tsp ground turmeric

½ tsp ground cinnamon

1 egg, beaten

2 tbsp gram flour

Sea salt and freshly ground black pepper

For the raita

250g (8¾oz) Greek yogurt

A handful of young borage leaves

A few mint leaves

1 tsp white wine vinegar

Sea salt and white pepper

To serve

Naan breads

Lemon wedges

Shredded lettuce

This recipe is based on the *chapli* kebab – a soft, flat kebab warmed with spices and flecked green by the copious amounts of herbs used. There are a lot of ingredients listed, but they are all very straightforward, with the exception of the pomegranate seeds. These add a slight sourness to the kebabs – if you can't get hold of them, sumac is a good substitute.

I serve this with a raita – but a raita with a difference. It is made from borage leaves instead of cucumber. They still offer succulence and the flavour is slightly sweeter and fresher. Borage self-seeds like crazy, so I am always looking for ways to use the leaves as well as the flowers. Pick them young and fresh before their hairs are too prickly, but don't worry too much, as once the leaves are shredded and stirred through the yogurt, the rough texture smooths out.

If you have one, put the lamb mince through a mincer attachment a couple of times – you want the texture to be very fine. A few blasts in a food processor will work.

Put the onion, tomato, chilli, garlic, ginger and herbs in a food processor and blitz until very finely chopped – you should end up with a coarse paste. Add this mixture to the lamb and add the spices, egg and gram flour along with lots of salt and pepper. Mix thoroughly – the best way to do this is to knead with your hands. The mixture will be very soft and sticky to start with but will firm up a little.

Chill the mixture in the fridge for as long as possible, preferably overnight. When you are ready to cook, divide the mixture into 8 pieces and flatten as much as you can – these kebabs are traditionally very flat and wide. Heat a griddle until it is too hot to hold your hand over, or heat some oil in a frying pan. Grill or fry the kebabs a few at a time – you need them to char slightly, not steam or boil in their own juices. Cook on the underside for 3–4 minutes, then cook for the same length of time on the other side.

To make the raita, simply stir all the ingredients together and season with a little salt and some white pepper.

Serve the kebabs with the raita, naan, lemon wedges, lettuce and extra coriander.

Stuffed Vine Leaves

Makes between 20–25

20–25 vine leaves, fresh or brined

2 tbsp olive oil

1 courgette (zucchini) (around 200g/7oz), finely diced

2 garlic cloves

50g (¼ cup) couscous

Zest and juice of 1 lemon

1 tsp dried mint

½ tsp ground cinnamon

2 tomatoes, finely chopped

A small bunch of basil, leaves finely chopped

A small bunch of dill, finely chopped

A few oregano leaves, finely chopped

A few lemon thyme leaves (optional)

50g (⅓ cup) pine nuts, lightly toasted

Sea salt and freshly ground black pepper

This is a fast and fresh take on stuffed vine leaves. It is one of those dishes in which temperature is very important – in fact, for a long time I did not like eating dolmas, simply because I was always served them chilled, and this adversely affects the texture. I like these crisp from the pan, as it means any slight stringiness in the leaves disappears.

You can use fresh or brined vine leaves for this. If you are using fresh, try to harvest early in the season when they are softer; the longer they stay in the sun, the tougher they become. Use medium-sized leaves – they will hold around a dessertspoonful of the filling.

I normally serve these as they are as a snack or hors d'oeuvre, but I do also eat them as part of a mezze. If you have any leftover filling, it makes a lovely salad.

First, prepare the vine leaves. Regardless of whether you are using fresh or brined leaves, wash thoroughly. Bring a large saucepan of water to the boil. Salt if using fresh leaves, then blanch for 5 minutes. Rinse in cold water.

Heat the olive oil in a frying pan and add the courgette. Season with plenty of salt and pepper, then cook, stirring regularly, until the courgette has browned and softened, around 8 minutes – when the colour of the oil deepens the courgette is usually ready. Add the garlic and stir for another couple of minutes, then remove from the heat.

Put the couscous in a bowl and cover with 4 tablespoons of just-boiled water. Cover with a plate. When it has absorbed all the liquid and is soft, fluff with a fork and add all the remaining ingredients. Season to taste.

To assemble, take a vine leaf and wipe it dry. Place it shiny-side down and remove the stem. Put a heaped dessertspoonful of the filling at the base of the leaf. Fold in the sides, then roll up quite tightly. Repeat.

To cook, heat 2 tablespoons olive oil in a cast-iron or non-stick frying pan over a medium heat. Fry the vine leaves for 5 minutes on each side until lightly browned and crisp. Serve immediately or allow to cool slightly.

Stuffed Flatbreads with Zhoug

Makes 8

For the flatbreads

500g (4¼ cups) strong white bread flour

1 tsp instant dried yeast

1 tsp salt

150g (5¼oz) plain yogurt

For the fillings

300g (10½oz) new potatoes, finely
diced

150g (5¼oz) hard goats' or ewes' cheese,
coarsely grated

150g (5¼oz) semi-soft goats' cheese,
coarsely grated

A small bunch of parsley, finely
chopped

A small bunch of coriander (cilantro),
finely chopped

A few sprigs of dill, finely chopped

½ tsp dried mint

Pinch of chilli flakes

1 x quantity Zhoug (see page 33)

**There are so many recipes for flatbreads, all of which
are variations on a theme. The dough for these is based
on a naan, as it contains yogurt, but the filling is closer
to the Turkish *gözleme*. You can either spread zhoug on
the flatbreads before folding them, or you can use it as
a dipping sauce – or you can do both.**

First, make the flatbread dough. Put the flour and yeast
into a bowl and mix. Add the salt. Mix the yogurt with
200ml (¾ cup) warm water, then gradually work this into
the flour. Knead until everything comes together in a sticky
dough that is smooth and no longer tacky – it should
take around 10 minutes. All of this can be done in a stand
mixer with the dough hook attachment, if you like.

Cover the dough with a damp tea towel and leave to
stand for an hour until it has increased in size and is
slightly puffy.

While the dough is rising, prepare the filling ingredients.
Put the diced potatoes in a saucepan and cover with water.
Bring to the boil and simmer until they are just tender –
probably 7–8 minutes. Drain and leave to cool.

Next, shape the dough. Knock it back and divide into
8 equal pieces. Roll out each one as flat as possible on
a floured work surface – you should end up with an oval
shape at least 20cm (8in) long. Sprinkle one half of each
of the flatbreads with the potatoes, cheese, herbs and chilli
flakes and spread with a little Zhoug, if you like, or save
for dipping. Fold the other half of the flatbread over the
filling and pinch the edges together, making sure you expel
any air as you do so.

To cook the flatbreads, heat a dry frying pan until hot.
Cook the flatbreads until they are speckled brown and
even lightly charred on one side before flipping over and
repeating. Keep warm under a tea towel while you cook
the rest.

Serve cut into strips with the Zhoug for dipping.

Herb Labneh with Leaves

Serves 4

For the labneh
1 tsp sea salt
1kg (2lb 3oz) Greek yogurt
Olive oil, to preserve

To decorate
A selection of finely chopped herbs,
   za'atar, dried herbs, dried rose
   petals, chilli flakes, sesame seeds,
   nigella seeds

To serve
A bunch of radishes
A selection of leaves, such as wild garlic
   if in season, carrot tops, parsley, mint,
   fennel, basil, dill, coriander (cilantro),
   radish leaves, young beetroot (beet)
   leaves, young chamomile fronds and
   French sorrel
A drizzle of olive oil

In the Middle East there is a dish called *sabzi kordhan*, which is simply a platter of herbs, perhaps with a few other bits and pieces to pair them with. It will often remain on the table throughout a meal, the leaves offering a mouthful of palate-cleansing freshness whenever necessary. I love this idea, and am in the habit of having some raw leaves to nibble on at mealtimes.

This is a celebration of the first leaves that come through in spring, both foraged and from the garden. I have made these little labneh balls to give the leaves something to wrap around, but I would happily just serve with a pile of radishes, perhaps with some tahini to dip them in, and plenty of sea salt.

To make the labneh, sterilise some cheese cloth or muslin by pouring boiling water over it and wringing it out. Use this to line a large sieve, then sit the sieve snugly over a bowl, making sure both will fit in your fridge.

Crumble up the salt and stir through the yogurt. You can also add any fresh or dried herbs at this point if you like – I prefer to leave additions to the coating. Pour the yogurt into the lined sieve and loosely cover with the overhang of the cloth.

Put in the fridge and leave to drain. For a very soft labneh, the texture of curd cheese, you only need to leave this for around 12 hours – for a firmer texture for rolling, you will need to leave it for up to 48 hours, but check after 24 – it really does depend on the yogurt you use. Remove the bowl from the fridge. Do not discard the whey, as it is a useful ingredient in its own right – I like to use it in breadmaking.

Shape tablespoons of the labneh into balls, then roll in your choice of coating. If I am going to use these straight away, I might use fresh herbs, otherwise I will use any or all of those listed. You can also leave them unadorned if you like. These will sit in the fridge, covered with a damp cloth, for a day or so – any longer and you should put them in a sterilised jar and cover with olive oil, kept in the fridge.

To serve, arrange on a board or platter with the radishes, salt and a generous selection of herbs and leaves.

Bagnetto with Bitter Crudités

Serves 4

40g (1½oz) flat leaf parsley

A few sprigs each of tarragon, basil and chervil (optional)

50g (1¾oz) capers

A few caper leaves (optional)

1 small tin of anchovies and their oil

2 tbsp Dijon mustard

2 tbsp tomato purée

1 tbsp red wine vinegar

1 tsp dried thyme or a few dried thyme flower heads

½ tsp chilli flakes, plus a little more to taste, if desired

½ tsp freshly ground white pepper

4 tbsp olive oil

A pinch of caster (superfine) sugar (optional)

Sea salt (optional)

To serve

A few heads of Belgian endive, separated into leaves, or cut into thin wedges, or any other kind of crisp winter leaves, such as slender, curling tardivo (fiori d'Inverno) or puntarelle

I was smitten by this dip when I first discovered it in Kate and Giancarlo Caldesi's *Gentle Art of Preserving*, **and I've been making variations on it ever since. The flavour really is incredible – richly savoury, spicy, salty, tinged with sweetness – so, to completely satisfy the palate is to serve it with something succulent and bitter.**

A few tasting notes: the seasoning for this very much depends on the ingredients you pick. I use my favourite Greek capers, which are preserved in olive oil (and so less vinegary/acidic). I also use anchovies in oil too, so I do sometimes need to add salt at the end. If you use the salted sort of either, it is likely you will not need to. As the sauce should also have a hint of sweetness, I have included basil, tarragon and chervil to add this in place of sugar – if you don't include these, you might want to add a pinch. But allowing the dip to stand briefly and tasting, tasting, tasting, are key.

Finely chop all the herbs, capers, caper leaves, if using, and the anchovies. Put in a bowl and add the mustard, tomato purée, vinegar, thyme, chilli flakes and white pepper. Stir to combine, then whisk in the olive oil.

Leave to stand for a few minutes, then taste. If you haven't used the sweeter herbs you may need to add a pinch of sugar, and if you haven't used salted capers or anchovies, you may want to add salt. Adjust according to your taste and transfer to a serving bowl, or for future use, a sterilised jar.

Arrange the endives on a platter and serve with the dip.

If you have any left, store in a sterilised jar in the fridge, covered with a little olive oil.

Patra

Serves 4

12 colocasia leaves, or alternatives
(see introduction)

3 tbsp olive or vegetable oil

1 tsp mustard seeds

A few coriander (cilantro) leaves,
to serve

A few wedges of lime, to serve

For the paste

150g (1¼ cups) gram flour

1 tsp ground cumin

1 tsp ground coriander

1 tsp chilli powder (or to taste)

½ tsp ground turmeric

½ tsp ground cinnamon

½ tsp asafoetida

1 tsp jaggery or light soft brown sugar

1 tsp sea salt

2 garlic cloves, grated or crushed

5cm (2in) piece ginger, peeled
and grated

1 tbsp tamarind purée

This is one of the few traditional dishes I haven't messed around with too much, but please see the variation for a more European-centric version. These rolls are usually made with elephant ear leaves that can be found in many Asian shops. Here in the UK they are labelled *patra*, which is really the name of the dish, not the leaf. The leaf is elephant ear or colocasia, which is the giant leaf of various giant tubers, also called dasheen and taro.

These leaves are not easy to find, but you can substitute any very large, long leaf, such as chard or collards, or follow chef and author Jane Baxter's advice and use large spring green leaves.

These are sometimes diced and stir fried, but I prefer to leave them in rounds.

First, prepare the leaves. Wash and dry thoroughly, or wipe over with a damp cloth. Remove any very thick veins. Leave under a damp tea towel until you are ready to use them.

Make the paste. Mix the gram flour with the spices, sugar and salt. Work in enough water to make a paste that is quite liquid but still thick enough to spread and stick to the leaves. Start with 100ml (scant ½ cup) and add more if necessary. Stir in the garlic, ginger and tamarind.

To assemble, take a leaf with the underside facing upwards and the tip of the leaf facing you. If you have had to remove much of the centre vein, pull the two sides together so they overlap slightly. Spread a thin layer of the paste over the leaf, making sure it is completely coated. Take another leaf and this time make sure the tip is facing away from you. Lay on top of the first leaf, cover with paste and then do the same for 2 more leaves, making sure you lay them in the opposite direction each time.

Next fold and roll. Fold in the sides to create two straight lines, then start rolling up from the bottom. Add a little paste as you roll, so the leaf is completely covered. Continue with the remaining leaves until you have 3 rolls.

Put the rolls into a steamer – you may need to cut them in half for them to fit, this is perfectly okay. Steam for around 20–25 minutes – this will both cook the leaves and bind the rolls together so they will not break apart during the next stage of cooking.

Cool the rolls, then cut into 1cm (½in) slices. Heat the oil in a large frying pan and add the mustard seeds. When they start to pop, start adding the patra slices. Fry until golden brown on each side – you will probably have to do this in 2–3 batches. Drain on kitchen towel and serve sprinkled with coriander leaves and lime wedges on the side.

Variation
This works pretty well with a slightly different flavour, more herbal than sour. You can substitute the gram flour for split green pea flour (easily available or grind your own) and replacing the spices to include black pepper, cinnamon, allspice and a pinch of clove. Keep the garlic and replace the fresh ginger with 1 teaspoon ground ginger and add 1 teaspoon Dijon mustard. Use the juice of 1 lemon in place of the tamarind, then proceed as above and serve with lots of chopped parsley instead of coriander, and lemon wedges in place of lime.

Panisse with Green Mayonnaise

Serves 4

A small bunch of parsley, leaves only, very finely chopped

200g (1¾ cups) gram flour

Olive oil, for frying

Sea salt

For the green mayonnaise

2 tbsp finely chopped parsley

2 tbsp finely chopped tarragon

1 tbsp finely chopped chervil

1 tbsp finely chopped dill

1 egg yolk

1 small garlic clove, finely grated or crushed

1 tsp Dijon mustard

1 tsp white wine vinegar

250ml (1 cup) neutral-tasting oil, such as sunflower

A small bunch of watercress, leaves only, blanched, squeezed dry and very finely chopped

A squeeze of lemon juice

Sea salt

A favourite snack from the south of France, panisse are traditionally left to set in rounds on saucers, but I've always shaped them in a large rectangle so they are easier to cut into chips rather than uneven-shaped wedges. The joy of these is their lightness – if made correctly, the crust will be thick, cracked and crisp, and the centre will be almost hollow. Try to serve these immediately as they can quickly turn leaden. I serve them in the kitchen, turning out batches so people can eat as I fry.

Put the herbs, egg yolk, garlic, mustard and vinegar into a food processor or bowl with a pinch of salt. Start adding the oil, a few drops at a time until you have an emulsion, then keep adding the oil very gradually, whisking constantly or keeping the motor of your food processor running, until all the oil is incorporated. Add the watercress then taste and adjust for seasoning with lemon and salt. Set aside.

Lightly oil a 30 x 20cm (12 x 8in) roasting tin.

Put the parsley into a small food processor and add 100ml (scant ½ cup) tepid water. Blitz until finely flecked. Add a further 650ml (2¾ cups) tepid water and swill to combine.

Sift the gram flour into a saucepan and add 1 teaspoon salt. Start whisking in the water, trickling it in gradually; the odd lump will not be an issue here; this is a very forgiving batter. When you have a thick paste, add the remaining water at a faster pace, still whisking all the time, until you have a smooth, runny batter. When all the water has been incorporated, put the saucepan over a medium heat and stir constantly. Be patient; the batter will suddenly thicken. Continue to whisk until a spoon stands up in it.

Remove from the heat and scrape the mixture into your oiled tin and spread evenly. Cover with a damp tea towel or plastic wrap and leave to stand for around half an hour, until it has cooled and set. It will be firm to touch.

Cut the panisse into strips the size of thick chips. Pour olive oil into a large frying pan to a thickness of around 1cm (½ in). Fry in batches, flipping them over until they are a deep golden brown – the texture will be rough and slightly cracked in places, but this is part of their charm. Sprinkle with salt and serve immediately with the mayonnaise.

Fragrant Pork and Prawn Balls
Wrapped in Pandan Leaf

Serves 4

200g (7oz) minced (ground) pork

100g (3½oz) peeled and cooked
cold water (North Atlantic) prawns
(shrimp), very finely chopped

1 lemongrass stalk, white inside only,
finely chopped

2 garlic cloves, grated

15g (½oz) piece ginger, peeled and
grated

10 laksa leaves, finely chopped

A few coriander (cilantro) or saw-
toothed coriander leaves, finely
chopped

2 tbsp cornflour (cornstarch)

1 egg white

3 tbsp pandan extract (see below)

12 pandan leaves, for wrapping

Sea salt and freshly ground black
pepper

For the extract

6 pandan leaves, finely chopped

For the dipping sauce

2 tbsp fish sauce

1 tbsp kecap manis

Juice of ½ lime

½ tsp chilli flakes or 1 tsp hot sauce

**These little meat and prawn balls rely on a double
whammy of pandan – the whole leaves do provide a
subtle flavour and aroma during the cooking process,
but it is the extract that really ramps it up. These balls
are wonderful on their own as a snack, but they are
also really good in a pandan-flavoured broth.**

**I have done my best to describe exactly how to wrap
the pandan leaves around the balls, but I recommend
you do an internet search for pandan-wrapped chicken
– there are some excellent demonstrations available
that will make the whole process much clearer.**

First, make the extract. Finely chop the pandan leaves
then put in a blender or food processor with 100ml
(scant ½ cup) water and blitz until you have a bright
green, runny paste. Push through a sieve to extract as
much liquid as possible.

To make the balls, mix the pork, prawns and aromatics
together with plenty of salt and pepper and the cornflour.
Whisk the egg white and pandan extract together and add
this to the pork mixture. Combine thoroughly, preferably
mixing with your hands in a kneading motion until the
mixture is soft but well combined. Chill for half an hour
to firm up a little, then divide into 12 balls and chill again.

Take a pandan leaf and hold it shiny-side down with the
base end on your left. Bringing the two ends towards you,
cross the ends over, creating a loop. The base end should be
on top and kept quite short – around 10cm (4in). Take the
longer end and tuck it through the base of the loop – this
will create a pocket. Drop the prawn ball into the pocket,
then pull the rest of the leaf through until quite snug. Turn
the pocket over and tuck the same length in through the
back, then over and through the front. Pull it quite tight
and then trim. Repeat with the rest of the leaves.

Bring a saucepan of water to the boil and set a steamer
over the top. Add the balls and steam for 10 minutes.

While the balls are cooking, make the dipping sauce.
Mix all the ingredients together. Season to taste. Leave
to stand until ready to serve, then unwrap and eat.

Mushroom 'Larb' with Shiso Leaves

Serves 4

1 tbsp basmati rice

2 tbsp groundnut oil

200g (7oz) field mushrooms, finely chopped

2 garlic cloves, finely chopped

3cm (1¼in) piece ginger, peeled and finely chopped

1 tbsp light soy sauce

1 tbsp lime juice

1 tsp smooth peanut butter

4 spring onions (scallions), finely chopped

2 tbsp peanuts, finely chopped

For the garnishes (all optional)

A few coriander (cilantro) leaves

A few mint leaves

A few Thai basil leaves

Baby shiso leaves or shredded salted shiso leaves (see page 22)

1 green chilli, finely chopped

I often find myself confounded by the myriad flavours that I taste in shiso leaves. I detect something different every time – sometimes the floral, spicy notes of mint, basil and cinnamon are the most pronounced, sometimes I can taste blackcurrant. Green shiso in particular has a deep note of peanut about it that is almost meaty; the red shiso in contrast has a Szechuan-esque lift to it, providing that mouth-tingling freshness. Consequently, it isn't always easy to figure out what to pair with them. The savouriness of this larb works really well, and suggest you try your first one without any of the garnishes so as not to mask it. I have started growing my own shiso and use their microleaves when very young – they add an extra intensity.

Shiso leaves look like plump nettle leaves and have a similar texture. When eating raw, make sure they are fresh and not dry, or they will feel tickly in the mouth and throat. If you just have a few and would rather use them in the larb, use lettuce leaves for wrapping.

If you are not vegetarian, you might want to use fish sauce in place of the soy sauce. I also think that shiso leaves work well with beef, so if you want to finely dice a piece of steak in place of the mushrooms, be my guest.

Put a non-stick frying pan over a medium heat. When it is hot, add the rice and toast until it smells rich and nutty, then remove from the heat and cool. Crush lightly with a pestle and mortar and set aside.

Heat the oil in a large frying pan. When it is hot to the point that the air is shimmering above it, add the mushrooms, making sure they are well spread out – you need them to brown and crisp, not to wallow in a pool of their own making. Stir fry for several minutes, then add the garlic and ginger. Mix the soy sauce with the lime juice and peanut butter until you have a smooth, runny paste, then pour this over the mushrooms. Continue to cook until there is no visible liquid in the pan. Remove from the heat and stir in the spring onions, peanuts and toasted rice.

Arrange on a platter with any of the garnishes and the shiso leaves. Eat by piling a spoonful onto a shiso leaf and eating in one mouthful.

Cime di Rapa and Scamorza Croquetas

Serves 4

1 large bunch of cime di rapa (broccoli rabe), roughly chopped

600ml (2½ cups) whole (full-fat) milk

2 bay leaves

1 slice of onion

A few peppercorns

7 tbsp butter

100g (¾ cup) plain (all-purpose) flour

1 ball of smoked scamorza

Olive oil, for frying

Sea salt and freshly ground black pepper

For the coating

100g (¾ cup) plain (all-purpose) flour

2 eggs

100g (½ cup) fine, dry breadcrumbs (not panko)

It is hard not to risk a mouth burn by eating these straight out of the fryer but, if you can, wait for them to cool a little – you will better appreciate the flavours. I love how the soothing béchamel wraps itself around the bitter, vegetal cime di rapa and smoky cheese.

Bring a saucepan of water to the boil and add salt. Add the cime di rapa and cook until tender, around 4–5 minutes. Drain thoroughly and leave to cool. Squeeze as much water out as possible – this is important, as if it is too wet it may cause the croquetas to burst. Chop finely and set aside.

Put the milk in a saucepan with the bay, onion and peppercorns. Warm to almost boiling then remove from the heat and leave to infuse until cool. Strain. Melt the butter in a saucepan, then add the flour. Stir over a medium heat until combined and the flour has lost some of its raw flavour, then start adding the milk gradually. Pour in a ladleful, leave it to sit until it starts to bubble, then stir like crazy. You'll end up with a thick but pourable béchamel.

Season the béchamel with salt and pepper. Stir in the cime di rapa and the cheese. Line a shallow baking dish with plastic wrap, then lightly oil it. Spread the mixture over this then put another piece of oiled plastic wrap directly on top to prevent a skin forming. Leave to cool, then chill in the fridge for several hours, or preferably overnight.

When ready to cook, either preheat your oven to 220°C (440°F/Gas 7) and lightly oil a couple of baking (cookie) sheets or fill a fryer with oil and heat to 180°C (375°F).

Remove the top layer of plastic wrap, then flip the béchamel over onto a work surface. Remove the other layer of plastic wrap, then cut into around 30 squares. Put half the flour, eggs, and breadcrumbs onto separate plates. Take each square, roll roughly into a ball, then dip in the flour. Pat off any excess, dip in the eggs, then roll in breadcrumbs. Repeat with the remaining mixture.

If baking, drizzle the croquetas with oil and cook for around 15 minutes. Alternatively, deep fry a few at a time for 3–4 minutes – either way they should be brown and crisp. Drain on kitchen towel, cool slightly and serve.

Baked Cheese with Thyme and Honey

Serves 4

400g (14oz) baby new, salad or
  fingerling potatoes

2 tbsp olive oil

1 tsp mixed dried thyme, rosemary,
  oregano

1 large, ripe, rinded cheese – choose
  anything from Camembert, Brie,
  Baron Bigod (my favourite but
  expensive), preferably boxed

2 garlic cloves

A few firm sprigs of thyme and/or
  rosemary

Thick stems from a bunch of chard,
  trimmed

1 tbsp lemon juice

100ml (⅓ cup) honey, preferably
  thyme honey

Sea salt

**This is an excellent way of using up chard stems if
you are making a separate dish that only requires the
leaves. Try also cooking the same way and eating with
Bagnetto (see page 64), Anchovy Dressing (see page
130) or Buttery Anchovy Sauce (see page 225).**

Preheat the oven to 180°C (350°F/Gas 4).

Bring a saucepan of water to the boil, then add the
potatoes. Boil for 5 minutes, then drain thoroughly. Put
in a large roasting tin and drizzle with 1 tablespoon of
the olive oil and the dried herbs. Roast for 25 minutes.

Prepare the cheese as soon as you've put the potatoes in
the oven. Make slits in the top rind and push in slivers
of garlic and sprigs of thyme and or rosemary, reserving
one to infuse the honey. Leave the cheese in the base of
its box if it has it, otherwise wrap it in a single layer of
foil, leaving the top exposed. Place in the middle of the
potatoes and bake for around 20 minutes, until you can
tell that it is very soft and melted when you press it.

Meanwhile, prepare the chard. Bring a saucepan of water
to the boil and add plenty of salt, the lemon juice and the
trimmed chard stems. Cook for around 2 minutes. Drain
and dry thoroughly. Heat a griddle pan until it is too hot
to hold your hand over. Add the chard stems and griddle
until they are lightly charred.

Dress the chard in the remaining olive oil. In a small
saucepan over a low heat, warm the honey through with
the thyme or rosemary sprig, and either leave on the side
or drizzle over the baked cheese. Serve the cheese with
the potatoes and chard around it.

Cabbage Potstickers

Makes around 45 dumplings

150g (1¼ cups) strong white flour

150g (1¼ cups) plain (all-purpose) flour, plus extra for stacking and rolling

½ tsp sea salt

OR a packet of 50 gyoza wrappers

Oil, for frying

For the filling

100g (3½oz) Chinese cabbage, shredded

100g (3½oz) Kimchi or any other fermented green (see pages 30 and 27), finely chopped

200g (7oz) pork mince

4cm (1½in) piece ginger, peeled and grated

2 garlic cloves, grated

2 long Chinese chives or 4 spring onions (scallions), finely chopped

1 egg

Sea salt and freshly ground black pepper

For the dipping sauce

2 tbsp soy sauce

1 tbsp rice wine

1 tsp rice wine vinegar

1 tsp sesame oil

1 tbsp chilli oil, preferably with chilli flakes

A handful of laksa leaves (optional)

I am always fascinated by the connections between different cultures and cuisines – how they overlap, develop similar ideas to one another, independently or through copying and adapting. The treatment of cabbage is a good example of this – we are told that the process of fermenting cabbage into sauerkraut is a Chinese one, reaching Europe via the Mongols and Genghis Khan, but there is no such route with the similar kimchi. Likewise dumplings – did all the Eastern European versions originate in China, or did they develop independently? There is no doubt that all the Asian variants – the Japanese *gyoza*, the Korean *mandu*, the Chinese *jiaozi* – have a lot in common with the Eastern European *pierogi*, and not just because of the simplicity of the wrappers, but because the traditional ingredients frequently include pork and both fresh and fermented cabbage.

I have flavoured these dumplings with kimchi, but I would use any of the fermented greens – wild garlic sauerkraut is particularly good. Although the laksa leaf is not a regular ingredient of a dumpling dipping sauce, I love it.

A note on the wrappers. I am afraid I do often just buy them. I find the filling and sealing of dumplings a pleasant if time-consuming job, but the making and rolling of the dough often seems a step too far, especially when it is so easy to buy perfectly round ones. So I have provided a recipe for the dough, but have used an inauthentic and straightforward rolling and cutting method for the wrappers.

Start with the wrappers, if making. Put the flours into a bowl. Dissolve the salt in 150ml (⅔ cup) just-boiled water and gradually work into the flour, cutting in with a knife until it is all combined into a dough. Cover with a damp cloth and leave to stand for 10 minutes then knead for 10 minutes, until it is smooth and elastic. Cover again and leave to rest for 1 hour.

When you want to form the wrappers, cut the dough into 4 even pieces and roll out thinly on a floured work surface. Using an 8cm (3in) diameter cutter, cut rounds. You can stack these dusted with flour until you need them – wrapped in plastic wrap they store very well in the freezer.

To make the filling, put the cabbage in a colander and sprinkle with salt. Leave to stand for an hour, then squeeze out any excess liquid and finely chop. Put in a bowl with the remaining ingredients with plenty of seasoning and mix well.

To assemble, take a wrapper and put a heaped teaspoon of the mixture into it. Moisten the edges with water, then close firmly together, pleating on one side as you go. Place on a baking tray until you are ready to cook them.

Mix together the dipping sauce ingredients and set aside.

To cook, put a thin layer of vegetable oil in a cast-iron or non-stick frying pan over a medium heat. When hot, add a batch of the dumplings, being careful not to over-crowd the pan. Fry until a good crust has developed on the underside of the dumplings, then pour in water – just enough to cover the base of the pan, no more – then cover and steam for up to 5 minutes, until the dumplings are glossy and all the water has evaporated. Cook uncovered for another minute to make sure the bottoms of the dumplings are crisp.

Serve with the dipping sauce.

Variations

I can't resist playing around with these – in my house they are different every time. I like a vegan version, 100 per cent cabbage, which is easily done if you take out the pork and so double the amount of both cabbage and kimchi – or just use cabbage. Or replace the pork with mushrooms: chop very finely, cook in a tablespoon of oil until the mushrooms are dry, then mix with the cabbage.

And if you want to make them with sauerkraut, take out the ginger and chives/spring onions. Fry a finely chopped onion in butter. Soak a few dried mushrooms in warm water, then strain, reserving the liquid and finely chop. Add to the onions with their liquid and cook off until dry. Mix with the pork and sauerkraut, or just the sauerkraut and proceed as above, cooking in exactly the same way (non-traditional, I know, but I like the crisp underside). To serve, melt butter and add to it finely chopped dill or parsley, or both.

Herb Pies

Serves 4

1 x 375g (13oz) block all-butter puff pastry

3 hard-boiled eggs, shelled and very finely chopped

Leaves from 4 bunches of tarragon – you need 60g (2oz) in total, or replace half the tarragon with a mixture of chervil, parsley, dill, basil or mint

4 spring onions (scallions), very finely chopped

Beaten egg

Sea salt and freshly ground black pepper

These little pies are inspired by the Georgian tarragon pie. I have taken the simplicity from this dish – the filling is literally tarragon, hard-boiled eggs and spring onions – and adapted to make small puff pastry pies instead. This makes them very portable and perfectly suited for picnics and lunchboxes. And while I love the all-tarragon pies, I do mix it up with other herbs sometimes, so you might want to replace some of the tarragon with a mixture of chervil, parsley, dill, basil, perhaps a touch of mint. As long as the end quantity is the same, it really is up to you.

Preheat the oven to 180°C (375°F/Gas 4).

First roll out two thirds of the pastry on a floured work surface and cut out 12 circles, 8cm (3in) in diameter. Use these to line a 12-hole muffin tin, making sure you push the pastry right into the corners. Set aside.

Reserve 12 leaves or fronds for decoration, then finely chop all the herbs and mix with the hard-boiled eggs and spring onions. Season well with plenty of salt and pepper. Spoon the mixture into the pastry cases, making sure you leave a border at the top.

Roll out the remaining pastry and cut 12 rounds, this time smaller, around 6.5cm (2½in). Brush egg wash around the rim of the filled pastry and top with the smaller rounds, crimping the edges together. Place a leaf on top of each pie, then brush the whole thing with egg wash. Make a small incision in each pie to allow steam to escape during the cooking process.

Bake in the oven for around 20–25 minutes, until the pies are well risen and a deep golden brown. Leave to cool in the tin. Eat at room temperature.

BASIL

Oh dear, basil. Basil is the herb above all others that I have struggled to like. It amazes me even now how much it is beloved; how the pickiest of young children seem to eat basil-rich pesto with absolutely no trouble at all (I still don't much like basil-based pesto. There, I said it). I attribute my dislike to early experiences. I have worked hard over the past 35 years to overcome these erroneous early impressions. I say erroneous, but I am not sure, because really, I feel a bit bullied by basil. I always have. Because it is always there, hard to ignore if you love Italian food (I do). We, as a nation, wholeheartedly embraced it when we fell in love with all things Italian, and it has been ubiquitous ever since. Why? How did this happen?

My first experience of basil was as a potted herb, and it was overwhelming. I think I was around 12 years old. Basil at that stage was not part of the culinary landscape of early eighties Lincolnshire. I don't think I'd ever knowingly seen it draped over a pizza, and I certainly hadn't eaten it dried in a jarred pasta sauce – what was that? We were staying with friends and there was a strange smell emanating from their kitchen. It was tenacious and overpowering, and no one else seemed to notice it. I can smell it now – cloyingly sweet, sickly, unpleasantly spicy – not quite cloves, not quite cinnamon. It clung to the inside of my nose and would not leave. It made me feel sick and I hated it. I looked forward to escaping from it.

This was a pot of basil. Not the tender, mildly perfumed basil we buy these days, all floppy and unthreatening, but a proper plant, with flowers and spikier, lighter-coloured leaves. I now know that it had spent some time outside. I also now know that the scent of basil does change when it flowers – for the worse, as far as I'm concerned. I have never really overcome it. I think the final straw came a year or so into actively disliking it, when I read Keats' poem 'Isabella, or the Pot of Basil', and for the longest time couldn't look at basil without seeing a decaying head underneath it, 'vile with green and livid spot', roots entwining round Lorenzo's hair and poking out through his eye sockets. Basil, opportunistic and lush, flourishing on all that organic matter. I clearly had an overactive imagination.

It wasn't long after this first encounter that my mother started growing basil and making both pesto and pizza regularly. Fortunately, in our household there was no question of the dried stuff in artificial jarred sauces – we didn't do that. However, it did feel that basil was suddenly everywhere. It was chopped (or torn if we're going to be precious about its poor tender leaves) with abandon into our tomato sauces. The Italians must think we're mad – as the food stylist for this book, Marina Filippelli, told me – a leaf or two added towards the end for a hint of flavour is all that is necessary. And thanks to the *tricolore* salad, we treat it as the only herb we can serve with tomatoes. I aim to put a stop to that nonsense (see pages 139–40).

I understand basil better these days. I like the bursts of flavour it gives as a microherb, and I quite like the regular sweet, Genovese basil in moderation when the leaves are soft and rounded and nowhere near to bolting. I know that if I grow it outside it will become tough and spikier, both in appearance, and flavour and that if it flowers, forget it – I don't want to be anywhere near it. I know that if I want basil raw in salads, I am better off with the small leaves of bush basil, and that my favourite of the lot is Thai basil. I also know that at least a couple of times a year, I will catch a whiff of that smell from decades ago and wish I hadn't.

Samphire with Courgettes, Basil and Brown Shrimp

Serves 4

1 tbsp olive oil

1½ tbsp butter

4 small courgettes (zucchini), thinly sliced into rounds

1 garlic clove, finely chopped

Zest of ½ lemon

A few small basil leaves

150g (5¼oz) samphire

100g (3½oz) small brown shrimp

Grated nutmeg

Sea salt and freshly ground black pepper

Eat this as a very light lunch or starter, or you could add it to spaghetti or linguine. If you wanted less of a salty punch – and samphire can pack a punch, as the intensity of its salty bitterness varies enormously – you can reduce the amount of samphire and double the amount of courgette (zucchini). You can also try this dish with agretti (also known as monk's beard), cooking in exactly the same way, or sea spaghetti, which will need soaking time if dried, and will take longer to cook.

Heat the olive oil and butter in a large lidded frying pan over a medium heat. Add the courgettes and season generously with salt and pepper. Cook the courgettes slowly, stirring regularly, until they take on a luscious, velvety texture and are almost, but not quite, on the point of collapsing, then stir through the garlic, lemon and basil.

While the courgettes are cooking, bring a saucepan of water to the boil. Salt the water then add the samphire – cook for a scant minute. Drain thoroughly then add to the courgettes. Stir through very gently then scatter over the shrimp and grate over a little nutmeg. Serve on its own with some bread, or serve over linguine or spaghetti.

NOTE: if you want to serve this with spaghetti or linguine, cook the pasta as you would normally, but then add the samphire for the last minute. This will save on water, fuel and washing up.

Herb Tempura

Serves 4

50g (scant ½ cup) plain (all-purpose) flour

50g (scant ½ cup) cornflour (cornstarch)

1 egg

175ml (¾ cup) chilled sparkling water

A selection of herbs, including sage, thyme, lemon thyme, dill, parsley, chives, fennel, lovage and oregano

Neutral-tasting oil, such as sunflower, for deep frying

Lemon wedges, to serve (optional)

Sea salt

These can be gutsy, flavour-packed mouthfuls or something much more ethereal, depending on what type of herb you choose. The choice of herb and how you prepare it is quite important. Some herbs are best fried as single leaves – sage, basil, parsley, perhaps larger lovage leaves or young sorrel. Others should be fried as sprigs, but if you do this, make sure you have soft, tender stems, nothing woody – be especially careful with the thymes and rosemary.

I usually resist serving these with anything, but a squeeze of lemon would be just about okay. You can also serve them at the other end of the meal, sprinkled with caster (superfine) sugar.

Whisk the flour to remove any lumps and season with salt. Work in the egg, then the water, being careful not to over-mix, until you have a consistency between double (heavy) and single (light) cream.

Heat the oil to 180°C (375°F) in a deep saucepan, wok or fryer. Dip the herbs (leaves or sprigs, see the introduction) in the batter, shaking off any excess, and fry a few at a time until lightly golden brown and floating at the top of the oil.

Drain on kitchen towel and serve immediately, sprinkled with salt and lemon wedges, if you like.

SOUPS

Herb Soup

Serves 4

2 tbsp olive oil

1 large onion, thinly sliced

3 garlic cloves, finely chopped

1 tsp ground turmeric

½ tsp ground cinnamon

1 tsp dried mint

1 litre (4 cups) vegetable or chicken stock

300g (10½oz) frozen chopped spinach, defrosted

150g (5¼oz) parsley, leaves only, finely chopped

100g (3½oz) coriander (cilantro), leaves only, finely chopped

50g (1¾oz) dill, leaves only, finely chopped

300g (10½oz) broad (fava) beans, blanched and peeled

200g (7oz) cooked green lentils

Juice of 1 lemon, to taste

Sea salt and freshly ground black pepper

To serve

A few tbsp yogurt

A few tsp Green Harissa (see page 34)

Lamb Meatballs (optional, see Variation)

Possibly the most important thing I have learned from Middle Eastern cooks is that herbs are more than just flavouring – they should be an integral part of the dish. In some greengrocers or corner-shops, you can buy generous bunches of all kinds of herbs at a fraction of the price of the mean-looking offerings available in most supermarkets. It this abundance that you need here.

I limit the spices in this soup so the combined flavours of the herbs really come to the fore, but I do like to pep it up with the Green Harissa on page 34. If you add this, you may not need a squeeze of lemon. I find adding citrus hard to resist, so I have both.

This soup also works as a sauce when reduced down, and I will use it to enrobe various things, including lamb meatballs or pieces of spiced, lightly grilled fish.

Heat the olive oil in a large casserole dish (Dutch oven) or saucepan. Add the onion and cook over a gentle heat until it is very soft and translucent, around 10 minutes. Add the garlic and cook for a further couple of minutes, then stir in the spices and mint. Pour over the stock and season with plenty of salt and pepper. Bring to the boil, then turn down and simmer for 5 minutes.

Add the spinach and two thirds of the herbs. Simmer for around 10 minutes – this seems counter-intuitive, but it is traditionally cooked for much, much longer. Add the broad beans and lentils. Continue to simmer until everything is heated through, then add the rest of the herbs. Check for seasoning, add lemon juice to taste and serve.

Variation

If you want to add meatballs to this, you can do so either as a soup, or you can use half the amount of stock and serve it as a sauce. To make the meatballs, mix 250g (8¾oz) lamb mince with 50g (⅓ cup) breadcrumbs, 3 grated garlic cloves, 1 teaspoon dried mint and 3 tablespoons finely chopped coriander (cilantro) stems. Bind together with an egg yolk and 25g (¾oz) soft goats' cheese. Make sure you season generously. Form into walnut-sized balls, then fry in plenty of olive oil, before heating through with the sauce. Sprinkle with sumac or pomegranate seeds.

Leek, Chard and Tarragon Soup
with Wild Garlic Pesto

Serves 4

1 tbsp olive oil

1½ tbsp butter

2 leeks, thinly sliced

1.5 litres (6 cups) well-flavoured chicken stock

A large pinch of saffron, soaked in 2 tbsp hot water

1 strip of lemon zest

A small bunch of tarragon, stems and leaves separated

A small bunch of baby chard leaves

3 small courgettes (zucchini), sliced into rounds

75g (2½oz) baby broad (fava) beans, blanched and skinned

50g (1¾oz) fresh peas

200g (7oz) cooked chicken (optional)

For the pesto

100g (3½oz) wild garlic (a mixture of leaves, stems and buds)

50g (1¾oz) Cornish Yarg, crumbled

50g (1¾oz) blanched hazelnuts or cobnuts, lightly toasted

Zest and juice of ½ lemon

Olive oil

To serve

A few small leaves of wild garlic

A few wild garlic flowers (optional)

Black tahini paste (optional)

I have always loved the combination of tarragon and garlic, and I have come to believe that tarragon with wild garlic is even better. It is one of the best butters you can make every spring (see page 20) and the combination also works well in this soup. It is a challenge to get the flavour of wild garlic into a soup like this as the flavour does disappear with heat (more on this on page 151) – the solution is to stir in this pesto just before serving.

The wild garlic pesto can be used in myriad ways, just like a regular pesto, but I would avoid using it in anything that involves much cooking – the flavour is much better fresh and raw, or just warmed through.

To make the pesto, roughly chop the wild garlic and put in a food processor. Blitz for a few seconds until it is starting to break down, then add the cheese, hazelnuts and lemon zest. Blitz again until everything is ground down to the texture of coarse breadcrumbs. Add the lemon juice, then with the motor running, drizzle in olive oil until you have the texture you like. I prefer it thick enough to stay on a spoon, so I only add 2–3 tablespoons, but add as much as you like. Transfer to a sterilised jar if you want to store it – it will be fine in the fridge for several weeks.

To make the soup, put the oil and butter in a large casserole (Dutch oven). Heat gently. When the butter has melted and started to foam, add the leeks. Cover and leave to braise for around 10 minutes, stirring and checking every so often, until the leeks are just tender.

Pour over the chicken stock, along with the saffron and its soaking water, the lemon zest and the tarragon stems. Simmer for 5 minutes, uncovered, then add the chard leaves, courgettes, broad beans and peas. Continue to simmer until the vegetables are still al dente and have retained their bright, fresh green, another 5 minutes. Add the cooked chicken, if using, and allow it to heat through in the broth.

Finely chop the tarragon leaves and stir through the soup. Remove the tarragon stems from the soup, then serve garnished with a few wild garlic flowers and leaves, with the pesto and the black tahini paste on the side, to be added at the table.

Pea and Lettuce Soup
with Sorrel Cream

Serves 4

1 tbsp olive oil

1 tbsp butter

3 leeks, white parts only, sliced into
rounds

100ml (scant ½ cup) vermouth

1 garlic clove, crushed or grated

4 little gem lettuces, thoroughly washed
and cut into thin wedges

500g (1lb 1½oz) petit pois

850ml (3½ cups) vegetable stock

A few mint leaves

For the sorrel cream

A handful of sorrel leaves

200ml (¾ cup) whipping (heavy) cream

Sea salt and freshly ground black
pepper

This a soup perfect for late spring, when lemony sorrel comes to life, the peas are small and sweet, and the lettuce has yet to become bitter with milk.

There is a temptation to blend a soup such as this, but if you do, you lose the benefit of the silky texture of the wilted lettuce and the tenderness of braised leeks and peas. However, as I do think the soup needs some thickening, I compromise and purée some of the peas before adding them to the pan.

Put the olive oil and butter in a large saucepan or casserole (Dutch oven). Add the leeks and cook over a medium heat for 5 minutes, then add the vermouth and cover. Turn down the heat and leave for 15 minutes to braise gently until soft.

Add the garlic and cook for a minute, then add the little gems. Turn up the heat a little and add two thirds of the petit pois and 700ml (2¾ cups) of the stock. Blitz the remaining petit pois and stock together and add to the soup. Simmer until the little gems are tender.

Finely chop the sorrel leaves and put in a small saucepan with the cream and a little seasoning, to taste. Heat very gently, swirling the herbs around the cream.

Serve the soup with the sorrel cream and a few mint leaves.

Variation

The base of this soup will also make a side dish, with or without the peas. Follow the recipe until you get to the point when you add the peas. Add two thirds of the peas (you won't need the rest) with just 100ml (scant ½ cup) stock. Simmer until the little gems are tender, then either add 100ml (scant ½ cup) cream, or make a half portion of the sorrel cream and stir that through at the end. Any sweet herb will work really well with this in place of the mint – try tarragon or chervil or even something more aniseedy like fennel fronds or anise hyssop.

French Sorrel Soup

Serves 4

1 tbsp olive oil

A thick slice of butter

1 onion, very finely chopped

1 large bunch of sorrel, around 400g (14oz), very finely chopped

1 litre (4 cups) vegetable or chicken stock

3 egg yolks

Juice of ½ lemon

Borage Leaf Raita (see page 58) or sour cream, to serve

A few sprigs of dill, to serve

Salt and freshly ground black pepper

Sorrel grows like a weed in my garden – one sowing and it just keeps coming back. So does borage, which is why I like to pair them here and is the reason, instead of plain sour cream, I serve it with a dollop of Borage Leaf Raita (see page 58). This soup is based on the Eastern European/Jewish soup *schav* (sorrel) or 'green borscht', and is often served chilled. On a scorching summer's day, there are few things more refreshing. However, as my sorrel patch keeps going all year long, I will serve it hot in the colder months, too, but with plain sour cream if the borage has died back.

This method will work with other soft greens, such as lettuce, watercress or nettles. It is like a green version of *avgolemono*.

One last note – this is a very tart soup, and many traditional recipes temper this with sugar. I don't like to do so, but if you want to taste after you have added the egg yolks and lemon juice and feel it needs it, you can add a little at this point.

Heat the olive oil and butter in a saucepan over a medium heat and add the onion. Cook until the onion is very soft and translucent, then stir in all but a handful of the sorrel. Pour over the stock, season with salt and pepper and bring to the boil. Turn down the heat and simmer for a few minutes until you are confident the onions are tender.

Whisk the egg yolks and lemon juice together until smooth and well combined, then take two ladlefuls of the broth and strain it. Add the greens back to the soup, then from a height, pour the broth over the egg and lemon mixture, whisking constantly as you do so. Pour this back into the soup, stirring, then leave on the lowest of heats (do NOT let it boil or even come up to a simmer from this point on). Let the soup cook gently for 3–4 minutes, stirring constantly, then remove from the heat. You can blitz in a blender or food processor until smooth, if you like. Stir in the extra handful of sorrel and let it wilt down, then serve, hot or cold, garnished with the raita or sour cream and a few snips of dill.

Classic Cabbage Soup

Serves 4

1 tbsp olive oil

1½ tbsp butter

1 onion, finely chopped

2 garlic cloves, finely chopped (optional)

1 medium floury potato, peeled and diced

500g (1lb 1½oz) cabbage, shredded

1 litre (4 cups) vegetable or chicken stock

3–4 tbsp single (light) cream

Salt and white pepper

Remember the Cabbage Soup Diet? I had friends who used to follow it, living on cabbage soup all week, then blow out (sometimes literally) at the weekend. The soup itself was as unappetising and soulless as you might imagine – watery, worthy, boiled into oblivion – real sackcloth-and-ashes stuff. This soup bears absolutely no relation to it whatsoever.

I am almost embarrassed to include this as a recipe – there really isn't anything to it at all. But, it does serve as a very useful blueprint, as it will work with virtually any robust green. I use primarily white or green cabbage, watercress, or my absolute favourite (I am waiting for the day when my children appreciate it) endive or witloof. I once had witloof soup served with a sweetbread garnish and it was my idea of heaven.

There are no herbs in this soup, but – and this works best with the white cabbage – you can use it as a base and add leaves from large bunches of herbs if you wish. Try parsley or dill or, best of all, chervil – I did this when I cut back the chervil patch in my garden last summer and it was divine.

Heat the olive oil and butter in a large saucepan or casserole (Dutch oven). Add the onion and cook over a gentle heat until it is very soft and translucent – this will take a while, around 10 minutes, so don't try to hurry it. Add the garlic, if using, and potato. Cook for another 2–3 minutes, stirring to coat with the buttery onions. If you are using a white cabbage or endive or anything particularly tough, stir in at this point, then cover with the stock. Season with salt and white pepper, bring to the boil, then turn down and simmer until the potato and cabbage is completely cooked. This can take up to 15 minutes. If you are using a softer green – for example, chard leaves, spinach, watercress leaves – wait until the potato is cooked enough that it will break down when you squash it with the back of your spoon. Cook for a further 5 minutes.

Purée the soup, preferably with a hand-held blender, then taste for seasoning. Stir in the cream.

Lentil and Spinach Soup
with Curry Leaf Vinegar

Serves 4

2 tbsp olive oil

1 onion, finely chopped

3 garlic cloves, finely chopped

2cm (¾in) piece ginger, peeled and finely chopped

1 tsp ground cumin

1 tsp ground cinnamon

1 tsp ground turmeric

½ tsp ground cardamom

¼ tsp cayenne pepper (optional)

3 tbsp coriander (cilantro) stems, finely chopped (optional)

200g (1 cup) red lentils, well rinsed

1 litre (4 cups) vegetable or chicken stock or water

400ml (1¾ cups) coconut milk

500g (1lb 1½oz) fresh spinach or chard leaves, shredded

Salt and freshly ground black pepper

To serve

2–3 tbsp curry leaf vinegar (see page 32)

A few coriander (cilantro) leaves

I've kept this soup fairly neutral in terms of the spicing, because what I am most interested in is the garnish. I love the mellow, earthiness of this type of soup and would normally add a squeeze of lemon or lime at the end, but what I wanted to do with this one is showcase how well herb vinegars can work. So instead, I have drizzled over some of the curry leaf vinegar mentioned on page 32.

I know it is a stretch for most people to have curry leaf vinegar, but if you can get fresh curry leaves, even if you don't make the vinegar proper, but infuse muddled curry leaves in a few tablespoons of vinegar for a few hours, it is worth it for this dish alone. The vinegar brings out all that is good in the curry leaf.

If you don't want to go down this route, there are plenty of other sauces and condiments in this book which will work well too. Try the Green Harissa on page 34, up the chilli content in the soup and cool it down with the Borage Leaf Raita on page 58. Add zing with the Coriander and Mint Chutney on page 35.

Heat the olive oil in a large saucepan or casserole (Dutch oven) and add the onion. Cook until very soft and translucent, then add the garlic and ginger. Continue to cook for a couple of minutes, then add the spices and coriander stems. Pour in the lentils, then stir until they are coated with the oil and spices. Season with plenty of salt and pepper.

Pour over the stock or water, then bring to the boil. Skim away any foam if it forms, then turn down the heat and leave the lentils to simmer until they have completely collapsed and thickened the cooking liquid. This will take 25–30 minutes. Add the coconut milk, then the spinach or chard leaves and continue to cook until they have completely wilted and are tender. The chard leaves will take a few minutes longer than the spinach.

Serve with a drizzle of the vinegar over each bowl and a few coriander leaves, if you like, or alternatively use one of the sauces mentioned in the introduction.

Herb and White Fish Broth

Serves 4

2 sea bream or sea bass, filleted, head and bones reserved for stock

200ml (¾ cup) white wine

1 leek, white parts only, sliced

1 carrot, chopped

1 bay leaf

A few peppercorns

1 small bunch of tarragon

A few sprigs of fennel, lemon thyme, parsley, chervil

A few chives

A handful of baby borage leaves and flowers

Salt

This is a very delicate dish – the fish and the herbs aren't cooked before serving, just arranged in bowls before the broth is poured over. It's a good thing to serve if you want something elegant, as there's no risk of the fish breaking up into your soup before you get it to the table.

The most economical way to prepare this dish it to buy two fish, ask the fishmonger to fillet them, and keep the head and bones to make the broth. If you are time-pressed, you can use a decent fresh fish stock instead.

Cut the fish into thin, flat slices – having the skin as an anchor helps to do this evenly. Chill until half an hour before you want to serve the broth, then remove from the fridge to come to room temperature.

Next, make the broth. Wash the head and bones thoroughly, then put in a saucepan with 750ml (3 cups) water and the white wine. Bring to the boil and skim off any brown foam collecting on the surface. When this has turned white, turn down the heat to a very gentle simmer and add the leek, carrot, bay leaf and peppercorns. Remove the leaves and tender tips of the tarragon, fennel, lemon thyme, parsley and chervil. Reserve these and put the stems in the stock. Simmer for a further 20 minutes.

Strain the stock through a sieve and then again through kitchen towels or a coffee filter. Transfer to a clean saucepan and taste for seasoning. Add salt, then heat until piping hot.

Warm shallow soup bowls, then arrange the fish on the base of them. Top with all the reserved herbs, along with the chives and borage leaves and flowers.

Put the fish broth into a jug and pour over the fish at the table – the hot broth will gently poach the fish.

Callaloo

Serves 4

2 tbsp olive oil

100g (3½oz) salt pork or smoked bacon, cut into lardons (optional)

1 onion, finely chopped

1 ripe (yellow) plantain, peeled and finely chopped

3 garlic cloves, finely chopped or grated

2cm (¾in) piece ginger, peeled and finely chopped

1 tbsp medium curry powder

1 litre (4 cups) chicken or vegetable stock

1 Scotch bonnet chilli, left whole but pierced with a sharp knife

1 sprig of thyme

600g (1lb 5oz) any soft fresh greens – chard (leaves not stems), spinach, amaranth or elephant ears, if you can get them, roughly chopped

Squeeze of lime, to serve

Hot sauce, to serve

Sea salt and freshly ground black pepper

There are as many versions of callaloo in the Caribbean as there are cooks. A slender book I own on the traditional dishes in Dominica, the island I know best, has five recipes for it, all using dasheen leaves, the large, elephant ears found all over the Caribbean, but you can use any greens including amaranth (used in Jamaican callaloo), spinach or water spinach, or even watercress. Callaloo can be a smooth soup or a very hearty stew, often including salt pork and seafood – or in Dominica, land crabs or freshwater crayfish.

The plantain is not traditional – I don't think I've ever seen it in a callaloo recipe – but it gives the soup a sweet, nuttiness to offset the gentle heat from the chilli pepper.

Put 1 tablespoon of the olive oil in a saucepan or casserole (Dutch oven). Add the bacon and fry over a medium heat until plenty of fat has been rendered out and the bacon is crisp. Remove half with a slotted spoon and set aside.

Add the onion and cook until soft and starting to caramelise, around 8–10 minutes. Add half the plantain and turn the heat to high, continuing to cook until it is browning. Add the garlic and ginger and cook for another minute. Stir in the curry powder. Pour in the stock and season. Add the Scotch bonnet to the pan with the thyme. Bring everything to the boil, then simmer for 10 minutes.

Add the leaves and press into the soup until they have completely wilted down, then simmer for another 10 minutes. Taste for seasoning and check the texture of the greens – they should be very soft and silky. Remove the thyme and Scotch bonnet, then blend to the texture you prefer – I blend to thicken the soup and homogenise while making sure there is still plenty of texture.

Once blended, make the garnish. Heat the remaining olive oil in a frying pan over a medium heat and add the remaining bacon. Cook until plenty of fat has rendered out and it is starting to crisp again, around 5 minutes, then add the remaining plantain. Continue to cook, stirring constantly, until the plantain has browned.

Serve the soup with the bacon and plantain, a squeeze of lime juice, and extra hot sauce.

A Seafood Laksa

Serves 4

500g (1lb 1½oz) North Atlantic
  prawns (shrimp) or similar, shells
  and heads on

2 tbsp vegetable oil

1 litre (4 cups) fish stock

400ml (1¾ cups) coconut milk

2 tbsp fish sauce

4 large kaffir lime leaves, shredded

300g (10½oz) firm-fleshed white fish,
  such as pollack, cut into chunks

400g (14oz) noodles, cooked

Sea salt

For the paste

3 lemongrass stalks, inner white part
  only, roughly chopped

2 red bird's eye chillies, roughly
  chopped

3 garlic cloves, chopped

3cm (1¼in) piece fresh galangal,
  chopped

2cm (¾in) piece ginger, peeled and
  chopped

2 shallots, sliced

1 tbsp shrimp paste

1 tsp palm sugar or light soft brown
  sugar

1 tsp ground turmeric

To serve

A large handful of laksa leaves

A handful of coriander (cilantro) leaves
  (optional)

A few mint leaves (optional)

A few Thai basil leaves (optional)

Lime wedges

This is a dish I used to make with large, fat king prawns (jumbo shrimp) as big as my hand, but the days of consumer innocence are long past, and sustainable ones are either impossible to find or, usually, prohibitively expensive. Now I use North Atlantic prawns. I love these – always a treat at home (Saturday afternoon fish market, a pint of these and probably herring milts fried up for tea), then in my poorest, post-student days, they were a Sunday staple, when the pubs around me used to put mountains of them on the bar, free, along with roast potatoes. I think this was my version of Sunday roast for a year or so. They are vastly underrated as they have a superb flavour and make excellent stock, which is why I use them here.

First, peel the prawns. Pour half the vegetable oil into a large saucepan over a medium heat and add the heads and shells of the prawns. Fry, stirring constantly, until the shells darken from pale pink to coral, and you start seeing droplets of the same colour in the oil, around 5 minutes. Pour over the fish stock along with 200ml (¾ cup) water, bring to the boil, then simmer for 20 minutes. Strain and discard the heads and shells.

While the stock is simmering, make the paste. Put all the ingredients into a small food processor with a little water and pulse until almost smooth. You may need to add a little more water to help it along.

Heat the remaining oil in a large saucepan or casserole dish (Dutch oven). Add the paste and fry over a medium heat until it browns and smells very aromatic – this will take several minutes. Pour in the prawn stock and the coconut milk, along with the fish sauce and kaffir lime leaves. Bring to the boil, then turn down the heat and simmer for 10 minutes. Taste for seasoning and add salt or a little more fish sauce if necessary.

Add the fish and poach gently until almost cooked through – it will continue cooking at the table. Divide the noodles and the shelled prawns between deep soup bowls and top with the fish. Ladle over the soup, then top with the leaves. Serve with lime wedges.

SEAWEED

On the final day of a recent family holiday in Cornwall, we were delaying the dreaded drive back to London by visiting one last beach. The beach was small, hemmed in by steep, cave-pocked cliffs on one side, a freshwater stream feeding into slippery, winkle-spotted rockpools on the other. It was perfect for walking on, with hard, compacted sand below the high tide line, which was also a treasure trove of shells and driftwood for the children, and of seaweed for me.

We were there for about an hour, and in that time I must have seen or collected at least eight varieties of seaweed. There was everything from gossamer sea lettuce, bright green, crinkled and clingy, which we could rinse and eat raw, to the thick, rubbery strands of kelp, freshly washed up onto the beach and several metres long, which I gave up on trying to bunch up and carry, and eventually dragged behind me, trainlike. There were various types of wrack, including the postuled murky-olive bladder wrack, which my children loved to tread on for the snap, crackle, pop. There was squelchy gutweed, purple, frond-like carrageen (Irish moss). There was also (hooray!) dulse. We cut very little free of the rockpools and held handfuls at the top of the stream to rinse them clean of sand and any tiny creatures along for the ride. The current tugged on the seaweed and a few fronds escaped. The kelp stretched out towards the sea, fluttering under the water like a ragged standard in a high wind before we reeled it in, cramming it into bags.

This was all great fun, but also a great example of what our coastlines have to offer. On another beach I might have found any number of other types of seaweed – for example sea spaghetti (also fetchingly known as thong weed) or laver or wakame.

I don't think we eat nearly enough seaweed in the UK, and most of us come at it from very different perspective from the scenario I describe above. Japanese food has become increasingly popular in recent years, but I don't think the connection between the weeds we can find on our shorelines and some of our favourite Japanese dishes is immediately apparent. But the link is there; nori, for example, flattened and used to wrap sushi or sold in strips as a snack, is exactly the same seaweed as laver – the seaweed I associate strongly with the Welsh and their laverbread (cooked and chopped laverbread is mixed with oatmeal and fried, often served for

breakfast with bacon and cockles). Kombu, most associated with Japanese broths such as dashi, is Japanese for kelp.

I must admit that I was guilty of using seaweed primarily in Japanese broths and very little else. I tried to rectify this, and have found that one of the easiest ways to incorporate seaweed into your food is as a seasoning – I have bought and made seaweed salts and seasonings, from dried, crumbled or blitzed seaweed (see page 18). I am now in the habit of leaving a pot of this on the table for seasoning, just to get an idea of what it might work with. The most successful experiment has been with dulse – it is one of the most umami of seaweeds – very savoury and smoky with a hint sweetness at the end. It has been likened to a sweet-cure bacon, and I can understand why. I often guessed that if I was eating something to which I might add bacon, it would work: eggs, especially omelettes, sprinkled on a chowder, and with any kind of seafood. Try wrapping scallops or prawns (shrimp) in it before grilling, and you will see what I mean.

You can use seaweed in sweet dishes too. My stepdaughter has never forgotten the time when food writer Fiona Bird, author of *Seaweed in the Kitchen*, sent us 'Mermaid Biscuits' and 'Seaside Fudge', both using sea gut. From that time on, whenever I have asked her to guess the secret ingredient, she still says hopefully, 'Seaweed?' I usually buy it dried now – when rehydrated it will be three times its volume, so better value for money. I supplement pasta or noodles with it – if we can do this with courgette (zucchini), why not with thong weed?

Seaweed and Mushroom Broth

Serves 4

20 x 15cm (8 x 6in) kelp or kombu,
  cut into strips

A handful of dried mushrooms,
  such as shiitake

5cm (2in) piece ginger, sliced

2 garlic cloves, sliced

For the soup

A handful of wakame or other sea
  vegetable, soaked in warm water for
  10 minutes

1 tbsp sesame oil

400g (14oz) mushrooms, a selection,
  sliced if large

1 large bunch of greens – anything
  you like as long as it is a wilting sort
  (see introduction)

400g (14oz) cooked noodles, ideally
  udon

Furikake, for sprinkling (see page 18)

A few mint leaves, to serve

A few mitsuba (Japanese parsley)
  leaves, to serve (optional)

A few ramps or garlic or Chinese
  chives, chopped

You can use any greens you like in this soup. The easily available Asian greens include bok choy, Chinese (Napa) cabbage, kai lan (Chinese broccoli) and water spinach. But you don't have to limit yourself: there is no reason why you shouldn't use kale or chard, or – and this works brilliantly – wild garlic when it is in season. I sometimes like to see how far I can get using just local ingredients, and this has meant greens from the garden, seaweed I have foraged myself and tender green shoots from my ginger plant, which grows happily in the garden.

First, make the broth. Give the kelp or kombu a wipe with a damp cloth, then put it in a saucepan with the dried mushrooms. Cover with 1 litre (4 cups) water and bring to the boil. Turn down the heat and leave on the lowest possible setting for 20 minutes. Add the ginger and garlic, and simmer for a further 20 minutes. Strain, but do not throw away the seaweed and mushrooms – you can chop them finely and add them back into the soup, or you can save them for another meal.

Return the stock to the saucepan. Add the wakame and simmer until soft, around 10 minutes.

In a separate frying pan over a medium heat, while the seaweed is simmering, heat the sesame oil and cook the mushrooms until glossy and tender. Add the greens and garlic chives to the broth and simmer until they have wilted down. Arrange the noodles and mushrooms in bowls, divide up the greens too (easiest done with chopsticks), then pour over the broth. Garnish with the Furikake and the mint, mitsuba leaves and ramps or garlic chives.

Variations

For a non-vegan broth, add a handful of bonito flakes (*katsuobushi*) to the stock with the garlic and ginger.

For a lower-carb meal, replace all or some of the noodles with sea spaghetti (also called thong weed). This will need to simmer in the broth for around 20 minutes.

As this is seaweed based, fish and seafood are really good additions. Thinly sliced scallops or tuna are good added to the bowls just before the broth is poured in.

Melting Cheese, Bread and Cabbage Soup

Serves 4

3½ tbsp butter

3 onions, thickly sliced

2 tsp plain (all-purpose) flour

1 large sprig of thyme, or a few sage leaves

3 garlic cloves, finely chopped

250ml (1 cup) cider or white wine

1 large Savoy cabbage, roughly chopped

1 litre (4 cups) stock, such as chicken, vegetable or ham

200g (7oz) hard cheese (see introduction)

Sea salt and freshly ground black pepper

For the garnish

4 thick slices of sourdough bread or 8 slices of baguette

1 garlic clove, halved

50g (1¾oz) hard cheese, grated

50g (1¾oz) stretchy cheese, such as Ogleshield or raclette, grated

To serve

1 tbsp butter

2 garlic cloves, finely chopped

1 sprig of thyme or a few sage leaves, shredded

Inspired by Johanna Spyri's *Heidi* and anything Alpine – the sort of rib-sticking soup you need in the middle of winter and one to make when you are happy staying close to the stove, perhaps with something decent to listen to as you stir.

This isn't a melty, stretchy type of cheese soup, but the sort in which the cheese just disappears and gives it a very savoury, creamy richness – think along the lines of what happens to a Parmesan heel when you add it to minestrone. So you need a hard cheese, such as a good Cheddar or, again with *Heidi* in mind, a hard goat's cheese. Also – and I cannot stress this enough – it is very important that you do not boil the soup once you have added the cheese – it will cause the cheese to flocculate into rubbery clumps before it has had a chance to melt into the liquid.

Put the butter in a heavy-based casserole dish (Dutch oven) or saucepan. When the butter has melted, add the onions and cook over a low-medium heat, stirring regularly, until they have softened, but are still translucent and pale, around 8–10 minutes. Turn up the heat slightly and continue to cook until they have caramelised: it is up to you how far you take this. You can allow them to brown and still retain some texture, or you can let them go all the way and collapse into a sticky brown mass. The latter will probably take over an hour with regular stirring, but will give a wonderful sweetness to the soup. Sprinkle over the flour and stir to combine, then add the thyme or sage and garlic. Continue to cook for a couple of minutes.

Pour in the cider or white wine and allow it to bubble up, continuing to stir until it has reduced by half. Add the cabbage, packing it down into the casserole, then pour over the stock. Season well with salt and pepper. Bring to the boil, then turn down and cover. Cook for 30 minutes, or until the cabbage is very tender, stirring every so often, then add the cheese. Make sure that from this point on you do not allow the soup to boil, but keep it gently simmering, again, stirring once in a while, until the cheese has melted into the stock.

Heat your grill to its highest setting. Lightly toast the bread, then rub all over with the garlic. Divide the cheese between the toast and arrange over the soup, pushing down slightly. Put under the grill until the cheese is patchy brown and bubbling.

While the cheese is grilling, heat the remaining butter in a small frying pan. Add the garlic and thyme or sage. Drizzle this over the cheese when you remove it from the grill, then serve at the table for people to ladle into bowls themselves.

Variation

This is a great soup to add sauerkraut to. It will give quite a different flavour, as the sauerkraut will cut through the richness, so if you think this soup sounds a bit heavy, this is a good way to temper it. I would stick to the quantities above, adding 250g (8¾oz) white cabbage sauerkraut at the same time as the cheese.

Winter Minestrone
with Mixed Leaf Pesto

Serves 4

3 tbsp olive oil

200g (7oz) bacon lardons

1 large onion, diced

2 carrots, sliced

3 celery sticks, thickly sliced

A large bunch of cavolo nero, chard,
Savoy cabbage or similar, stems and
leaves separated and shredded

4 garlic cloves, finely chopped

2 bay leaves

1 large sprig of rosemary

200g (7oz) tinned tomatoes (or 2 large
fresh ones, if good)

1 litre (4 cups) well-flavoured stock,
such as ham, chicken or vegetable

1 Parmesan rind (optional)

3 leeks, sliced into thick rounds

300g (10½oz) cooked beans (try the
Cannellini Beans on page 227)

100g (3½oz) cooked grains or pasta

Sea salt and freshly ground black
pepper

For the pesto

100g (3½oz) mixture of young kale,
beetroot and turnip top leaves,
roughly chopped

1 small bunch of parsley

A few basil leaves

2 garlic cloves

1 tbsp of cider or herb vinegar (tarragon
or rosemary, for preference)

50g (1¾oz) hard cheese – I use
Lincolnshire Poacher for this one

50g (1¾oz) hazelnuts, lightly toasted

Olive oil, for drizzling

This is the sort of soup I cobble together midweek. I normally try to devote part of Sunday to batch cooking; stocks and soups, bags of grains, pasta and pulses to use as building blocks when assembling the week's meals. This soup will always have some kind of pre-cooked bean in it, and whatever grain I have to hand. It's also a good way of using up anything in the fridge – lots of vegetables, slightly past their prime, a few bacon lardons, or a hard piece of cooking chorizo.

First, make the pesto. Put all the greens and herbs into a food processor and blitz for a few seconds, just to get it started, then add the garlic, vinegar, cheese and hazelnuts. Blitz again until you have a roughly textured purée then, while the motor is running, start drizzling in olive oil until you have a thick, spoonable texture. Transfer to a sterilised jar.

To make the soup, heat the olive oil in a large casserole dish (Dutch oven). Fry the bacon lardons until crisp and brown, then remove with a slotted spoon and drain on kitchen towels.

Add the onion, carrots and celery and cook over a medium heat until the vegetables are well on their way to softening and have started to caramelise around the edges – give them at least 20 minutes. Add the stems from whatever greens you are using and the garlic. Stir for a couple of minutes, then add the herbs, the tomatoes and stock. Tuck in the Parmesan rind, if using, and return the bacon to the casserole.

Season with plenty of salt and pepper, then add the leaves of the greens. Bring to the boil, then turn down and cover. Leave to simmer for 20 minutes, then add the leeks. Continue to cook until the leeks are tender, then add half the beans. Mash the rest roughly – this will help to thicken the soup a bit, and add these along with the grains or pasta.

When everything is piping hot, serve with spoonfuls of the pesto stirred in.

Kimchi Soup

Serves 4

4 chicken wings

2 onions, roughly chopped

2 tomatoes, quartered

1.5 litres (6 cups) chicken stock

Cloves from ½ bulb of garlic

5cm (2in) piece ginger

2 bay leaves

A few peppercorns

3 cloves

For the soup

1 tbsp sesame oil

1 onion, thinly sliced

300g (10½oz) Kimchi (see page 30) made with white cabbage, shredded

2cm (¾in) piece ginger, peeled and finely chopped

4 garlic cloves, finely chopped

1 tbsp gochujang paste (optional)

2 tbsp light soy sauce

2 tsp honey

300g (10½ oz) bag of Chinese greens or broccoli, shredded lengthways

300g (10½oz) cooked noodles (I like glass noodles, use any you like)

Sea salt

To serve

3 spring onions (scallions), halved and shredded lengthways

1 tbsp black sesame seeds

Chilli oil (optional)

This is not a classic *jjigae* (Korean Kimchi Stew). Instead I am using kimchi to enhance my favourite cold remedy soup, which is always chicken-based. I also add noodles, which are a boon to eat when you have a cold as they slide down so easily. I don't bother with much more in the way of texture. This is an enhanced chicken broth, but please simplify when you need to make life easier – a bought chicken or beef consommé, instant noodles, kimchi with a dash of chilli paste or oil and a handful of greens is also a good meal.

A note on chilli: sometimes I like the sweetness of gochujang, sometimes I want chilli oil at the end, and sometimes I want both or neither. It does depend on the flavour and heat of the Kimchi, which varies from batch to batch. I cannot stress the importance of tasting, tasting, tasting as you go.

First make the broth. Preheat the oven to its highest setting. Put the chicken wings and onions in a roasting tin and drizzle with oil. Season with salt and roast for 45 minutes until well browned and charred in places, adding the tomatoes for the last 10 minutes.

Transfer the chicken, onions and tomatoes to a saucepan and deglaze the tin with a little water. Pour this over the wings. Add the chicken stock along with the other aromatics. Bring to the boil, then turn down and simmer for 1 hour. Strain, pushing through the some of the pulp from the tomatoes and garlic cloves. Strip the meat from the wings, if you have time, and set aside.

Heat the sesame oil in a large casserole dish (Dutch oven) or saucepan and add the onion. Cook over a medium heat until softened and starting to lightly brown, around 8–10 minutes, then add the kimchi, ginger and garlic. Continue to cook for a few minutes, stirring constantly, then add the gochujang paste, if using, and honey. Stir to coat, then pour in the strained stock. Add the soy sauce and honey. Taste for seasoning and add salt as necessary.

Bring to the boil, turn down the heat and leave to simmer for 5 minutes, then add the greens or broccoli. Cook until tender. Serve over the noodles, garnished with spring onions and black sesame seeds and chilli oil, if using.

SALADS

Grilled Vegetable and Herb Salad with Peanut Dressing

Serves 4

4 little gem lettuces, halved

Olive oil, for brushing

2 medium courgettes (zucchini), cut into thin ovals

1 bunch of spring onions (scallions), trimmed

½ crunchy lettuce, such as Cos, romaine, Chinese leaf cabbage, shredded

1 small carrot, julienned

½ red (bell) pepper, very finely julienned

A few baby sweetcorn, thinly sliced

A selection of herbs, such as coriander (cilantro), laksa leaf, kaffir lime (finely shredded), various mints, various basils

For the dressing

1 tbsp peanut butter

½ tsp palm sugar or honey

2cm (¾in) piece ginger, peeled and grated

1 garlic clove, grated

1 tbsp fish sauce

Juice and zest of ½ lime

A dash of hot sauce

A dash of sesame oil

Sea salt and freshly ground black pepper

This salad is an example of how seemingly disparate flavours can work well together. I made it when I had lots of bits and pieces to use up, supplemented by fresh produce from the garden. I grow several types of mint, and used ginger mint here. The trick is not to use too much of any one thing so every mouthful tastes different – the opposite of a chopped salad, where you expect a certain homogeneous quality.

The grilling does take some time, but it is worth it for the flavour, and can be done on an outside grill faster than on the hob.

First, whisk all the dressing ingredients together and thin with a little water, if necessary. Taste for seasoning and add salt and pepper as required.

Heat a griddle pan until it is too hot to hold your hand over. Brush the cut sides of the little gem with olive oil and season with salt. Grill the little gems, courgettes and spring onions until they have softened and have charred ridge lines. You will probably have to do this in more than one batch. Do not leave them and turn as soon as they easily come away from the griddle. Keep warm.

Assemble the salad by arranging all the raw ingredients on a large platter with half the herbs. Add the grilled vegetables and turn everything over together very gently. Add the remaining herbs and drizzle over the dressing. Serve immediately.

Warm Bean Tops Salad

Serves 4

6 apricots or loquats, halved

Honey, for brushing

400g (14oz) broad (fava) bean tops and leaves

1 bunch of radishes, with their leaves, sliced into rounds

30g (1oz) hazelnuts, lightly toasted

For the dressing

2 tbsp olive oil

1 shallot, very finely diced

30g (1oz) 'nduja

1 tbsp sherry vinegar

1 tsp honey

Sea salt and freshly ground black pepper

Broad (fava) bean tops and leaves are not normally available in shops – I don't think I've ever seen them for sale. However, most vegetable growers pick them out in early spring to guard against a black fly invasion, so if you have a friendly gardener or allotmenteer, get in quick. Pick the tops off and any tender leaves. The flavour is similar to broad beans, but slightly greener. If you want to substitute it, you can use any salad leaves, but make sure you include something tart or peppery – rocket (arugula) or mitsuba (Japanese parsley), for example. I also like very young vine leaves, blanched for a couple of minutes and shredded.

First, make the dressing. Heat the olive oil in a small pan and add the shallot. Cook over a medium heat until very soft and translucent, around 5 minutes – it should almost dissolve into the oil. Remove from the heat and stir in the 'nduja until it has melted into the oil. Whisk in the sherry vinegar and honey, and season with salt and pepper. Thin out with a very little water if necessary.

Heat a griddle until it is too hot to hold your hand over. Brush the apricots or loquats with honey and grill quickly – you don't want to cook them through, just get char lines on the cut edges.

Wash the broad bean tops thoroughly, and remove any really small, delicate leaves to garnish. Put the remaining leaves into a large colander. Boil a kettle and pour the contents over the leaves – they will wilt down but still keep their shape. Drain thoroughly.

Arrange the cooked and reserved raw leaves on a plate with any nice radish leaves, the radishes, apricots or loquats and the hazelnuts. Drizzle over the salad dressing and serve immediately.

Fattoush

Serves 4

2 large pitta, or an equivalent amount of flatbread

1 small red onion, thinly sliced

3 small cucumbers, diced, cut into crescents

200g (7oz) cherry tomatoes, halved

200g (7oz) radishes, sliced

1 bunch of summer purslane, leaves only

A few small borage leaves (optional)

100g (3½oz) lamb's lettuce (corn salad)

1 small bunch of parsley, leaves only

A few mint leaves

A few sprigs of coriander (cilantro)

A few sprigs of oregano

Sea salt

For the dressing

3 tbsp olive oil

Juice of ½ lemon

1 tbsp adjika or Zhoug (see page 33; optional) or 1 garlic clove, crushed

1 tsp sumac

Sea salt and freshly ground black pepper

To serve

Sumac

Za'atar

A few microleaves (see introduction; optional)

Purslane, a succulent, is the traditional salad leaf to include in fattoush; each leaf bursts with a pleasant citrus flavour. I've included borage leaves too as they have a similar effect, but this time with hints of sweetened cucumber. I think they complement one another well.

I prefer to use the firmer, smaller cucumbers found in Middle Eastern shops here – if you use a larger variety, it might be wise to scoop out the seeds. It is up to you whether you peel them.

If you have them (I grow them on cotton wool on my windowsill), microleaves are really good in this salad – think basil, fenugreek and coriander (cilantro).

First, toast the pitta or flatbread. You can either do this in a dry frying pan or in your toaster. Leave to cool, then tear or cut into pieces. Meanwhile, put the red onion in a small bowl, toss in ½ teaspoon salt and cover with cold water. Leave to stand for 20 minutes, then drain thoroughly.

Put all the salad ingredients, including the herbs and the bread, into a large bowl. Whisk the dressing ingredients together and taste – if using the adjika it will be quite salty, so you may not need to add more. Add pepper.

Dress the salad and mix everything together. Serve on a large platter, sprinkled with sumac, za'atar and a few microleaves, if you have them.

Winter Panzanella

Serves 4

500g (1lb 1½oz) Brussels sprouts, trimmed and halved

250g (8¾oz) squash (I like an onion squash), peeled and sliced into wedges

2 red onions, 1½ sliced into wedges, ½ thinly sliced

4 tbsp olive oil

2 tsp rubbed sage leaves

1 tbsp fresh thyme leaves

4 garlic cloves, finely chopped

3 slices of sourdough bread, cubed

200g (7oz) curly kale or cavolo nero, leaves stripped from stems

Sea salt and freshly ground black pepper

For the dressing

1 tbsp olive oil

200g (7oz) bacon lardons

1 shallot, finely chopped

2 garlic cloves, finely chopped

1 tbsp sherry vinegar

1 tsp Dijon mustard

1 tbsp maple syrup (optional)

A handful of young beetroot (beet) or chard leaves (optional)

A panzanella is usually a summery affair – gluts of overripe tomatoes left to marinate with stale bread. I prefer a warm version though, which bridges the gap between autumn and winter. I've deliberately used several cooking methods to show how different-textured greens can come together.

Preheat the oven to 200°C (400°F/Gas 6).

Bring a saucepan of boiling water to the boil and add plenty of salt. Add the Brussels sprouts and blanch for 2 minutes. Drain thoroughly. Put the Brussels sprouts, the squash and the onion wedges into a roasting tin and season with salt. Drizzle over 1 tablespoon of the olive oil and toss so everything it is well covered. Season and sprinkle in the sage and thyme. Roast for 25 minutes. Stir in the garlic, then toss the bread cubes in the rest of the olive oil and add these to the roasting tin. Roast for a further 15–20 minutes. By this point the vegetables should be lightly charred and the bread crisp and brown.

While the vegetables are roasting, sprinkle the onion slices with salt and cover with cold water. Leave to stand until you are ready to assemble the salad.

Next make the dressing. Put the olive oil into a frying pan over a medium heat and add the bacon. When the bacon is crisp and has rendered out plenty of fat, add the shallot. Continue to fry until the shallot has also taken on some colour, around 5 minutes, then add the garlic. Cook for 2 minutes. Deglaze the pan with the vinegar then stir in the mustard and maple syrup. Add the leaves, wet from just being washed, and wilt them into the dressing.

Put the kale leaves into a bowl with a pinch of salt, then 'massage', by which I mean just rub the leaves between your fingers until the kale starts to wilt; make sure you stop as soon as this happens, as it will quickly become too soft. Roughly chop or tear.

To assemble, put the kale, drained red onion, vegetables and bread into a large bowl and add the dressing. Toss until everything is well coated, then serve straight away, while still warm. You can also serve directly from the roasting tin – I often do this to save on washing up.

Salad of Bitter Greens and Bacon

Serves 4

300g (10½oz) bitter salad greens
 (see introduction)

2 tbsp olive oil

1 shallot, very finely chopped

200g (7oz) thick-cut smoked bacon,
 pancetta or guanciale, diced

2 tbsp sherry vinegar

Freshly ground black pepper

This deliberately simple salad is based on the classic French salad of *frisée aux lardons*, which is like a cultivated version of foraged dandelion leaves with bacon, so it will therefore work with any type of bitter leaves. In early spring, when dandelion leaves are young (and plentiful in my garden), I will use these; later in the year I will use wild chicory, which has similar pointed leaves to dandelion or perhaps frisée or any kind of soft-leaved chicory. In winter I can buy so many varieties – tardivo, castelfranco, grumolo or blowsy, rose-like radicchios: beauty belied by bitterness.

For me this is a winter/spring salad. It feels good for you while still waking up the taste buds. One word of warning though – if you do use dandelion or wild chicory for this and have a nibble, you will probably find them unpleasantly bitter. But the magic of food pairing means that as soon as you add the bacon and dressing, the bitterness will work seamlessly into something more than palatable.

Finally, if you want to turn it into something substantial, consider adding some small cubes of fried potato and a poached egg.

Pick over the leaves and wash thoroughly. Dry roughly and set aside.

Heat the olive oil in a frying pan and add the shallot. Cook over a medium heat until softened and just starting to change colour, around 5 minutes, then add the bacon. Turn up the heat and continue to cook until the bacon has rendered out some fat, has crisped up and is brown around the edges, another 2–3 minutes.

Deglaze the pan with the sherry vinegar and add a crack of black pepper. Remove from the heat and add the greens. Toss them gently in the contents of the pan and then transfer to plates as soon as possible before they have had a chance to wilt down much. Eat immediately.

Winter Salad of Red Leaves, Mackerel and Orange

Serves 4

250g (8¾oz) red cabbage, finely shredded

2 heads of red chicory, roughly chopped

1 large carrot, preferably purple, julienned

2 celery sticks (plus leaves from the centre of the bunch), sliced

1 red onion, thinly sliced

½ tsp caster (superfine) sugar

1 tsp white wine vinegar

1 blood orange

400g (14oz) smoked mackerel, skinned, deboned and roughly broken up

2 tbsp capers, rinsed

1 small bunch of dill, finely chopped

1 small bunch of mint, leaves only, finely chopped

A few sprigs of tarragon, finely chopped

A handful of baby beetroot (beet) leaves

A few purple kale leaves, destemmed and massaged (see page 112)

A few horseradish, mustard green or mitzuna leaves (see introduction; optional)

Sea salt

For the dressing

1 heaped tbsp crème fraîche

2 tsp wholegrain mustard

1 tbsp sherry vinegar

1 tbsp hazelnut or walnut oil

Orange juice from the blood orange (see method)

Sea salt and freshly ground black pepper

This is just the sort of salad I want to eat when I am coming out of the winter stodge phase and need something fresher – just in time for the end of the blood orange season. It is a good salad to prepare ahead and will keep well in the fridge as long as you follow the salting instructions below – if you skip this step, the vegetables will go soggy.

There are other greens that work well in this salad. I grow horseradish, and the leaves, when young, give a bit of a kick. Shred some finely and add to the serving greens. Mustard greens will give a similar effect; mitzuna is also mustardy but much milder.

Put the red cabbage, chicory, carrot, celery and red onion into a large colander and sprinkle with 1 teaspoon sea salt, the sugar and the vinegar. Mix thoroughly and set over a bowl or stand in your sink. Cover with a tea towel and leave to stand for an hour.

Transfer the vegetables to a serving bowl. Prepare the orange by topping and tailing it, cutting away the skin and outer membrane, then dicing the remaining flesh, flicking out any seeds or large pieces of pith. Squeeze juice from the discarded skin into a small bowl.

Make the dressing by adding the crème fraîche, wholegrain mustard, sherry vinegar and oil to the orange juice. Season with salt and pepper and whisk together.

Pour the dressing over the salad, then add the mackerel, capers and orange. Fold over gently to combine everything, then add the herbs and the celery leaves. Fold over once more.

Serve on a bed of the remaining leaves.

Grilled Chicken and Little Gem Salad

Serves 4

2 tsp dried oregano

2 tbsp olive oil

2 skin-on chicken breasts, butterflied

1 bunch of spring onions (scallions), trimmed

2 little gem lettuces, cut into wedges

A few tomatillos, cherry tomatoes or physalis, roughly chopped

A selection of salad leaves, including purslane

75g (scant ½ cup) cooked quinoa

Leaves from a few small bunches of herbs, such as basil, coriander (cilantro) or mint, or snipped chives

A few pumpkin seeds, lightly toasted

Sea salt and freshly ground black pepper

For the dressing

1 small bunch of tarragon, leaves only

1 small bunch of parsley, leaves only

A few sprigs of coriander (cilantro)

A few sprigs of basil

1 jalapeño or other green chilli, deseeded and roughly chopped

1 garlic clove, peeled and chopped

Juice of 1 lime

2 tbsp yogurt

1 tsp red wine vinegar

1 tsp honey

4 tbsp olive oil

There are a lot of ingredients here, but I do this because the joy of a salad like this is that every mouthful will be different. You can choose if you want a piece of chicken with a chunk of tomatillo and a sprig of coriander (cilantro) – or with some grilled lettuce and tarragon. It will never be dull.

First, heat a griddle pan until it is too hot to hold your hand over. Mix the oregano with salt and pepper and the olive oil and rub all over the chicken. Griddle the chicken for a few minutes on each side until char lines appear and it is just cooked through. The pieces with the skin will take longer, skin-side down – make sure the skin is crisp and papery, not soft and flabby.

Remove the chicken from the griddle pan and rest for a few minutes before cutting or tearing into strips.

Add the spring onions and little gems to the griddle pan. Grill until lightly charred and softened, turning regularly. Remove from the griddle pan.

Make the salad dressing. Blitz the herbs, chilli and garlic with the lime juice, adding a little water if they are reluctant to come together. Add the yogurt, vinegar, honey and olive oil. Whisk together – you need the dressing to be quite thin, so add more water if necessary. Season well and taste – adjust the vinegar and honey if necessary.

To assemble the salad, toss the chicken, vegetables, baby leaves and quinoa together and drizzle with the dressing. Garnish with the herbs and pumpkin seeds.

WATERCRESS

Sometimes I experience a jolt when I see an ingredient out of its normal (for me) context, and it makes me realise how limited my repertoire has been thus far. This has happened a few times, but it had the most impact with watercress, an ingredient that I associated strongly with England – and worse, a certain type of Englishness. You know, that particular kind of 'safe', pastoral, green-and-pleasant land where you know the postman by name, you have *Wind in the Willows* picnics by lazily meandering streams, and the only occasional sounds on a Sunday afternoon are the buzzing of bumblebees and the low-key thwack and desultory clap when ball meets bat. All very St Mary Mead. In this fictional land watercress grew in abundance and was picked upstream and transported on the Hampshire watercress train to be piled into a steak sandwich for 'him', or chopped into a sauce for poached salmon for 'her'. It is the kind of ingredient considered so quintessentially English that the *Daily Mail* would probably go to war to defend it. In terms of culinary use, I don't think I ever gave it a great deal of thought.

Then I went to Dominica. The overriding colour in Dominica is also green, but it is stronger, deeper and brighter. The island is largely undeveloped, with rainforest-covered mountains and allegedly a different river or stream for every day of the year, many of which cascade down to the sea. These water sources are often the focal point of daily life – people wash their

clothes in them, swim in them, catch crayfish in
them and land crabs by them. It should not have surprised
me to find that an island with such an abundance of fresh
water should be a haven for watercress, but it did. Walking
up through the peaceful and well-cared-for terraced vegetable
gardens, following the stream up to where the cultivated
land met the lower reaches of the rainforest, I was taken to
the point where the water was no longer visible, hidden as
it was by a dense covering of healthy, flourishing green. It felt
like a single moving entity, spilling over the rocks, swaying
back and forth as it was pulled at gently, and itself in turn
resisting the current. It was as plentiful as anything you
might see in Hampshire.

I had persuaded a co-worker to take me up to see these banks
of watercress. She, like most of the locals who worked in the
same kitchen as me, pretty much ignored it as a foodstuff. In
the kitchen it was neglected too, relegated to being a garnish
and left uneaten by most of our customers. Nevertheless, just
seeing it grow in situ made me revaluate it as an ingredient.

We value watercress for its punch – that peppery, mustardy
hit that makes it such a good foil for richer ingredients, and
which is one of the reasons we match it with oily fish. I now
know that watercress grows all over the more mountainous
Caribbean islands and is used extensively as a salad green.
I do love it raw, and often use it to round off a saltfish salad
(see page 120) where its peppery notes balance the salt,
sweet, sour, heat of the other ingredients. But I also like it as a
cooked vegetable – it can cut through the richness of coconut
milk and cream, so is good to add alongside or in place of
spinach in curries. It can offset the sickliness of sweet potato
in purées and fritters. It will make a fine soup, especially
when garnished with butter-fried, garlicky freshwater crayfish.
And the stems have the same succulent, cooling property of
cucumber, borage and purslane – they can be chopped into
salsas and raitas to temper the heat of the ubiquitous Scotch
bonnet. It works.

Caribbean Saltfish Salad
with Watercress

Serves 4

300g (10½oz) saltfish fillet

1 tsp allspice berries

A few sprigs of dried thyme

1 bay leaf

A few strips of pared lime zest

Juice of 2 limes

Sea salt and freshly ground black
  pepper

For the salad

1 firm mango, peeled and finely diced

1 green (bell) pepper, finely diced

1 bunch of spring onions (scallions),
  finely chopped

1 Scotch bonnet, deseeded and
  deveined, very finely chopped

1 small bunch of parsley, leaves only

A few celery leaves

1 bunch of watercress

Sea salt and freshly ground black
  pepper

For the salad dressing

2 tbsp groundnut oil

2 tsp sherry vinegar

Juice of ½ lime

1 tsp honey

A dash of hot sauce

¼ tsp medium curry powder

1 small garlic clove, crushed

Sea salt and freshly ground
  black pepper

This salad is all about the layering of flavours. It is the main reason I have prepared the saltfish in this fast way rather than the cold-soak method, as it means aromatics can be introduced under heat. If you can, get a semi or just-ripe mango – you want something that will hold its shape when diced, not turn to mush, with a hint of sourness about it. The watercress is the main green here and works well with the heat because of the cooling nature of the stems.

First, prepare the saltfish. Rinse off as much of the surface salt as you can, then put it in a saucepan. Cover with hot water and bring to the boil. Leave to boil for 25 minutes, then drain. Give the saucepan a quick wash if there is starchy foam clinging to the sides. Peel off the fish skin and return it to the saucepan along with the aromatics and the juice of 1 of the limes. Cover with water and boil again – this time for 20 minutes. Drain and flake the fish as soon as it is cool enough to handle. It is now ready to use. Squeeze over the remaining lime juice. Taste and check for seasoning – it sounds perverse, but you may need to add salt, and you will definitely need to add black pepper.

Mix the saltfish with the mango, pepper, spring onions, Scotch bonnet and most of the parsley and celery leaves. Pick over the watercress – separate the small sprigs and leaves from the large stems, then finely chop the stems and add to the salad. Stir the leaves through too and taste once more for seasoning.

Make the dressing by whisking together all the ingredients and seasoning generously with salt and pepper. Pour over the salad and toss to combine. Garnish with the remaining leaves.

Castelfranco Salad with Pear and Blue Cheese

Serves 4

1 large head or 2 small heads of castelfranco, roughly torn

200g (1 cup) cooked farro, spelt or barley

3 fat or 4 slender pears, peeled, cored and cut into slim wedges

Juice of ½ lemon

150g (5¼oz) blue cheese, such as Roquefort, cubed

For the dressing

½ tsp Dijon mustard

1 tbsp sherry vinegar

4 tbsp hazelnut oil

Sea salt and freshly ground black pepper

This is one of those classic combinations I usually shy away from, but the sum of the three main parts is perfect – as long as the quality is just so. You need a blue cheese that is creamy but not bland, as it needs a bit of sharpness about it. Likewise, the pear must be only just ripe – sweet, but still with a hint of crispness. As for the castelfranco, you want one that is still tightly furled in the centre; start breaking into it and you will see a deeper contrast between the claret red and the pale buttermilk yellow.

This is a good starter without the farro, and is enough for a light meal with it.

Put the castelfranco in a large salad bowl or arrange over a platter. Sprinkle over the farro, allowing plenty of it to fall under the leaves.

Drop the pear wedges into the lemon juice and toss so the exposed surface of the pear is lightly coated – this will stop oxidisation and browning. Arrange the pear slices and the blue cheese over the leaves and farro.

Make the dressing. Whisk the mustard and vinegar together with plenty of seasoning, then gradually add the oil. Drizzle the dressing over the salad just before serving.

Variations

Castelfranco is at its best when blood oranges are in season, and these make an excellent substitute for pears, offering a slightly sharper foil to the leaves and creamy cheese. Cut the peel off two oranges and cut out the orange segments, leaving the membrane and central core behind. Squeeze the juice from the membrane and the peel into the salad dressing.

Onglet Steak Salad
with Mustard Green Chimichurri

Serves 4

500g (1lb 1½oz) piece onglet (hanger) steak, split along its central vein

1 tsp dried thyme

1 tsp dried oregano

½ tsp ground black pepper

Sea salt

For the salad

1 x quantity Chimichurri (see page 34)

1 small bunch of young mustard greens, shredded

A few herbs, such as 2 sprigs of thyme, 2 sprigs of tarragon, leaves only, or a small bunch of parsley

200g (7oz) tomatoes, roughly chopped

200g (2¾ cups) cooked black beluga lentils

2 tbsp olive oil

200g (7oz) salad leaves, such as watercress, mizuna, spinach, lamb's lettuce (corn salad)

This is like a green equivalent of steak with horseradish. It is all best prepared a day ahead – the chimichurri is much better after it has been sitting for a while, the steak will benefit from a dry marinade in the fridge. The lentils can be cooked any time really, but it won't do them any harm to sit.

The night before you want to eat, remove the onglet from its packaging. Mix the dried thyme, oregano and black pepper with salt and rub it all over the steak to rest overnight, on a plate, loosely covered by kitchen towel. This is what I would do in an ideal world – but if you can only give it a couple of hours to marinate, don't worry, anything helps. When you are 1 hour away from wanting to cook your steak, remove it from the fridge so it can return to room temperature.

Make the chimichurri as on page 34, adding the mustard greens along with your chosen herbs.

Put a griddle pan on to heat. When it is too hot to hold your hand over, add the meat. Cook to your own taste, but do not try to lift it off and turn until it is ready to and comes away clean – you want a deep, charred crust to develop for maximum flavour. Cook the other side, then turn a couple of times if you wish. Remove from the heat and leave to rest.

Assemble the rest of the salad ingredients on a large platter, then thinly slice the steak crossways and add this, along with any meat juices. Toss gently together, then drizzle over the chimichurri and serve.

Roast Red Cabbage
and Camargue Rice Salad

Serves 4

1 branch of rosemary

3 tbsp olive oil

1 red cabbage, cut into thin wedges

75g (¾ cup) Carmargue red rice

1 small bunch of dill, roughly chopped

1 small bunch of mint, leaves only

1 small bunch of parsley, roughly
  chopped

Seeds from ½ pomegranate

Sea salt and freshly ground black
  pepper

For the dressing

4 x 5cm (2in) sprigs of rosemary

2 tbsp olive oil

2 tbsp tahini

2 tsp pomegranate molasses

Sea salt

Roasting red cabbage in this way is perfect for a warm salad, as you get a variety of textures. The core will be sweet and tender, the leaves closest to the core will still have a little bite, and the outer leaves will crisp up. I have also become a bit addicted to the flavour of roasted or grilled rosemary. It chars beautifully, becoming crisp and crumbly, and loses that tickly texture it shares with most spiky leaves.

I love this on its own as a salad, but it is also a really good side dish to roast lamb. Or, you could add a couple of lamb steaks to the roasting tin after the cabbage has had its first 20 minutes in the oven. If you do this, just make sure you give the lamb some resting time before slicing it thinly to add to the salad.

Preheat the oven to 200ºC (400ºF/Gas 6).

Toss the rosemary for the dressing in 1 tablespoon of the olive oil and put in a roasting tin. Roast for 5 minutes, or until the needles are crisp. Remove from the oven, then strip the needles from the stems and crush with ½ teaspoon sea salt – this is best done using a pestle and mortar.

Put the rosemary branch in the base of the roasting tin and place the wedges of cabbage on top. Drizzle with the remaining olive oil and sprinkle over plenty of sea salt and pepper. Roast for around 40 minutes, until the cores are tender when pierced with a knife and the leaves have a brown char around the edges.

While the cabbage is roasting, cook the rice according to the packet instructions (usually around half an hour) and make the dressing. Mix the rosemary with the tahini and pomegranate molasses. Add the remaining olive oil and enough water so you have a dressing somewhere between single (light) and double (heavy) cream.

To assemble, stir two thirds of the herbs and pomegranate seeds through the rice and divide between four plates. Top with the roasted cabbage, then drizzle over the dressing. Sprinkle over the remaining herbs and seeds and serve while still warm.

Gnudi with Pea Shoot Salad and Pistachio and Herb Vinaigrette

Serves 4

250g (8¾oz) ricotta

75g (2½oz) peas, lightly cooked and cooled

2 tbsp finely grated Parmesan

250g (8¾oz) fine semolina, for dusting

Olive oil, for drizzling

Salt and freshly ground black pepper

For the vinaigrette

2 tbsp pistachios

1 tbsp hard cheese – I like a ewes' cheese, such as pecorino

25g (¾oz) wild garlic, or ½ garlic clove

A few sprigs of tarragon

A few fronds of fennel

50ml (¼ cup) olive oil

1 tbsp lemon juice

Juice of ½ orange

Sea salt and freshly ground black pepper

For the salad

50g (1¾oz) pea shoots

10 asparagus spears, trimmed

A few basil, tarragon, chervil and fennel leaves or fronds

This is one for a late spring lunch, when the sun is shining, and you can feel the hope of summer in the air. You should plan a little in advance as the gnudi need resting time, but these are – dare I say it – foolproof compared with their trickier cousins, gnocchi. If the vinaigrette is also made ahead, then the last-minute assemblage is effortless.

First, make the gnudi; you will need to start this the day before, or at least several hours before you want to cook them. Drain the ricotta and put into a bowl. Crush the peas to a coarse purée, then stir through the ricotta along with the cheese. Season with salt and pepper.

Sprinkle half the semolina onto a roasting dish or a tray, then form heaped teaspoons of the ricotta mixture into small quenelles or rounds. If shaping into rounds with your hands, wet them first and dip into the semolina – this will stop the whole process descending into a sticky mess. Quenelles, shaped by scooping the ricotta from one teaspoon to another, is much easier. Drop the gnudi into the semolina, then sprinkle over the rest of it. Leave in the fridge for at least 8 hours, until the semolina has formed a light crust around the ricotta.

To cook the gnudi, bring a large saucepan of salted water to the boil. Add the gnudi in one large batch, then leave to simmer for 3–4 minutes. They will be done when they float to the top of the pan. Remove with a slotted spoon to a bowl and drizzle with a little olive oil.

To make the vinaigrette, put the pistachios into a small food processor. Pulse until finely chopped, then add the cheese. Pulse again, then add the herbs. Process until the herbs are finely chopped. Transfer from the food processor to a bowl and lightly whisk in the oil and citrus juice – you don't want an emulsion, more a suspension of ingredients in oil. If it is too thick, thin with a little water, then season with salt and pepper.

Shave the asparagus spears into strips, using a peeler, and put into iced water. When you are ready to serve, drain and arrange on a plate with the gnudi and pea shoots. Drizzle over the dressing and garnish with the herbs.

Green Papaya Salad

Serves 4

1 green papaya

1 carrot, julienned

4 spring onions (scallions), shredded

A handful of laksa leaves, shredded

A handful of coriander (cilantro) leaves

A few small mint leaves

2 tbsp roasted, salted peanuts, lightly crushed

2 tbsp dried shrimp, chopped

2 red or green Thai chillies, thinly sliced

For the dressing

2 tbsp fish sauce

Juice of 2 limes

1 tsp palm sugar, honey or light soft brown sugar

1 shallot, thinly sliced

1 garlic clove, grated

2cm (¾in) piece ginger, peeled and finely grated

This is by no means a traditional papaya salad, as it is very herby. I grow laksa leaves (also known as Vietnamese mint or rau ram) all year round, and I cannot get enough of their flavour and aroma. I am sure I now overuse them (they even find their way into toasted cheese sandwiches), but they are perfect in this salad.

First make the dressing. Mix the fish sauce, lime juice and sugar together until the sugar has dissolved, then stir in the remaining ingredients. Taste and adjust the seasoning to your liking – you might want to add salt, or more lime juice or more palm sugar.

Prepare the green papaya. Cut it in half lengthways and scoop out the white seeds and the papery layer of membrane in the hollow of the fruit. Peel the papaya then shred the flesh. I use a julienne peeler – a strip setting on a mandolin or even a coarse grater would also work.

Mix the papaya with the carrot, spring onions and herbs, then pour over the salad dressing and toss. Garnish with the peanuts, dried shrimp and chillies.

Puntarelle Salad

Serves 4

1 head of puntarelle

50g (1¾oz) Parmesan or similar hard
  cheese, shaved (optional)

For the dressing

2 garlic cloves, crushed

Juice of 1 lemon

4 anchovy fillets, finely chopped

4 tbsp olive oil

Sea salt and freshly ground black
  pepper

The first time I ate a puntarelle salad was on a
Christmas day when an Italian guest took over the
starters for me. He made *passatelli in brodo* and a
puntarelle salad with this traditional dressing. I feel
there are two ways to go when dressing anything bitter.
In my last book, *Citrus*, I took the sweet route with
oranges, but perhaps an even better foil is the intensely
savoury flavour from mashed anchovies.

There is a special tool for slicing the puntarelle into
what will eventually be slender curls – it is a wire,
crossed over a simple wooden frame, through which you
push the puntarelle lengthways – a bit like a green bean
shredder, and actually, you can use this tool for beans
too. I like using it, but a sharp knife will work well.
What is essential is a bowl of iced water to leave the
puntarelle in while you prepare the rest of the salad.

Puntarelle actually refers to the central core of this
vegetable, which is a type of chicory. It is this centre
of stems you need for the salad. The outer leaves are
much more bitter – you can finely chop them and add
them to the salad if you like, but you can also treat
them like dandelion leaves and use them in the salad
on page 113 or fry them with or without a tomato sauce
(see page 199).

Strip away the looser, outer leaves of the puntarelle. Pull
apart the hollow stems you will find in the centre of the
head – these will provide the bulk of your salad. Trim
away any stray leaves and set aside with the outer leaves.
Take each stem and slice it very thinly. Put in the iced
water and leave for 1 hour – they will curl up pleasingly
during this time.

While the puntarelle are soaking, start the dressing. Crush
the garlic and add it to the lemon juice. Leave to stand
until the puntarelle is ready. Then you can either strain it
or leave the garlic in – it is up to you how strong you want
it. Mash the anchovies and mix with the lemon juice, then
whisk in the olive oil. Taste for seasoning and adjust as
you like – it should be quite peppery.

Drain the puntarelle well and toss in the salad dressing.
Scatter with cheese, if using, and serve immediately.

Classic Wedge Salad

(in praise of crispheads)

Serves 4

1 tbsp olive oil

6 slices of streaky bacon

1 small shallot, very finely chopped

1 tbsp cider vinegar

1 iceberg lettuce (see method)

4 radishes, finely diced

Sea salt

For the blue cheese dressing

50g (1¾oz) creamy blue cheese
(gorgonzola works well)

100ml (scant ½ cup) buttermilk

50ml (¼ cup) sour cream

Up to 1 tbsp white wine vinegar

Crispheads are glorious lettuces to look at – tightly furled heads, surrounded by generous crowns of softly serrated leaves. In markets all over the world we see them at their best; invitingly abundant, glossy and green, used as everything from thirst quenchers to edible cups. In the UK, however, they – and by 'they' I mean mainly the iceberg, by far the most popular crisphead lettuce grown and a staple of industrialised agriculture – are untrendy, unless you are being ironically retro and making a prawn cocktail, and derided for their lack of flavour and nutritional content. But I like them. They stay crisp and sweet and juicy, and are as refreshing as a cucumber. I can crunch through wedges of them like an apple – unadorned or drizzled with another retro ingredient that fills me with joy – salad cream. I am not going to introduce anything earth-shatteringly new here (although perhaps you haven't tried it stir fried – see page 201), because I love a classic wedge salad, in which iceberg shows it is the perfect foil for anything tart, spicy, creamy. Type 'wedge salad' into Google and the most common 'people also ask' question is, 'What is the point of a wedge salad?' Do not be one of these people. Find out for yourself.

First prepare the bacon garnish. Put the olive oil in a large frying pan and add the bacon. Fry over a low-medium heat, slowly, as you want the fat to render out and the bacon to crisp without it burning. Transfer to some kitchen towel. When it has cooled, finely chop or crumble.

Next, cover the shallot in vinegar, diluted with 1 tablespoon water, and salt generously. Set aside.

Take the lettuce, trim the stem very slightly if it is brown, and cut through it to the top of the lettuce. Cut each half into 3 wedges, so the leaves are still attached to the core.

Make the dressing by mashing up the blue cheese and whisking with the buttermilk and sour cream. Add the white wine vinegar ½ teaspoon at a time until you have an acidity you are happy with and taste for seasoning. The dressing should be creamy with just a hint of acidity.

Arrange the wedges on a plate and drizzle with dressing. Sprinkle over the shallots, bacon and radishes.

Quick and Easy Salads

Tabbouleh Four Ways

Tabbouleh really is the ultimate in chopped salads. The concept – finely worked herbs, given texture by way of grains – is such an excellent one that I feel strongly that it shouldn't be confined by origin or ingredient. The classic is perfect, but there are combinations that I love just as much. As long as you get the basics right – and by this I mean you chop the herbs as finely as you can, and make sure the grains do not overwhelm the herbs, in fact, are barely visible – and keep it simple with additional ingredients, you can't go far wrong.

Tabbouleh is often relegated to a side salad or a small bowl as part of a mezze. I will quite happily eat it on its own, spooned into wraps of floppy lettuce leaves. Here are some options.

The classic contains mainly flat leaf parsley, but could also include coriander (cilantro), dill and mint. I prefer adding a bit of dried mint to fresh, as fresh always goes black too quickly, but it is up to you. Take a very large bunch of parsley and smaller ones of any other herbs you would like to add and chop as finely as possible. Soak 2 tablespoons bulgur wheat in boiling water for 30 minutes, then drain and mix with the herbs, a couple of finely chopped tomatoes, a chunk of peeled, deseeded cucumber and half a red onion, both finely chopped. Dress with a squeeze of lemon juice and plenty of olive oil and sprinkle with a little sumac if you wish.

Move **further east** and make the main herb coriander (cilantro). Add laksa leaves, Thai basil, garlic chives, mint and finely chop the lot. Mix with 2 tablespoons finely chopped cashew nuts (or quinoa if you'd rather use a grain), cucumber as before, 3–4 spring onions (scallions) and a piece of semi-ripe papaya, doused in lime, all very finely chopped. Dress with 1 teaspoon fish sauce mixed with the juice of a lime and plenty of olive oil as before. Serve in cups of iceberg lettuce.

This time think **English country garden**. Make the base watercress and sweet herbs such as borage, chervil, Genoese basil if it is soft and floppy, and tarragon, with a few spicy notes from chives or wild garlic. Stick with tomato and cucumber, but in place of the bulgur, use finely chopped hazelnuts. Dress in tarragon vinegar if you have it, cider vinegar if you don't, and plenty of olive oil.

Turn north and embrace dark, earthy bitter flavours from kales, mustard greens and pungent herbs. Destem some kale (massage if you like, but only very lightly) and chop it very finely along with mustard greens and beetroot leaves, including their jewel-coloured stems. Mix with dill and a few lovage leaves, a few caraway seeds and if you want to lift the mood, mint. Add cucumber and cooked beetroot and a wholegrain such as spelt or buckwheat groats – this one is very robust, but entirely edible, promise – and toss in a dressing of wholegrain mustard, red wine vinegar and oil.

Summer Garden Salad

This is the best of my garden at the height of summer. I walk around and pick out tender leaves and flowers, then jumble them together in a salad that is pretty and a bit messy, with every mouthful giving you a burst of something unexpected. I am not going to suggest you buy all of these herbs if you don't have them, but try to pick out 3–4 and if you don't already do this, it is really worth growing a few on your kitchen windowsill.

Take a large bunch of runner beans. De-string them (run a peeler down both sides), then shred with a sharp knife or bean slicer and blanch in salted water until just tender. Drain and rinse under cold water. Take some very small, young courgettes (zucchini) and slice them finely into rounds. Add to a bowl with the runner beans, a few handfuls of baby salad leaves, and a selection of herbs – I will include tender leaves and flowers from tarragon, chervil, fennel, dill, lemon verbena, lemon myrtle, various mints, thymes, basil, borage, sorrel, chives and marigold. Toss them together and dress with olive oil and tarragon vinegar. You could also finely grate in some Parmesan, if you like.

Dressed Floppy Lettuce

You can use any kind of soft-leaved lettuce for this – the floppy green sorts that are as cheap as chips in the supermarket, a butterhead or an oak leaf. They will all work well.

Make a vinaigrette with 4 tablespoons walnut oil, 1 tablespoon red wine vinegar, ½ teaspoon Dijon mustard and 2 thinly sliced shallots. Whisk together and season generously. Roughly tear the leaves from 1–2 heads of lettuce, depending on their size, leaving whole the smaller ones closer to the heart. Toss the lettuce in the dressing and serve immediately before it wilts.

Raw Kale Salad with Pomegranate and Almonds

I never imagined in a million years I would want to eat a raw kale salad, and yet there are two of them in this chapter. This one is based on a recipe by Danish cook Trine Hahnemann. I don't think I would ever have made it if it hadn't been put in front of me, but it was, and I did, thus I was converted.

Take a large bunch of curly kale and remove the stems. Shred the leaves as finely as you can – this is important, as it will stop the leaves being scratchy when you eat them. Lightly toast 2 tablespoons flaked almonds then remove to cool. Remove the seeds from a pomegranate. Combine everything in a bowl, then dress with 2 tablespoons olive oil, a squeeze of orange juice, a squeeze of lemon juice and plenty of salt and pepper. Toss and serve immediately.

Lightly Spiced Mixed Leaf and Lentil Salad

This salad relies on a good old-fashioned mango chutney. A really sweet one. Take half a cucumber, deseed and finely dice it. Thinly slice an onion and dice a red or green (bell) pepper. Put them all in a colander and sprinkle with salt. Leave to stand for 30 minutes. Mix with 200g (1 cup) cooked lentils – it doesn't matter what sort. Make a dressing – take 2 tablespoons mango chutney and chop it as finely as you can. Add to it a crushed garlic clove, a finely chopped red chilli or some chilli powder, 1 tablespoon cider vinegar and 2 tablespoons nut oil. Whisk together and taste – add seasoning if needed. Thin down with a little water if you like, then stir through the vegetables and lentils. Finally, pick over a large bunch of fenugreek leaves (methi) – you can finely chop some of the stems and add to the vegetables. Mix the fenugreek leaves with any other leaves you fancy – think any type of spinach, baby amaranth, rocket (arugula), watercress – along with a few coriander (cilantro) leaves. Mix everything together. Drizzle over a tiny amount of Curry Leaf Vinegar (see page 32) if you have any, and serve. This is good on its own or with some grilled paneer.

Shredded White Cabbage and Crab Salad

This is another example of the sublime crab/chervil combination. It is a based on a salad I ate at Fergus Henderson's St John restaurant, and I hope it retains all his trademark simplicity. I normally salt cabbage before using it raw, as it keeps it crisp, but the cabbage here is at its best almost wilting down, and this is not a salad you are going to want to leave hanging around for long – it is best fresh.

Take half a white cabbage and shred it as finely as you can. The thinnest setting on a mandolin will give you the best results if you dare to use one, otherwise a very sharp knife and patience. Take a large bunch of chervil and pick off half the leaves. Add these to the cabbage along with 125g (4½oz) crab meat, then finely chop the rest. You want them almost chopped to a purée so they will leach out colour into the oil. Mix with 3 tbsp olive oil, and the zest and juice of 1 lime – you should have a bright, intensely green dressing. Season generously with salt and pepper, then pour over the cabbage. Mix thoroughly.

Cucumber with Shiso and Szechuan Pepper Leaves

The Szechuan peppercorn tree is a wonderful thing to grow. Mine arrived no more than a bare twig, and within a couple of years was taller than me and throwing out any number of leaves which – wonder of wonders – had the same mouth-numbing, refreshing quality of the peppercorns. The tree is a spiky one and so are the leaves, so I just use the very soft, young ones that haven't had time to grow claws. I use them here to ramp up the coolness of the shiso – but if you don't have any, add a few crushed Szechuan peppercorns instead, or just miss them out entirely.

Take a large cucumber. Peel it if you wish (I usually do) and scrape out the seeds with a spoon. Slice into crescents and put in a colander. Sprinkle with a teaspoon of salt, toss to combine and leave to stand for half an hour. After this time some liquid will have drained away from the cucumber and it will be crisp. Put into a bowl. Mix a dressing with 1 tablespoon light soy sauce or tamari, 1 tablespoon lime juice, a few drops of sesame oil and a pinch of caster (superfine) sugar. Pour over the cucumber. Shred a large handful of shiso leaves (preferably a mixture of red and green), and mix with the cucumber. If you have them, add a few tiny Szechuan pepper leaves too. Sprinkle over 1 tablespoon sesame seeds and a fine dusting of a red chilli powder.

Coriander and Spring Onion Salad

This is something I have adapted from my local Korean restaurant, expanding a coriander (cilantro) salad to use the greens from spring onions (scallions). I hope it is in the spirit of the dish. I also use it as a sauce to go with noodles.

Take a large bunch of spring onions, preferably long with plenty of greens at the top. Separate into white and green. Finely slice the whites, and leave the greens intact. Take a large bunch of coriander, separate into stems and sprigs of leaves and discard the stems – you can use them for something else. Make a dressing from 1 tablespoon each of dark soy sauce, rice wine vinegar and sesame oil along with mild Korean chilli powder to taste (between 1 teaspoon–1 tablespoon). Heat 1 teaspoon oil in a wok and quickly fry the spring onion whites. Add a finely chopped garlic clove and a small piece of ginger, also finely chopped, and fry for another minute or two. Remove from the heat and add the spring onion greens. Leave it to wilt down and cool to room temperature, then add the coriander. Toss everything together with the dressing and sprinkle with sesame seeds. Serve at room temperature.

Spicy Noodle Salad

The greens in this are all about the dressing – a pesto-like concoction, using laksa leaves. This, incidentally, could be turned into a soup – just heat a little stock and coconut milk and swirl everything in. This is great to have in the fridge for summer lunches and picnics.

Take a couple of large handfuls of cooked noodles – any you like – and put into a bowl with a dash of sesame oil. Julienne a large courgette (zucchini) and carrot into long noodles – you can use one of those new-fangled spiralizers if you like, but I use an old-fashioned metal cutter (like a peeler but with ridges). Add a few finely chopped spring onions (scallions), a few chopped radishes if you like, and handfuls of mint, coriander (cilantro) and Thai basil. Make a paste with a large handful each of coriander and laksa leaves, 4 kaffir lime leaves, 50g (1¾oz) cashew nuts, a medium-hot green chilli, a garlic clove, 1 tablespoon fish or soy sauce and the zest and juice of 1 lime. Pound or blitz together with a little water to thin it out, toss in the noodles and garnish with sesame seeds.

Quick Avocado and
Blue Cheese Salad

I'm not sure anyone needs another avocado salad, let alone one with blue cheese, and yet, it is a wonderful combination. I even used to eat them baked together, inspired by a starter in an old-fashioned Italian restaurant. I know this will upset some people. Sorry.

Juice a lime into a bowl and add 1 teaspoon sea salt. Scoop the flesh from two avocados into the bowl, leaving it fairly chunky, and toss immediately. Add 150g (5¼oz) blue cheese – a creamy one like gorgonzola, preferably – roughly cubed. Toss with plenty of coriander (cilantro), mint and tiny basil leaves, and sprinkle with smoked chilli flakes. You can pile over lightly dressed leaves if you like. I promise it is good.

Tomato Salads

I put a tomato salad on the table probably at least a couple of times a week throughout most of the year. It means in the winter months I spend silly money on winter varieties (such as the superb Iberica Black tomatoes, which to me are better than most tomatoes at their summer peak). I think it's fair to say that most people might just throw some basil at it and think job done. There is nothing wrong with that. I make a tomato and basil salad on occasion using tips from tiny-leaved bush basil in favour of large, blowsy leaves that turn black as soon as look at you (cut or torn, they don't seem

to care). I also make the classic *tricolore* from time to time – although I am more likely to break open a large burrata, drizzle over some basil oil, and top with finely chopped tomatoes. Regardless, as tomatoes feature so frequently in my household as a side salad, I don't often want basil. Here are three options, but don't limit yourself – try tomatoes with the charred rosemary dressing on page 125, mixed with shredded laksa leaves and Thai basil and dressed with oil and a squeeze of chilli, or simply throw at them any tiny leaves from your garden. They will all work.

Tomatoes with Tarragon Cream Sauce

If you are in a hurry, just dress the tomatoes with finely chopped tarragon – or even chervil – and you will see how good they can be together. But for the sauce, take 1 tablespoon tarragon vinegar and put it in a small saucepan. Reduce down to 1 teaspoon, then add around 150ml (⅔ cup) single (light) cream, along with some sprigs of tarragon. Bring up to close to boiling, then remove from the heat and leave to infuse. Reheat gently, then remove the sprig and whisk in an egg yolk if you want the consistency of the sauce richer and creamier – this is entirely optional, but you must make sure you don't allow the sauce to boil from this point. Add lots of finely chopped tarragon and season with salt and pepper. Taste and add a few more drops of the vinegar if you like, bearing in mind the acidity of the tomatoes.

Tomatoes with Agretti and Capers

I don't know why I wish that agretti was a summer vegetable, but it isn't, and I've never managed to grow it successfully – the seeds are viable for about 2 minutes before they won't germinate. However, it does provide a good, cooling foil for the salty-sweet astringency of winter tomatoes during those months when there isn't a great deal salady around, so I should not grumble. You could replace the agretti with rocket (arugula), but don't blanch it, obviously.

Take a bunch of agretti. Trim off the roots and wash thoroughly. Bring a saucepan of water to the boil and salt generously. Cook the agretti for no longer than a minute, then strain and immediately cool in ice-cold water. Drain thoroughly. Roughly chop 400g (14oz) tomatoes and add to the agretti along with 1 tablespoon capers and 1 tablespoon sliced olives (optional). Dress with olive oil and either a squeeze of lemon juice or a drizzle of sherry vinegar.

Madhur Jaffrey's Tomato Salad with Curry Leaves

This is a really quick way of getting something fresh on the table as a side to any type of curry. Even quicker would be if you've made the Curry Leaf Vinegar on page 32 – you could just whisk that with oil and dress, perhaps with a few coriander (cilantro) leaves as garnish.

Thickly slice or halve tomatoes depending on size, and season with salt and pepper. Heat 2 tablespoons olive oil in a pan, add 1 teaspoon mustard seeds, a dried red chilli and 12 curry leaves. Cook until the curry leaves have stopped crackling at you and are looking dry and crisp. Pour over the tomatoes and serve immediately.

Coleslaws

Years ago, a dentist told me that one of the best things you could do for your dental health was put a crunchy coleslaw-type salad on the table at every mealtime. I don't go this far, but I do like having coleslaw in the fridge. It's the sort of thing I might eat on its own, or with some grated cheese or smoked fish, when I am in full writing flow and I don't want to stop. It is worth more than that of course, but all the same, there is value in having healthy, crunchy snacks ready to go – it keeps the salt and vinegar crisps at bay.

I don't go in for very creamy, mayonnaise-laden coleslaws, which I often find a bit cloying – I pretty much always want something zingier. I find buttermilk makes the best dressing. Here are a few I like. Assume that everything is shredded as finely as you can get it – I use a mandolin on its thinnest setting, but if you don't trust yourself with one, use your sharpest knife.

A Summery Coleslaw

Take a small, green, tightly furled cabbage and finely shred it. Shred also a fennel bulb, a courgette (zucchini) and a peeled green apple (I like something with the tartness of Granny Smith). Put into a colander and toss in 1 teaspoon sea salt and the juice of ½ lemon. Leave to stand for 1 hour. Squeeze very gently and transfer to a bowl. Add the zest of ½ lemon and a few finely snipped chives, some fennel fronds, a few snips of tarragon and some small basil microleaves or leaves from bush basil (I don't like using large leaves here – they go black if torn or cut and this needs to stay fresh). If you have any, add some finely chopped wild garlic or 1 tablespoon fermented wild garlic (see page 27). Make a dressing from 50ml (¼ cup) buttermilk, 1 tablespoon sour cream, juice of ½ lemon, 1 tablespoon finely chopped tarragon and a pinch of caster (superfine) sugar. Season and pour over the vegetables. Stir to combine.

Sauerkraut Coleslaw

Any of the sauerkraut/ferments in this book will be good in coleslaw – in moderation, just to add depth and a slight funkiness to all the fresh ingredients. Here's a simple one to get you started. I like this with smoked cheese or cold cuts.

Finely shred a small white or red cabbage. Add 2 celery sticks, thinly chopped, 1 small white onion, very finely sliced and 1 carrot, julienned. Put into a colander, sprinkle with salt and leave to stand for 1 hour. Squeeze the liquid out of any type of ferment or sauerkraut and chop finely – I will probably use around 100g (3½oz) white cabbage sauerkraut (see page 24), less of anything with a more pronounced flavour. Add this to the other vegetables. Whisk together 50ml (¼ cup) buttermilk, 1 tablespoon sour cream, 1 tablespoon wholegrain mustard and ½ teaspoon honey. Pour over the vegetables and stir to combine, then add any herbs you like – dill is good.

Brussels Sprout Caesar Coleslaw

A raw Brussels sprout salad is a stretch too far for me, but I do like salting them as I would for a coleslaw. The method also means you end up with a variety of textures.

Trim the Brussels sprouts. Leave whole any of the outer leaves which may fall off after trimming and finely shred the rest. Sprinkle with 1 teaspoon sea salt and massage in until they start to feel wet, then leave to stand for 30 minutes. Add any other vegetables you like, for example a thinly sliced shallot, some carrot or any other greens, or just leave it plain.

Meanwhile, make the dressing. Finely chop 6 anchovy fillets and mix with a crushed garlic clove, juice of ½ lemon, 1 teaspoon Dijon mustard and 4 tablespoons olive oil. Squeeze out the salted Brussels sprouts and put in a bowl with plenty of finely chopped parsley. Pour over the dressing, then sprinkle in 25g (¾oz) grated Parmesan and mix thoroughly.

VEGETARIAN
MAIN COURSES

Braise of Kale and Mushrooms with Sage and Apple Dumplings

Serves 4

1 tbsp olive oil

2 tbsp butter

2 medium red onions, sliced into wedges

6 portobello or field mushrooms, thickly sliced

250g (8¾oz) chestnut mushrooms, halved

2 garlic cloves

1 sprig of thyme

1 sprig of rosemary

A few fresh sage leaves

150ml (⅔ cup) red wine

200ml (¾ cup) vegetable or mushroom stock

500g (1lb 1½oz) any type of kale such as buttonhole, variegated, cavolo nero or curly, destemmed if very woody and roughly chopped

For the dumplings

150g (1¼ cups) self-raising flour

75g (2½oz) suet or well-chilled butter

2 crisp eating apples, peeled and diced

2 tsp dried sage

50g (1¾oz) hard cheese, such as Cheddar, grated (optional)

Sea salt

I am susceptible to suggestion, and when I was developing this recipe I was reading Hilary McKay's *The Skylarks' War*, which mentioned apple dumplings. It meant the dessert type of dumpling, which is pastry-wrapped apples, but it did put me on the path to thinking a savoury apple dumpling would work well here, and it does.

This is proper autumnal food. It's a vegetarian version of a classic *boeuf Bourguignon*. Now, I have to admit that when I serve this with dumplings, I will favour beef suet from my butcher, rather than a vegetarian one, as these are all made from palm oil. A good alternative to both is to use chilled butter, which will make a softer, fluffier dumpling. If you want to forget about the dumplings entirely, you might consider serving the braise with the Parsley and Garlic Cannellini Beans on page 227.

I use red wine in this dish, but for a sweeter flavour, which carries through the apples in the suet dumplings, you could use cider instead.

Heat the olive oil and butter in a wide, lidded frying pan or casserole dish (Dutch oven). Add the red onions and cook over a medium heat until starting to soften, around 10 minutes. Turn up the heat and add the mushrooms, garlic and herbs. Cook for another few minutes to lightly brown the mushrooms, then pour in the red wine. Bring to the boil and reduce by half, then add the stock. Return to the boil and then add the kale. Allow to wilt into the sauce for a few minutes while you make the dumplings.

Put the flour, suet, apple and sage into a bowl with plenty of salt. Add just enough water to make a slightly sticky dough. Pull into 8 pieces and try to roughly approximate a spherical shape – I say roughly as the mixture will be sticky and recalcitrant. Dot around the braised vegetables and cover. Cook for around 15–20 minutes until the dumplings are well risen and slightly glossy.

You can serve this dish as it is, or you can add the cheese. If doing so, sprinkle the cheese over the dumplings, once cooked, and put under a hot grill until melted and starting to brown.

Pici Verdi with Parsley and Breadcrumbs

Serves 4

200g (7oz) spinach, well washed

300–350g (2½–scant 3 cups)
  '00' pasta flour

Sea salt

For the sauce

3 tbsp olive oil, plus extra for drizzling

2 garlic cloves, finely chopped or
  crushed

½ tsp dried chilli flakes

1 piece of pared lemon zest, very thinly
  sliced

50g (1 cup) fresh breadcrumbs

1 small bunch of parsley, leaves only,
  finely chopped, plus extra whole to
  serve

A few basil leaves, finely chopped, plus
  extra whole to serve

200g (7oz) any leaves, including rocket
  (arugula), baby leaf salads, spinach,
  baby chard and beetroot (beet),
  to serve

Sea salt and freshly ground black
  pepper

I was so sceptical about this as every time I have tried to make eggless pasta at home, the results have been a bit grim. However, this one is amazingly quick, easy and the texture is just perfect. It's also a great to make with children, as they like rolling out the pasta into snakes.

The sauce is deliberately vegan, but of course there are plenty of non-vegan ingredients you could add if you wanted – you can mash anchovies into the sauce, or add a sprinkling of Parmesan at the end, if you like.

To make the pasta, shake off the excess water from the spinach and put into a food processor with 300g (2½ cups) flour and a pinch of salt. Blitz together until the spinach has completely broken down and formed a dough with the flour. You may need to push everything down the sides once or twice. Check the dough – if it is very sticky, add more flour. It should be soft and slightly tacky.

To roll out the pasta, pull off small balls (around the size of a large marble) and start by rolling between your hands. Then lay the pieces out on a work surface and roll lightly with both hands, moving from the centre outwards. If it is very sticky, coat the palms of your hands with a little flour, but try not to use too much as it makes the pasta much harder to roll – it will slide away from you. The length of the pasta doesn't really matter here, but it is advisable to make it all roughly the same thickness, 5mm (¼in) diameter.

The pasta can be cooked right away, in plenty of salted water, or it can be dried out. If you are cooking from fresh, it will take 5 minutes. If it is dry, 8–10 minutes.

To make the sauce, heat the oil in a large frying pan. Add the garlic and chilli and cook for a minute or two, then add the zest and breadcrumbs. Cook, stirring regularly, until crisp and brown, then add the herbs. Season.

Cook the pasta according to the instructions above. If you have leaves to use up, add them just as the pasta is ready. As soon as they have wilted, drain, reserving a ladleful of the cooking water. Add the pasta to the sauce, and toss to coat. Drizzle with oil and if it feels dry, add some of the cooking water. Serve with parsley and basil leaves.

Green Parmigiana

Serves 4

4 aubergines (eggplants) or large courgettes (zucchini), sliced lengthways

500g (1lb 1½oz) greens (see introduction), well washed

½ x quantity Tomato Sauce (see page 199)

75g (2½oz) ricotta

Zest of 1 lemon

Leaves from a small bunch of basil, finely chopped

Leaves from a small bunch of tarragon, finely chopped

A few sprigs of lemon thyme, finely chopped

2–3 balls of mozzarella

50g (1¾oz) Parmesan or vegetarian equivalent, grated

Salt and freshly ground black pepper

This is like a green version of melanzane parmigiana, with the option of using courgettes (zucchini) when there is a glut of them. You could replace either with sheets of lasagne if you wanted – it does speed up the preparation time considerably. My preferred method of cooking the aubergines (eggplants) or courgettes for this dish is to cook them over a griddle or an outside grill.

You can use any greens in this recipe. I like the bite of rocket (arugula) and watercress with a handful of lemony sorrel. You can also use chard, spinach, lettuce – anything that will wilt down well.

First cook the aubergines or courgettes: if you have the time, griddling is the best way as you get char lines and a smokier flavour. Heat a griddle until it is too hot to hold your hand over. Arrange the vegetable slices over the griddle and cook until dark lines have appeared on the underside and they easily lift off. Flip over and repeat. Alternatively, preheat the oven to 200°C (400°F/Gas 6), lightly brush baking (cookie) sheets with olive oil and arrange the slices over them. Brush with olive oil then roast for 20 minutes, until soft and lightly browned.

Put the greens into a saucepan with enough water to cover the base – the greens will still be wet from washing so you don't need much. Set over a high heat and cook until the greens have wilted. Transfer to a colander and run under cold water, then wring out the excess liquid. Finely chop. Mix the greens with the Tomato Sauce.

Preheat the oven to 200°C (400°F/Gas 6).

In a small bowl, break up the ricotta with a fork and add the lemon zest, basil, tarragon and lemon thyme and stir through the ricotta, then season with salt and pepper.

To assemble, brush a large ovenproof dish with olive oil. Arrange a layer of the grilled veg on the base, then top with a ladleful of tomato sauce. Dot teaspoonfuls of the ricotta mixture over the top. Repeat twice, then cover with mozzarella. Grate over plenty of Parmesan and bake for 35–40 minutes, until bubbling and piping hot. Leave to rest for 10 minutes.

Freekeh and Vine Leaf Pilau
with Baked Feta and Tomatoes

Serves 4

2 tbsp olive oil

1 onion, finely chopped

2 garlic cloves, finely chopped

Zest of 1 lemon

½ tsp ground cinnamon

½ tsp ground allspice

150g (5¼oz) cracked freekeh, well rinsed and soaked for 5 minutes

300ml (1¼ cups) vegetable stock or water

A handful of brined vine leaves, shredded

1 small bunch of parsley, finely chopped

50g (1¾oz) pine nuts

Sea salt and freshly ground black pepper

For the baked feta and tomatoes

Olive oil, for drizzling

200g (7oz) tomatoes and/or watermelon, thickly sliced or cut into chunks, respectively

150g (5¼oz) cucumber, peeled, deseeded and cut into crescents

A few sprigs oregano or rosemary

2 tbsp black olives

1 tbsp capers

200g (7oz) piece feta

A few mint leaves

Sea salt and freshly ground black pepper

The smoky bite of freekeh provides an excellent backdrop here to sweet spices, and the slightly fermented, tannin flavour of the brined vine leaves in this dish. If you want to use fresh vine leaves, blanch them in plenty of salted water first, to soften.

I much prefer the taste and texture of feta when it is baked – it mellows to a much less astringent creaminess, a perfect foil for the tomatoes or watermelon, both of which should be ripe, sweet and juicy.

Heat the olive oil in a large casserole dish (Dutch oven) or saucepan, then add the onion. Cook slowly over a medium heat, stirring regularly, until the onion is soft and translucent, around 10 minutes. Turn up the heat and allow the onion to start browning for a few minutes, then add the garlic, lemon zest, spices and drained freekeh. Fry for a few minutes so the freekeh is lightly toasted, then add the stock. Season with salt and pepper. Bring to the boil, then turn down the heat, cover, and leave to simmer for 5 minutes. Remove the lid, add the vine leaves, and continue to cook for a further 10 minutes.

Meanwhile, bake the feta. Preheat the oven to 200°C (400°F/Gas 6).

Take a small ovenproof dish and drizzle the base of it with olive oil. Add the tomatoes and/or watermelon and the cucumbers and season with salt and pepper. Sprinkle over the oregano or rosemary, olives and capers. Put the feta on top, left whole, and drizzle with more olive oil. Bake in the oven for around 20 minutes, until the feta has softened and puffed up very slightly.

Stir the parsley and pine nuts through the freekeh, then serve the two dishes together, with a few mint leaves scattered over the baked feta.

Spinach and Pomegranate Pie

Serves 4

500g (1lb 1½oz) spinach

500g (1lb 1½oz) other greens, such
  as chard, nettles, amaranth, rocket
  (arugula) or horta

2 tbsp olive oil

1 onion, finely chopped

2 garlic cloves, finely chopped

½ tsp ground cinnamon

½ tsp ground turmeric

150g (5¼oz) feta

100g (3½oz) pomegranate seeds

75g (2½oz) pine nuts

1 small bunch of mint, leaves only,
  finely chopped

A mixture of parsley, dill and tarragon
  leaves, finely chopped

6 large sheets of filo pastry

100g (3½oz) butter, melted

Sesame seeds, for sprinkling

Sumac and za'atar, for dusting

Sea salt and freshly ground black
  pepper

**One of the staples I eat whenever I am visiting my
parents in Greece is *spanakopita*. Every bakery has
several versions – some are very plain, some replace
the spinach with *horta*. This pie is a little bit different;
I wanted to create something that celebrates many of
the flavours and textures I associate with Greece, but is
more substantial.**

Wash the spinach thoroughly and transfer to a saucepan
without bothering to shake off the excess water. Cook until
wilted, then drain thoroughly. When it has cooled, squeeze
out as much liquid as you can, then finely chop.

If using chard, cut the stems away from the leaves. Finely
dice the stems and shred the leaves, making sure you keep
them separate. Shred any other greens you are using.

Heat the olive oil in a large frying pan. Add the onion and
chard stems, if using, and cook over a medium heat until
the onions are soft and translucent, around 10 minutes.
Add the garlic and spices, then the greens. When the greens
have wilted down, season with salt and pepper and remove
from the heat to cool. Add the spinach, feta, pomegranate
seeds, pine nuts and herbs to the pan and combine.

Take a sheet of filo pastry and lay it on top of a damp tea
towel. Brush generously with butter, then lay another sheet
on top. Brush with butter again. Take the next sheet and
overlap it with the first two sheets, so it covers a third of
the pastry. Butter, top with another sheet and butter again.
Finally do the same with a further two sheets.

Spread the green mixture along the bottom of the filo
pastry, leaving a border the same width as the filling on
the bottom and on each side. Fold the border over the
filling, then brush with butter. Fold in the side borders,
then roll up, not too tightly, brushing with butter as you go
until the filling is contained and you have a long snake.

Gently roll the snake into a coil. If it splits at any point,
do not worry – you can patch it with any remaining filo.
Transfer to a lined baking (cookie) sheet. Brush with
more butter and sprinkle with sesame seeds. Bake in the
preheated oven for around 25–30 minutes, until golden.

Dust lightly with sumac and za'atar, then serve.

FORAGED LEAVES

I am not a confident forager. I should be – I grew up in the countryside with the kind of mother who picked all kinds of edible things. There were regular blackberrying jaunts, puffballs grew in the field out the back, elderflowers, and later, their berries, were prolific. I knew to suck the nectar out of honeysuckle, and which flowers were edible. But as a child, I wouldn't voluntarily go near nettles, and most of the leaves we could pick were either too bitter for my palate (dandelions) or had that slightly tickly, peppery flavour profile, similar to nasturtiums, that I didn't love. The exception was sweet, aniseedy cicely.

These days, I still have a limited number of leaves I look forward to foraging. I pick and dry nettles (blanching first to get rid of the sting), and don't have to go far at all for these as I have allowed (ahem) a couple of patches to grow in the garden. Like most country children, I have a healthy respect for nettles. I knew their blistering sting and never found a dock leaf helpful – in fact, I always wondered whether looking for a dock leaf was just a way of distracting oneself from the pain of the nettle. This meant that I read with appalled fascination the fairytale about the poor girl who had to knit nettle shirts for her enchanted swan brothers, without the protection of gloves – and worse, Maid Maleen of Grimm Brothers fame, who was so hungry she was forced to eat them raw:

'I have known the time
When I ate thee unboiled
When I ate thee unroasted.'

Imagine! Anyway, with nettles you need to be careful of the sting, and you also need to be careful about which part of the nettle you pick and when. Always go for the pea green tips you can pinch out – nothing darker – and make sure you harvest before the nettles flower. This is normally in early spring during the 'hunger gap', which is very handy, but if you cut them back you might get a second growth later in the season.

Nettles are a useful green to have around and make nice tea with mint, but I really look forward to wild garlic and three-cornered leeks for a subtler hint of flavour, and Jack-by-the-hedge, also know as garlic mustard. I start looking out for them in early February and expect a decent harvest by early March, and hope this will last until the end of May. Wild garlic is one of those things that if you have any sense of smell at all, you will never confuse it with anything else. I have my spots in London – locations generously shared by locals when I cried out for help – generous, because these are small patches, not the swathes of ground cover I see plastered all over Instagram every spring. This abundance has me green with envy, because the thing about wild garlic is that for it to be much use in the kitchen, you need a lot of it. A whole bagful will wilt down to nothing in no time – it is worse than spinach for that. It means I need to fill two bags just to make one small jar of wild garlic ferment, which is my favourite thing to do with it.

continued overleaf

I read all kinds of things written about wild garlic, which –
not to mince words – I believe are just wrong. What especially
annoys me is when people say that it comes into its own when
it is cooked, and that through the spring and early summer
you can use it as a replacement for garlic in all your recipes.
It doesn't work like that. Despite throwing out a very strong,
pungent scent, this doesn't carry through to cooking. If you
put wild garlic into a dish at the beginning of the cooking time,
at the same time as you would normally add garlic, you may as
well not bother – the flavour will dissipate into nothing as fast
as it hits the heat. Raw, it is a cross between garlic and spring
onion (scallion) – unsurprisingly fresh and green-tasting, so
use it with abandon in salads or as a garnish. But the trick, I
have found, if you want it in anything warm or hot, is to allow
it to wilt right at the end of cooking, and make sure you use
enough of it. Any gentle heat will mellow the flavour. Turn it
into pesto (see page 88) and add it at the last minute to soup
or stir through pasta; wilt it in melted butter just taken off
the heat as a dressing for new potatoes; add it chopped to an
omelette that has almost finished cooking, but don't cook it
any longer than that. And if you want a wild garlic soup, use
twice the amount you think you need. Wilt it into the soup
right at the last minute and blitz. Otherwise it is just a waste.

Orzo with Foraged Spring Greens

Serves 4

2 tbsp olive oil

1½ tbsp butter

4 small (baby) leeks, cut into rings

2 garlic cloves

Zest of 1 lemon

400g (14oz) orzo (or Greek equivalent, trahana)

100ml (scant ½ cup) vermouth or white wine

25g (¾oz) kefalotyri or Parmesan cheese, grated, plus extra to serve

For the greens

Around 150g (5¼oz) in total of nettle tips, young dandelion leaves, wild garlic

1 tbsp butter

A few sprigs of any anise-flavoured herbs – anise hyssop, sweet cicely, fennel fronds

Sea salt and freshly ground black pepper

By this recipe title I mean greens that are available in spring, not 'spring greens'.

There is a type of pasta in Greece that is very similar to the Italian orzo, in that it is quite dense and rice-shaped. I like to cook it in the same way as a risotto by absorption method, using ingredients I use when in Greece – horta (the earthy, bitter wild greens found everywhere), fresh lemons and Greek cheese such as *kefalotyri*, which most closely resembles Parmesan. As I am in the UK though, I will normally make this in spring with a mixture of nettles, wild garlic, perhaps even a few dandelion leaves.

Heat the olive oil and butter in a large, lidded frying pan. When the butter has melted, add the leeks. Allow to cook gently for around 10 minutes over a medium heat, covered, until almost tender, stirring every so often, then add the garlic, lemon zest and orzo. Stir for a couple of minutes so the orzo looks glossy with butter, then turn up the heat. Pour in the wine or vermouth and allow it to bubble up and reduce to almost nothing.

Boil a kettle of water and add enough to the pan so the orzo is just covered and season with salt and pepper. Bring to the boil, then turn down the heat and leave to simmer until most of the liquid is absorbed and the pasta is just cooked – this should take around 10 minutes. You do need to check on it a couple of times just to make sure it isn't catching on the bottom, but you do not need to stand and stir the entire time.

While the pasta is cooking, prepare the greens. Make sure they are washed thoroughly, and shake off any excess water. Melt the butter in a saucepan, add the greens, and wait for them to wilt down in the heat – you want to keep the cooking to an absolute minimum here. When they are just collapsed, strain through a colander, then squeeze out any excess liquid. Chop finely so it's almost a purée.

When the orzo has finished cooking, beat in the cheese, then gently stir through the greens and the herbs. Serve with more cheese and plenty of pepper.

Radicchio Risotto

Serves 4

1.2 litres (5 cups) vegetable or chicken
stock

500g (1lb 1½oz) radicchio, a robust red
sort such as Treviso

50g (1¾oz) butter

1 onion, very finely chopped

A sprig of rosemary, leaves very finely
chopped

300g (1½ cups) arborio rice

150ml (⅔ cup) red wine, preferably
Barolo

30g (1oz) hard cheese, such as
Parmesan or vegetarian alternative

Sea salt and freshly ground black
pepper

For the radicchio garnish

1 tbsp olive oil

A squeeze of lemon juice

A few radicchio leaves (see method)

Sea salt

**Depending on your tolerance for bitterness, you can use
any type of radicchio for this risotto. You needn't limit
yourself to rice, either; farro, spelt and barley all have
an earthy nutty flavour that works really well with bitter
leaves, rosemary and red wine – they will take double
the time to cook.**

Put the stock in a saucepan, bring to the boil, then turn
down so it is just simmering gently.

To prepare the radicchio, pull off a couple of handfuls of
leaves for the garnish and shred the rest. I always prepare
the garnish at this point so it just needs to be reheated
once your risotto is ready to serve. Heat the oil in a small
pan and add the leaves. Cook over a high heat until lightly
caramelised and wilted, around 3–5 minutes, then season
with salt and a squeeze of lemon juice. Leave in the pan.

Heat half the butter in a frying pan with a large surface
area, then add the onion. Cook over a medium heat until
the onion is soft and translucent, then add the shredded
radicchio, the rosemary and the rice. Stir to make sure
every grain of rice is coated and season.

Turn up the heat and pour in 125ml (½ cup) of the wine.
Allow it to hiss and bubble up while stirring constantly
– it will soon disappear to nothing but a rich coating for
the rice. Now you can start adding the stock, a ladleful at a
time. Stir until each ladleful of stock has been absorbed by
the rice, making sure you keep the pan at a steady simmer,
until you have included it all. This should take around
15–20 minutes and by the end the rice should still have a
little bite to it. The texture as a whole should still be quite
loose – when you push your spoon through it, you should
see the risotto slowly but inexorably fall back in its wake.

Remove from the heat and beat in the reserved wine,
then the remaining butter and cheese. Lightly reheat the
caramelised leaves and serve as a garnish.

Chard Galette

Serves 4

1 tbsp olive oil

1 tbsp butter

400g (14oz) chard, stems and leaves
separated, finely shredded

3 garlic cloves, finely chopped

2 sprigs of rosemary, finely chopped

200g (7oz) new or waxy potatoes,
sliced, or cooked beetroot, cut into
wedges

100g (3½oz) Cheddar cheese, grated

For the pastry

300g (2½ cups) wholewheat spelt flour

175g (6oz) butter

1 egg, beaten

Sea salt

For the rosemary oil

4 tbsp olive oil

A few sprigs of rosemary

**This is something I make frequently as it is a very
good receptacle for leftovers – heels of cheese, roasted
root vegetables, and of course, any greens. It is very
quick if you have enough cooked greens and a packet of
vacuum-packed beetroot, though of course, the flavour
is better if you roast fresh beetroot and then use their
leaves in the galette. The rosemary oil at the end isn't
essential, but it does add an extra depth and smokiness.**

Start with the filling. Heat the olive oil and butter in a
large frying pan and add the chard stems. Cook for 5–10
minutes over a medium heat until lightly coloured, then
add the garlic and chard leaves. Pour in 50ml (¼ cup)
water, then cover and leave the chard to wilt. Stir in the
rosemary and cool. At the same time, cook the potatoes in
salted boiling water until tender. Drain and cool.

Next, make the pastry. Put the flour into a bowl with a
pinch of salt. Add the butter and rub in until the mixture
resembles fine breadcrumbs. Alternatively do this in a food
processor or in a stand mixer using the beater attachment.
Add the egg and work in just enough iced water to bring
together into a smooth, slightly tacky dough. Form into a
ball, then cover in plastic wrap and chill for 30 minutes.

Preheat the oven to 200°C (400°F/Gas 6). Roll out the
pastry on a floured surface to a round of approximately
30–35cm (12–14in) diameter.

Transfer the round to your largest baking (cookie) sheet –
you will probably find that it will overlap slightly, but it is
still much easier to assemble in situ. Mix the chard with
the potatoes or beetroot, then pile onto the pastry, leaving
a border of around 4–5cm (1½–2in). Sprinkle with the
cheese. Fold in the borders so they cover the outer limits
of the filling – don't worry about the pastry pleating and
overlapping; it will have to in places. Brush with beaten
egg. Bake for 35–40 minutes, until well browned.

Meanwhile, make the rosemary oil. Put the rosemary on
a baking sheet and brown in the oven for a few minutes.
Crush in a pestle and mortar, then mix with the olive oil.

Drizzle the galette with the rosemary oil. It is best served
on the warm side of room temperature with a green salad.

Aubergines with Curry Leaf

Serves 4

2 tbsp oil

30 curry leaves

2 large aubergines (eggplants), thickly
   sliced, or 8–10 baby aubergines

1 tbsp mustard seeds

1 onion, thickly sliced

5cm (2in) piece ginger, peeled
   and grated

5 garlic cloves, crushed or grated

1 green chilli, very finely chopped

¼ tsp ground turmeric

¼ tsp ground cinnamon

400ml (14fl oz) tin coconut milk

150g (5¼oz) cooked chickpeas
   (garbanzo beans; optional)

A handful of wilting greens, such as
   baby chard or spinach (optional)

1 lime, cut into wedges

Sea salt and freshly ground black
   pepper

To serve

Coriander and Mint Chutney (see
   page 35)

Curry Leaf and Coconut Quinoa
   (see page 215)

I am not subtle when it comes to cooking with curry leaves, and use as many as I can. This is because while the aroma is strong, the flavour can be quite elusive. I always want to ramp it up and layer the flavour in several different ways. I have deliberately limited the spices – the result is very mellow and comforting, with a double whammy of smoky depth from the curry leaves and aubergines (eggplants). Serving with Coriander and Mint Chutney (see page 35) isn't essential – I will usually eat at least half a bowl of the curry before I add any. If you decide not to make it, the curry will benefit from a hint of lime juice instead.

If you want to add carbs to this, try some plain steamed rice, or the Curry Leaf and Coconut Quinoa on page 215.

In a large casserole dish (Dutch oven) over a medium heat, warm through the oil and add the curry leaves. When they start to crackle and brown, remove them with a slotted spoon and set aside. Add the aubergines and quickly brown on all sides, then remove and set aside (you may need to do this in batches).

Add the mustard seeds and when they start to pop, add the onion. Cook over a medium heat until the onion has started to soften, about 8–10 minutes, then add the ginger, garlic, chilli and spices. Return the curry leaves to the casserole and season with salt and plenty of pepper. Cook until everything is well combined and quite dry-looking, then return the aubergine to the casserole. Pour over the coconut milk and add the chickpeas, if using. Bring to the boil then turn down the heat, cover and simmer until the aubergines are just tender – you don't want them to collapse. This will take up to 20 minutes. Wilt in the greens if using, then serve with the lime wedges, Coriander and Mint Chutney and Curry Leaf and Coconut Quinoa, if you like.

Caramelised Endive Gratin

Serves 4

2 tbsp olive oil

6 white or red endives (chicory)

1 tbsp butter

50ml (¼ cup) orange juice (optional)

2tsp thyme leaves

100g (3½oz) cheese, such as Gruyère

Sea salt and freshly ground black pepper

For the béchamel

600ml (2½ cups) whole (full-fat) milk

1 onion

3 cloves

1 mace blade

A few peppercorns

2 bay leaves

2½ tbsp butter

40g (⅓ cup) plain (all-purpose) flour

My all-time favourite comfort food; gutsier and more satisfying to the taste buds than cauliflower cheese. The orange juice is optional because it isn't strictly necessary – I just think that bitter leaves work so well with a hit of citrus, and orange is very good with thyme.

Preheat the oven to 200°C (400°F/Gas 6).

To start the béchamel, pour the milk into a saucepan. Stud the onion with the cloves and add this to the milk along with all the other aromatics. Heat until almost boiling, then remove from the heat and leave to cool and infuse.

Next, caramelise the endives. You may have to do this in 2 batches, depending on the size of your frying pan. Add the olive oil to your pan, and when it is hot, add the endives, cut-side down. Cook for several minutes until the endives have started to brown, then turn over and cook for a few more minutes. Repeat with the second batch. At this point you can put them all together. Add the butter and the orange juice, if using, and continue to cook until it looks a little syrupy. Season and set aside.

To finish the béchamel, strain the milk into a jug. Melt the butter in a saucepan over a medium-low heat and add the flour. Stir for 3–4 minutes to cook out the flour, then begin adding milk, a little at a time, stirring well between each addition. You will start with a thick paste and end with a sauce the consistency of double (heavy) cream.

Arrange the endives in an ovenproof dish that will fit them snugly and sprinkle over the thyme leaves. Cover with the béchamel and sprinkle with the cheese. Bake in the oven for around 30 minutes, or until the béchamel is bubbling under the golden brown cheese.

Variations

There are few things I like better than a side of endives, and if you want to make it more substantial but don't want to make béchamel, you can drizzle with double cream and top with cheese or just cover with cheese or breadcrumbs and grill. You can also make it heartier by cutting 6 slices of ham in half, spreading with mustard and wrapping around the endive and proceeding as above.

Wild Greens Tart

Serves 4

300g (10½oz) greens, stems removed
  if using chard or woody kale

1 garlic clove, finely chopped

A handful of herbs, left as small sprigs,
  such as tarragon, chervil or lemon
  thyme

100g (3½oz) hard cheese, such as
  mature Cheddar or Ogleshield

Nutmeg, for grating

4 eggs

200ml (¾ cup) crème fraîche

100ml (scant ½ cup) double
  (heavy) cream

Sea salt and freshly ground black
  pepper

For the pastry

225g (scant 2 cups) plain (all-purpose)
  or spelt flour

½ tsp sea salt

130g (4½oz) butter, chilled and diced

1 egg yolk

This is a tart I have been making for years. It's a really good way of using up any greens – I will often add wilted lettuce, cooked kale or bitter leaves. I also like adding sweet herbs and leave them fairly intact to give little bursts of flavour. My favourite filling is chard, though this doesn't always go down well. I once served it up to a vegetarian friend, not realising that she had issues with most green vegetables, and she picked every little bit of it out and just ate the custard and pastry (yes, Amy, I'm looking at you).

If I use anything particularly bitter, I will normally add some bacon as well, as the fat does such a good job of tempering bitterness.

First, make the pastry. Sift the flour and add the salt. Add the butter and rub in or process until it resembles fine breadcrumbs. Add the egg yolk and mix, then add just enough water to bring it all together into a ball. Knead it together very briefly, then wrap in plastic wrap and chill for 30 minutes.

Preheat the oven to 200°C (400°F/Gas 6).

Roll out the pastry to line a deep, 25cm (10in) tart tin and prick lightly with a fork. Line with baking parchment, then cover the paper with baking beans. Bake for 15 minutes, remove the paper and beans and cook for 5 minutes.

Reduce the oven temperature to 180°C (375°F/Gas 4).

Wash the greens thoroughly, discarding any particularly woody stems, and put in a large saucepan. Wilt over a high heat, pushing the greens down until they collapse, then drain thoroughly. Squeeze out any excess liquid and chop.

Mix the greens with the garlic, herbs (reserving some for decoration) and half the cheese. Season with salt, pepper, and a few rasps of nutmeg then sprinkle over the pastry base. Beat the eggs, then mix with the crème fraîche and cream. Pour over the greens, then sprinkle with the remaining cheese. Bake in the oven for around 30–35 minutes – you may find that it will soufflé up if you have vigorously beaten the eggs, but it will subside as it cools.

Serve warm or at room temperature.

Brussels Sprout Christmas Tree

Serves 4

500g (1lb 1½oz) Brussels sprouts, trimmed and halved

2 x 320g (11oz) sheets of ready-rolled all-butter puff pastry

2 tbsp wholegrain mustard (optional)

200g (7oz) cheese, such as Cheddar, grated

1 egg, beaten

1 tbsp olive oil

Sea salt

I thought this recipe might encourage some friends of my son to eat Brussels sprouts. No such luck, but the rest of us loved it. There are so many different things you could add to this – for example, the marsala-soaked cranberries on page 226 could be added for the last few minutes of cooking time – but I do think simple is best.

Oh, and just in case you were in any doubt, Brussels and cheese go brilliantly together. You can simply roast them (pretty much as below – blanch first, roast for half an hour, tossed in oil), transfer to an oven dish, cover with grated cheese and grill. And crumbled blue cheese is good too, especially if you add in the cranberries.

Preheat your oven to 200°C (400°F/Gas 6).

First blanch the Brussels sprouts – bring a saucepan of water to a rolling boil and add salt. Add the sprouts and blanch for 2 minutes. Drain and immediately plunge into ice-cold water to cool down. This will help them retain their colour.

Take a large baking (cookie) sheet and unroll the first sheet of puff pastry out onto it. Cut the pastry into a symmetrical Christmas tree shape, making sure you cut a small trunk at the base. You can cut yourself a template for this first if it makes it easier. I also find it is much easier to cut the pastry with a pizza wheel, rather than a knife. Keep the trimmings – you can use these for cheese straws or similar.

Spread the entire tree with the mustard, if you are using it, then sprinkle over all the cheese. Unroll the other sheet of pastry and place it over the top, then cut to size.

Next, leaving a central 'trunk', cut horizontal lines at 3cm (1¼in) intervals down both sides of the tree – you will end up with around 10 branches on each side. Twist these around, fairly tightly – you will see some of the cheese escaping, but this doesn't matter. Brush the whole tree with beaten egg.

Drain the Brussel sprouts thoroughly and toss in the olive oil. Arrange these over the tree. Bake in the oven for around 30 minutes, until the pastry is well risen and brown, and the Brussel sprouts are lightly coloured in places. Serve immediately.

MEAT AND FISH MAIN COURSES

Agretti with Cockles and Linguine

Serves 4

1 large bunch of agretti

1kg (2lb 3oz) cockles in their shells

300g (10½oz) linguine

1 tbsp olive oil

2 garlic cloves, thinly sliced

100ml (scant ½ cup) white wine

1 sprig of tarragon, finely chopped

A few fennel fronds, finely chopped

Pared zest of ½ lemon

Sea salt and freshly ground black
  pepper

I am fascinated by the texture of agretti (also known as Monk's or Friar's Beard). It grows in clumps of spiky, chive-like leaves – you expect it to have that same ticklish feeling you get from a single long chive or one of the stringier kales or rocket (arugula), but it is soft and succulent with a flavour that makes me think it should be grown on salt marshes – a subtler, less salty and bitter version of rock samphire.

The agretti season is short – late winter to early spring. I buy it in paper-wrapped bunches from decent greengrocers who import it from Italy. It is possible to grow it, but only if you have very fresh seeds, as they lose their potency quite quickly.

Agretti is often paired with seafood, frequently crab (an Italian classic) or clams. I've used cockles here because they are much cheaper than clams and just as good – if you find clams easier to get hold of, use them instead.

Wash the agretti thoroughly and trim off any discoloured roots from the base of the clumps. Pick it over carefully – I find sometimes that there is the odd brown shoot in the middle of the bunch.

Next prepare the cockles. Give them a good wash in cold water, and, as with all bivalves, tap any open ones to make sure they close immediately. Discard any that do not do this, they will be dead and not suitable for eating.

Bring a large saucepan of water to the boil and add plenty of salt. Add the linguine and cook for 10–12 minutes until al dente. Add the agretti for the last minute, then drain.

While the pasta is cooking, steam the cockles. Heat the olive oil in a large casserole dish (Dutch oven) and add the garlic. Cook for a minute or two, over a medium heat, making sure it doesn't colour, then pour in the white wine. Allow it to bubble up, then add the herbs and lemon zest. Add the cockles and cover, shaking regularly, until they are all open.

Make sure the agretti is well distributed through the linguine and divide between four large pasta bowls. Top with the cockles and their cooking liquid and season with plenty of black pepper.

Fish Wrapped in Fig Leaves

Serves 4

2 sea bream or similar, gutted and cleaned

1 tsp dried oregano or a few sprigs of fresh

A few strips of pared lemon zest

4–6 medium-sized fig leaves, washed

Sea salt and freshly ground black pepper

For the potatoes

500g (1lb 1½oz) new or salad potatoes, diced

2 tbsp olive oil

A few sprigs of rosemary or oregano

For the Greek salsa verde

1 small bunch of parsley, finely chopped

A few fronds of fennel (optional)

1 garlic clove, finely chopped

2 tbsp capers, chopped

1 tbsp preserved sea fennel (optional)

Zest of ½ lemon

2 tsp red wine vinegar

1 tsp ouzo

4 tbsp olive oil

Sea salt and freshly ground black pepper

It is my theory that few people, especially urban dwellers, are far away from a fig tree. Keep your eyes peeled as you walk around, and you will see what I mean. I have my favourite spots where I can pick the odd leaf, otherwise I rely on the generosity of friends who have figs on their allotment, and whenever I am visiting Greece, I strip leaves from the tree outside my mother's bedroom. A fig tree is a good tree to grow in a small space – you need to contain the roots anyway so they do okay in large pots, and being able to use the leaves is some compensation in the early years when they might not bear much fruit.

The fig leaves in this dish add a sweet, gentle fragrance to the fish – this will hit you when you remove it from the oven, so make sure you get it to the table quickly. The sea fennel (marsh samphire) can be replaced by a few thinly sliced capers or caper leaves, which have a similar astringency.

Preheat the oven to 200ºC (400ºF/gas 6).

First cook the potatoes in salted boiling water until they are just tender, then drain thoroughly. Put in a roasting tin large enough to hold the potatoes and the fish, then toss in the olive oil. Add salt, pepper and the rosemary or oregano. Roast for 20 minutes, or until starting to brown and crisp up around the edges.

Cut 3–4 slashes on the sides of each fish. Sprinkle the inside cavity and the skin of the fish with salt and pepper, then tuck in the herbs and lemon zest. Wrap in the fig leaves, making sure the sides are underneath the fish so they stay in place. I like to use quite skinny leaves that mean a few patches of the fish are left exposed. Place the fish on top of the potatoes and return the roasting tin to the oven. Roast for 15–20 minutes, until the fish is just cooked through.

To make the salsa verde, stir all the ingredients together and season with salt and pepper.

Serve in the roasting dish with the salsa verde and a green vegetable on the side.

Aromatic Fish Baked in Banana Leaves

Serves 4

½ tsp ground cardamom

½ tsp ground white pepper

½ tsp ground turmeric

¼ tsp ground cinnamon

½ tsp salt

4 thick fish fillets, skinned and patted dry

8 tbsp coconut milk

Thai basil, kaffir lime and laksa leaves

For the paste

1 small bunch of coriander (cilantro) leaves

2 garlic cloves, finely chopped

1 shallot, finely chopped

5cm (2in) piece of ginger, finely chopped

2 red chillies, medium strength, finely chopped

Zest and juice of ½ a lime

Sea or rock salt

To serve

Steamed jasmine rice

Sweet Lime Pickle (optional)

1 large semi-ripe mango

Zest and juice of ½ lime

The joy of these parcels is in the opening. You will immediately get a jumble of leaf smells hitting you first, then it will give way to the sweet spices and the paste – layer upon layer of flavour and aroma. This is a very hot and sweet dish, and what I really like to serve with it, besides some steamed jasmine rice, is a sweet and sour lime pickle. If you have my book *Citrus*, the recipe for the Sweet Lime Pickle is what I would use here. Alternatively, dress a semi-ripe mango with plenty of lime zest.

This dish also works well on a griddle or outside grill. Cook for 15 minutes, turning regularly, until the banana leaf has blackened in places.

Preheat the oven to 200°C (400°F/Gas 6).

Mix the spices with the salt and rub into the fish fillets. Set aside while you make the curry paste.

You can either pound everything together with some coarse sea or rock salt using a pestle and mortar, or you can use a food processor. If taking the latter approach, pulse until everything is well combined but coarsely textured. You might need to scrape down the sides a couple of times and add a little water, if necessary.

Smear 1 teaspoon paste over each of the fish fillets. Place each fillet in the centre of a piece of banana leaf. Pour over 2 tablespoons coconut milk, then top with a mixture of the Thai basil, kaffir lime and laksa leaves. Fold in the sides of the banana leaves, then the top and bottom and seal together with a cocktail stick. If you wanted to make a real effort with presentation, you could cut wider slits and use lemongrass stalks. This is fiddly and probably a step too far for me.

Put the parcels on a baking (cookie) sheet and place in the oven. Roast for 20 minutes, until the banana leaf is browning. Pierce through the side of one of the parcels into the fish with a skewer – the tip should feel almost too hot to touch if the fish is done.

Remove from the oven and place onto 4 plates. Serve with rice and either the pickle or the lime-dressed mango.

Squid, Chorizo and Cabbage Stir Fry

Serves 4

500g (1lb 1½oz) small prepared squid, with tentacles

2 tbsp olive oil

200g (7oz) cooking chorizo, sliced

1 onion, cut into thin wedges

2 garlic cloves, finely chopped

A few sprigs of rosemary or ginger rosemary

500g (1lb 1½oz) white or green cabbage, shredded

A few celery leaves, finely chopped

A few parsley or coriander (cilantro) leaves, finely chopped

This recipe came about because I asked my son what he wanted for dinner and he said 'squid with cabbage'. I ran with it (I usually do if I can) and found that actually, this is a very good combination. Stir fried cabbage, especially a white or green-pointed cabbage, is nutty and sweet, and really complements everything else in the dish.

First prepare the squid by cutting down one side each of the tubes so they will open up into one piece. Lay them flat, then score shallow criss-cross lines across the top side.

Heat half of the olive oil in a wok. When it is hot, but not yet smoking, add the chorizo. Fry for a couple of minutes, stirring constantly, until it is browned on all sides. Remove from the wok with a slotted spoon.

Allow the wok to heat up again, then add half the squid. Fry for a couple of minutes until they curl up and turn opaque. Remove from the wok and set aside. Check the oil – if you think you need to add a little more, do so now. Again, let the wok heat up and add the remaining squid, cooking as before, and remove.

Add the onion to the wok. Cook for several minutes until it has started to soften and turn translucent, then add the garlic, rosemary and cabbage. Fry for several minutes until the cabbage looks glossy and is starting to brown around the edges – you want it to retain some bite, so do not overcook it. Add the squid back into the wok with the chorizo and stir to combine. Sprinkle over the celery leaves and parsley or coriander leaves and toss briefly before serving.

Cime di Rapa and Anchovy Pizza

Serves 4 (2 pizzas)

300g (2½ cups) strong bread flour

1 tsp instant dried yeast

1 tsp sea salt

1 tbsp olive oil, plus extra for oiling

For the topping

2 tbsp olive oil, plus extra for drizzling

1 large bunch of cime di rapa
  (broccoli rabe)

2 garlic cloves, crushed

2 balls of mozzarella

12 white anchovies

A few fennel fronds

A few capers

A few chilli flakes

Sea salt and freshly ground black
  pepper

How I love a white pizza – and really, they are the best sort to make at home, as it is difficult to get a good crust on a homemade pizza. The addition of tomato sauce makes this harder and can lead to a soggy base.

Cime di rapa (broccoli rabe) is a green that loves other strong flavours – smoked meat, chilli and, here, white anchovies. I know some people will throw up their hands in horror at the idea of cooking the anchovies on the pizza, but I think they are better that way.

To make the pizza dough, put the flour and yeast in a bowl and mix together, then sprinkle over the salt. Do not add the salt and yeast together, as the salt can interfere with the effectiveness of the yeast. Make a well in the centre of the flour, then gradually work in 200ml (¾ cup) tepid water and the olive oil until it all comes together as a dough. Turn out onto a floured work surface and knead until the dough is smooth and springy and will pass the windowpane test (if you can stretch it until it is so thin you can see through it, without it tearing, it has enough elasticity). You can do all of this in a stand mixer with a dough hook if you prefer. Put the dough in a lightly oiled bowl and cover with a damp tea towel. Leave to stand while you make the pizza toppings.

Heat 1 tablespoon of the olive oil in a large frying pan and add the cime di rapa. Stir for 2–3 minutes over a medium heat, then season and add the garlic. Pour over 75ml (⅓ cup) water and continue to cook, partially covered, until the greens are tender and the water has evaporated.

When you are ready to assemble, preheat the oven to its highest setting – around 240°C (465°F/Gas 8). Put 2 baking (cookie) sheets into the oven to heat. Divide the dough into two equal pieces. Roll out each piece into a large round of at least 25cm (10in) and as thin as possible.

Remove the baking sheets from the oven and upturn them. Dust with flour or semolina and slide the rounds onto them. Divide the toppings between the pizzas. Bake in the oven for between 7–10 minutes, until crisp, patchily browned and searingly hot. Drizzle with a little olive oil, sprinkle with chilli flakes and serve immediately.

Red Cabbage and Duck Stir Fry

Serves 4

300g (10½oz) fingerling potatoes, quartered lengthways

1 tsp olive oil

2 duck breasts

½ red cabbage, shredded

2 garlic cloves, finely chopped

5cm (2in) piece ginger, peeled and finely chopped

½ tsp Chinese five spice

1 pear, cored and sliced into wedges

2 tbsp light soy sauce

1 tbsp Chinese wine vinegar

1 small bunch of mint leaves

Sea salt and freshly ground black pepper

This is probably one of the most 'fusion', cross-cultural dishes I've come up with in this book, but if you want to steer it back eastwards and speed up the cooking process too, you could replace the potatoes with cooked noodles and the red cabbage with Chinese cabbage or something leafy such as morning glory (water spinach) if you liked. It would be a very different dish, but would still taste wonderful.

In a large saucepan of salted water, parboil the potatoes until just tender, around 10–12 minutes. Drain thoroughly and set aside.

Heat the olive oil in a large wok. Sprinkle the duck breasts with salt and pepper, then cook skin-side down over a medium-high heat until plenty of fat has rendered out and the skin is crisp. Turn over and cook the duck for another couple of minutes, just to brown the flesh side, then remove from the wok. Leave to cool slightly then thinly slice.

If there is a lot of fat in the wok, drain off all but around 1 tablespoon then put back over the heat, reserving the excess in case you need it. When the air above it is shimmering, add the potatoes. Stir fry briskly until lightly browned, then remove with a slotted spoon. Add a little more fat if necessary and add the red cabbage. Stir fry for 4–5 minutes, then add the garlic, ginger, five spice and pear. Pour over the soy sauce and wine vinegar and allow it to bubble up and reduce for a moment. Put the potatoes and duck breasts back into the wok and warm through. Garnish with plenty of mint and serve immediately.

Sauerkraut with Sausages

Serves 4

1 tbsp olive oil

4–6 sausages, depending on size

2 crisp eating apples, cored and cut into wedges

150ml (⅔ cup) cider

3½ tbsp butter

2 onions, sliced

3 garlic cloves, finely chopped

1 tsp juniper berries, crushed

1 tbsp plain (all-purpose) flour

400ml (1¾ cups) chicken or vegetable stock

¼ Savoy cabbage, shredded

400g (14oz) sauerkraut

Sea salt and freshly ground black pepper

This is a very plain, homely dish – related to the classic *bigos*, but simplified for a quicker evening meal. The only time-consuming thing about it is the caramelisation of the onions. This is something that can be done in advance – or what I like to do is to cook a large batch of them at once to save time when I want a quicker meal in the evenings.

I buy free-range bratwursts from my local farmers' market and they are exactly the right thing here, but you can use anything – just make sure it is substantial and meaty. Or perhaps combine with a smoked sausage such as *kielbasa*. The sauerkraut can be any kind – homemade, shop-bought, and any flavour you like.

First heat the olive oil in a frying pan. Add the sausages and brown on all sides over a medium heat, then remove and slice thickly. Add the apple wedges and fry until brown, around 3–4 minutes. Remove from the pan then add the cider. Turn up the heat and deglaze the pan and cook until the cider has reduced by half. Transfer to a jug.

Melt the butter in a large casserole (Dutch oven) over a medium heat. When it has started foaming, add the onions. Cook gently until soft and translucent, about 20 minutes, then turn up the heat and allow the onions to brown, stirring regularly until they are an even colour, around 5 minutes. Stir in the garlic, juniper berries and the reserved sausage slices and cook for a few minutes to give the cut edges of the sausages a chance to brown, then sprinkle in the flour. Pour over the reserved cider and then gradually stir in the stock. Season with salt and pepper.

Add the cabbage and sauerkraut to the casserole and bring to the boil. Turn down the heat and cover. Simmer until the savoy cabbage is tender – around 20 minutes. Add the apples to the casserole to warm through then serve. I like this with mashed potatoes and lots of tarragon mustard.

Braised Chicken with Coriander, Chilli and Orange

Serves 4

1 tsp dried thyme

1 tsp sea salt

8 chicken thighs, skin-on, bone-in

1 tbsp olive oil

2 onions, thickly sliced

For the paste

1 large bunch of coriander (cilantro)

1 garlic bulb, cloves separated and
  peeled

150ml (⅔ cup) orange juice

100ml (scant ½ cup) lime juice

2–3 green chillies (I use jalapeño)

Sea salt and freshly ground black
  pepper

To serve

Coriander leaves

Sliced green chillies

The alchemic combination of coriander (cilantro), chilli, garlic and orange is one I can't seem to leave alone. It is central to one of my favourite lamb dishes, but here I use it with chicken. The flavours are taken from a Peruvian recipe, so I serve it with quinoa, but it would be just as good with rice or potatoes.

If possible, start the day before. Mix the thyme with the sea salt and sprinkle over the chicken thighs. Leave uncovered or loosely wrapped in paper towel in the fridge, then remove 30 minutes before you want to start cooking. If you don't have time for this, simply sprinkle with the salt and thyme before cooking.

Heat the olive oil in a large frying pan. Add the chicken thighs, skin-side down, and fry over a medium-high heat until they are a rich golden brown, around 15 minutes. This will take longer than you expect it to, and you shouldn't stint at this stage – you want crisp, thin, skin, nothing thick or flabby. Turn the chicken thighs over and spoon off some of the rendered fat if there seems a lot of it – you can store this fat and use it for frying some other time. Add the onions to the pan and continue to cook until the onions have softened and the chicken is just about cooked through, around 20 minutes.

Meanwhile, make the paste. Take two thirds of the coriander and put it in a blender with the garlic, juice and chillies. Remove the leaves from the remaining coriander and add the stems to the blender, reserving the leaves for garnish. Add salt and pepper, then blitz until fairly smooth – a very fine green flecking is fine.

When the chicken is just about cooked, pour two thirds of the paste around the chicken. Bring it to the boil and let it reduce by half – it should thicken and it will turn a murkier colour, but this cannot be helped – it will be worth it for the flavour.

When you are ready to serve, stir in the remaining paste to enliven the colour, then top with the coriander leaves and sliced chillies.

Fish with Parsley Sauce

Serves 4

4 fillets of white fish, skinned or not,
  up to you

1 tbsp olive oil

1 tbsp butter

A squeeze of lemon juice (optional)

Sea salt

For the sauce

600ml whole (full-fat) milk

1 bay leaf

A few peppercorns

1 mace blade

1 slice of onion

1 bunch of curly leaf parsley, leaves
  separated from the stems

1½ tbsp butter

1½ tbsp plain (all-purpose) flour

1 tsp lemon juice or white wine vinegar

Sea salt and finely ground white pepper

**This is a polarising dish if ever there was one.
I can't speak for the rest of the world, but when I was
growing up in the UK, the closest most people got to
this was the boil-in-the-bag version – either that or
an institutionalised gloopy and (oh, the horror) lumpy
sauce made with cornflour (cornstarch) served up
during school dinners. Very unpleasant. However, the
real deal is a beautiful dish – comforting and easy, but
still vibrant with a little punch from the parsley. On that
note, it is also just about the only dish that should be
made with the curly sort of parsley, not the flat leaf one.**

To make the sauce, put the milk in a saucepan with the
bay, peppercorns, mace and onion. Bruise the parsley
stems lightly with the back of a knife, then add to the
milk. Heat until almost boiling, then remove from the heat
and infuse. When the milk is cool, strain into a jug.

Melt the butter in a saucepan over a medium-low heat.
When it has melted, add the flour and stir until you have a
smooth roux. Keep cooking and stirring for a few minutes
to cook out the raw flavour of the flour, then gradually
work in the infused milk, making sure you stir thoroughly
between each addition, so the sauce stays smooth and
lump-free. When you have incorporated all the milk, add
the lemon juice or white wine vinegar and stir for another
minute or two. Taste for seasoning and add salt and finely
ground white pepper, then chop the parsley leaves as finely
as you can and stir into the sauce. Keep warm.

To cook the fish, season on both sides with a fine
sprinkling of salt. Heat the olive oil and butter in a large
frying pan. When the butter has foamed, add the fish
fillets – skin-side down if you have left it on. Fry on one
side until you can see that the edges are turning a golden
brown and the top side has almost lost its translucency. At
this point you should find it has enough of a crust on it
to easily come away from the pan with no tearing. If it is
resisting, leave it for a minute. If it still resists, take a little
knob of butter and melt around the fish to ease it off. Flip
the fish over and cook for another scant minute. Squeeze
over the lemon if you want an acidic bite. Arrange the fish
on warm plates, flood with the sauce and serve.

Bay Leaf Chicken

Serves 4

1 x 1.6kg (3lb 7oz) chicken

400g (14oz) baby new potatoes, parboiled

1 onion, cut into slim wedges

12 fresh bay leaves, lightly torn but still whole

1 garlic bulb, broken up into cloves

Juice of 1 lemon

300ml (1¼ cups) chicken stock

Sea salt

For the marinade

3 dried bay leaves, crumbled

1 tsp black peppercorns, lightly crushed

Zest of 1 lemon

3 garlic cloves, crushed

50ml (¼ cup) fino sherry

2 tbsp olive oil

This is based on my favourite way to barbecue chicken – on a bed of bay leaves for a smoky, herbal infusion. A spatchcocked chicken is a wonderful thing. Faster than a whole roast chicken, you get more crisp skin and deliciously sticky wings. It's all I can do to get it to the table without tearing it apart with my bare hands.

I used a mixture of dried and fresh bay leaves here. The dried work best crumbled into the marinade, and the fresh are best added during the cooking process.

This is a dish that will work equally well with other leaves that we use for flavour but don't traditionally eat. For example, you could swap out the bay leaves for fig leaves or lime leaves and leave all the other ingredients as they are, and you would still have a wonderful meal.

First, mix all the marinade ingredients together. Spatchcock the chicken by cutting down either side of the backbone (you can use this piece to make stock) and then turning it over, breast-side up, and pressing down hard on the breastbone. Season the chicken with plenty of salt and pour over the marinade. Transfer to the fridge and leave overnight if possible, turning regularly.

Preheat the oven to 200°C (400°F/Gas 6).

Arrange the potatoes and onion in a roasting tin and place the chicken on top, skin-side up. Tuck the bay leaves and garlic cloves around the chicken then pour over any marinade and the lemon juice and roast for 45 minutes– 1 hour, until the chicken and potatoes are crisp, brown and sticky underneath.

Transfer the chicken, onions and potatoes to a warm serving dish. Squeeze out the flesh from the garlic and add it to the roasting tin, then set the tin over a medium heat and deglaze with the chicken stock. Reduce the stock down by half and transfer to a jug. Serve with the chicken.

Beef, Lemongrass and Cha Plu Stir Fry

Serves 2–4

300g (10½oz) sirloin steak, trimmed and very thinly sliced

1 tbsp groundnut oil

2 red shallots, thinly sliced

2 chillies, thinly sliced on the diagonal

2 lemongrass stalks, white parts only, thinly sliced

2 garlic cloves, peeled and finely chopped

15g (½oz) piece ginger, finely chopped

100g (3½oz) radishes, sliced into rounds

1 tbsp fish sauce

½ tsp light soft brown sugar or palm sugar

A large bunch of cha plu, stems discarded, roughly chopped

A few laksa leaves, finely chopped

A few coriander (cilantro) leaves

Sea salt and freshly ground black pepper

There is a lot of confusion around cha plu, as many of the dishes in which it is used are referred to (in the West at least) as betel leaf. The two are closely related, but whereas betel leaf has quite an intense bitterness to it, cha plu (or bai cha plu – wild pepper leaf) has a very distinctive, fragrant sweetness to it. It will be instantly recognisable if you've ever wandered around a food market anywhere in South East Asia. The leaves are often used as wraps, but are also excellent as a stir fried green.

This recipe makes enough for four for a palate-enlivening starter, or two as a low-carb meal, but you could easily bulk it out by tossing in some cooked noodles or serving it with rice.

Finally, a note on the cooking – when the leaves look as they do in the photograph, this is when you should add the coriander and laksa leaves – then continue to wilt.

Put the steak in a bowl and season with salt and pepper. Toss and leave to stand for a few minutes.

Heat the oil in a wok. When the air above the oil starts to shimmer, it will be hot enough to use. Add the shallots, chillies, lemongrass, garlic, ginger and radishes and stir fry for a minute.

Add the beef and continue to cook for a minute or two, until browned around the edges. Sprinkle in the fish sauce and sugar, then add the cha plu. Continue to cook until the leaves have started to wilt, then toss in the laksa and coriander leaves. Cook for another minute or two, then serve immediately.

WRAPPING LEAVES

The use of leaves as receptacles – plates, wraps, even boats –
is surely an ingrained one. Every child who has cast around for
something to hold their mud pies, or their garden treasures, or
used a glossy, waterproof leaf to send a snail on an adventure
downstream (guilty) knows how useful they are. They can
hold and repel water (is there anything more beautiful than
droplets of water, running off a leaf?), so can make fine
umbrellas and cups; they can be woven into baskets and
cones; they even work as barriers to bacteria (think of cheeses
wrapped in the leaves of wild garlic, nettles or chestnut, for
flavour and protection). All this while providing flavour and
aroma, too.

There are edible leaves that make a fine job of displaying food
in lieu of a plate or bowl and eaten trencher-style. These are
wonderful in their own right, but also a boon for anyone on
a low-carb diet. Use endive leaves in place of crisps to scoop
up dips, cut rounds of large leaves or lettuces for tacos or
even sandwiches. I often do this impromptu fashion – a fridge
forage of cold chicken and condiments, piled between two
lettuce leaves, eaten at the kitchen counter. Pile spoonfuls of
salads – everything from larb to tabbouleh, anything chopped
– onto lettuce leaves, shiso, cha plu or into iceberg lettuce
cups. Roll wild garlic around choice morsels of meat or cheese.

Making edible parcels or rolls from lettuces and robust
greens is a method that crosses cultures. Lettuces work best
raw, greens and cabbages cooked, and you can use them
interchangeably. Vine leaves can be replaced with chard, or
– and I love this one, learned from forager Clare McQuillan –
native lime leaves before they become sticky with honeydew.
Cabbage, colocasia and collards encase as well as any
dumpling wrapper and steam beautifully. Finer-textured but
firm leaves such as chard or cha plu are wonderful deep fried,
and then there is seaweed, flattened into nori sheets for sushi.

There is also a raft of leaves we don't eat but are important for adding flavour and aroma. Some of these – pandan (screwpine), fig, even bay – can be dried and ground into powder or blitzed with water to make an extract, but sometimes the harsher tastes can take over. The effect of wrapping is much more subtle, and it suits all kinds of cooking methods and foodstuffs. For example, when roasting or grilling, the aroma will be apparent throughout the cooking process and when parcels are unwrapped, you realise that even with banana leaves, which don't smell of anything much before the heat gets to them, the food is imbued with their essence. Not only will you have added depth to your finished dish, but you will have kept in moisture and given protection from burning in a completely natural way. As well as the examples of this kind of cooking I have given in this book, try sandwiching cheeses such as paneer or halloumi or pieces of meat between bay, avocado, cinnamon, citrus leaves, then grill and see what it does to their flavour.

Perhaps one of the most dramatic ways to use leaves for wrapping works especially well with seaweed, or giant leaves such as banana, but also works with branches of pine or woody resinous herbs. This is pit or fire cooking, which feeds a sense of adventure when done on a beach (read James Morton's superb description of a Viking pit feast in his book *Shetland*), or even in a back garden if you are prepared to dig a hole or sacrifice a wheelbarrow. Stones are heated and placed in a leaf-lined pit with seafood (clams are especially good) or vegetables and/or meat, then covered. The leaves help keep moisture in and help everything steam, as well as adding flavour. I think it is worth doing for the aroma alone, smoky and spiked with ozone. There are many variations of this, including the Peruvian *pachamanca*, which uses banana leaves, but I think the seaweed ones are best, and just about as far as you can get from the precision and rigour of sushi-making.

Spiced Lamb with Spinach

Serves 4

1 tbsp olive oil

1 kg (2lb 3oz) lamb neck fillet, sliced into 5cm (2in) chunks

2 onions, thickly sliced

20 curry leaves

½ garlic bulb, cloves finely chopped or crushed

25g (¾oz) ginger, peeled and grated

Zest and juice of 1 lime

1 tbsp ground cumin

1 tsp ground cinnamon

1 tsp ground coriander

1 tsp ground fenugreek

1 tsp ground turmeric

1 tsp cayenne pepper

1 tbsp tomato purée

1 tbsp kecap manis

4 kaffir lime leaves

A few laksa leaves

A large bunch of coriander (cilantro), stems removed from leaves, both finely chopped

250ml (1 cup) chicken or lamb stock

500g (1lb 1½oz) frozen spinach or equivalent (see introduction)

Sea salt and freshly ground black pepper

To serve

A few coriander (cilantro) and laksa leaves

A few green chillies, sliced (optional)

Flatbreads or rice

This isn't a classic lamb *saag*, but a rich, oleaginous gravy flavoured with kaffir lime leaves, coriander (cilantro) and laksa leaf. It was an absolute joy to taste for the first time as it was exactly as I had imagined it would be. Serve with some steamed rice or perhaps the Fig Leaf Pilaf (see page 216) – the coconutty notes of the latter complement the citrus and chilli.

Spinach is the obvious green to add to this, but if you can get them, fenugreek leaves (methi) wilt down very well too and add a hint of that slightly smoky, bitter curry flavour to the dish. Methi can be bought in bunches or frozen into cubes like spinach.

Heat the olive oil in a large casserole dish (Dutch oven). Add the lamb, a few pieces at a time, and brown well on all sides over a medium heat. You should not have to add any more olive oil during this stage as the lamb should render out some fat as it cooks.

Remove all the lamb from the casserole and add the onions and curry leaves. Cook for several minutes until they have started to soften, then return the lamb to the casserole. Add the garlic, ginger, lime zest, spices and tomato purée and stir until the lamb is completely coated.

Add the kecap manis, lime leaves, laksa leaves and coriander stems to the casserole and pour in the stock. Add enough water to make sure the lamb is just covered and stir to loosen anything stuck to the base of the casserole. Season with salt and pepper.

Bring to the boil, then turn down the heat and cover. Simmer for 1½–2 hours, until the lamb is very tender.

At this point you have a choice – you can proceed with the rest of the recipe or you can pause to leave the lamb to rest overnight. The advantages of this are that the flavour will develop further and also if you chill it once it reaches room temperature, you will be able to remove some of the fat from the dish, as it is likely to be excessive. If you decide to do this, return the lamb to the boil before adding the spinach, coriander leaves and lime juice. Simmer for a further 15 minutes then serve in shallow bowls. Garnish with coriander leaves, thinly sliced laksa leaves and some green chillies.

A Hommage to Gumbo Z'Herbes

I have a long-standing crush on Louisiana and its food, and consequently this is a dish I care deeply about getting right. Gumbo is an investment of time and faith, and when it is made properly, it elevates often humble ingredients into something very special. I say faith is required, because taste it at any point during the first two thirds of the cooking process and you will be tempted to give up or start again. Then something miraculous happens and this unprepossessing, gloomy, dirty, muddy, swampy sludge turns into one of the most spectacular things you will ever eat.

In terms of leaves, what is wonderful about this dish is the way they are used to layer flavour upon flavour. The leaves are there in the form of herbs for seasoning and taste, while the greens form most of the bulk and texture. But in gumbo there is the final leafy element – the ground sassafras leaf, known as filé powder, which provides a slightly peppery flavour when added at the end, and will also help to thicken the gumbo cooking liquid.

Gumbo is a dish steeped in history and tradition and there are rules to follow, but as with many great dishes, those rules come with myriad hotly discussed variations within those rules. Understanding the rules allows you to be flexible around them. Here are my thoughts on the main elements of a gumbo z'herbes, and how you can vary them.

The Greens

You can use as many of these as you like, but local superstition insists on an odd number – lucky number seven, but as low as three and as high as 17. Anything goes. Choose from whatever is seasonal and plentiful (or even just what needs using up) and your gumbo z'herbes will never taste the same way twice.

I always add some kind of bitter leaves – this is in keeping with its position as a Good Friday/ Lenten dish – but I do moderate this, especially if I'm feeding my children. Be frugal – use the tops of your root vegetables, foraged greens, anything really you have to hand. I cannot give an exhaustive list of what to include, but mine would normally have any of the following: chard, spring greens, collard greens if I can get them, cime di rapa (broccoli rabe), in moderate amounts as bitter, mustard greens, rocket (arugula) , watercress, spinach, turnip, beetroot (beets) or carrot tops, any kind of kale or cabbage, lettuce, nettles or dandelions.

The Roux

To roux or not to roux? I always do – it is the most important element of the flavouring to me, adding those bitter, chocolate/coffee notes is so intrinsic to gumbo. I have seen recipes for gumbo z'herbes without roux, but I can't view this as gumbo, just a stew-down of greens. The character of a gumbo comes from the depth of flavour the roux adds. The paler your roux, the more it will thicken your final gumbo. As it darkens, it loses some of its thickening property, but adds more flavour. A roux is a flour and fat mixture – at its palest used for béchamel, but here it is a very different animal. The main variant is what type of oil or fat to use. Vegetable oil is the most common, but if you are European, you might want to use a combination of olive oil and butter. Or if you are not wedded to keeping it vegetarian, you might want to use bacon dripping or smoked ham fat or lard.

The Holy Trinity

In Louisianan cooking, these are onion, celery and green (bell) pepper. I have heard anecdotally that red pepper can be substituted to make the dish less bitter, but I have never seen this in a recipe, and it just feels wrong, not least because a hint of red would be jarring in the muddy green. What I will add when making gumbo z'herbes is the tougher stems from any of the greens I am using (chard, kale), as well as any finely chopped herb stems.

The main issue with the roux and the Holy Trinity is when and how to add them. It has always seemed strange to me that you cook the roux so gently and get it exactly the right colour, then add the Holy Trinity to it, raw. So many recipes say these should soften in anything between 5–20 minutes, but I find the Holy Trinity is very stubborn about this and just won't give when added to the roux. And the longer I leave it in the hope they will soften, the more nerve-wracking it becomes. And they do need to be soft – as my friend and Louisianan aficionado Nicola Miller was once told, they should be soft enough so 'they can be gummed by your toothless grandma'. So I cook the two separately, at the same time.

Meat

Traditionally, if this was to be cooked for Good Friday, it would have to be vegetarian, but many Louisianans have quite a flexible view on what constitutes a vegetarian dish – pieces of meat, no, a stock made with meat, perfectly okay. And Leah Chase's version, which she only cooked during Lent, flies in the face of this and includes all kinds of smoked meats.

I have made variations of both and have come to the conclusion that if you want to make a gumbo with roux and the Holy Trinity AND use any bitter greens, a smoked ham hock stock magically brings all the elements together and tempers the bitterness without dampening the flavour. So I include it. Many gumbos include sausage – usually andouille, which is hard (but not impossible) to find in the UK. Instead look for a garlicky French sausage or a fat, soft *kielbasa*.

Time

Gumbo z'herbes might be considered to be a dish of 'smothered' greens – greens, particularly collard, which are cooked long and slow, usually with some kind of bacon or pork. This length of cooking time is key. I was once sceptical about this, thinking this was just a Louisianan idiosyncrasy and it wasn't necessary. I was wrong, and I only realised this when I accidentally left my pot of gumbo z'herbes on a low heat and came back to it over an hour later. It isn't just about the texture of the greens; it's about the melding of flavours, the balance of bitter, sweet, earthy. It's essential.

Gumbo Z'Herbes

Serves 4

Bunches of leafy greens, preferably 7 types (see page 186)

6 tbsp oil, butter or bacon fat

200g (7oz) piece smoked sausage, thickly sliced (optional)

1 large onion, finely chopped

3 celery sticks, finely chopped

1 green (bell) pepper, finely chopped

4 tbsp plain (all-purpose) flour

3 garlic cloves, finely chopped

1 tsp garlic powder

1 tsp allspice berries, crushed

3 bay leaves

A large sprig of thyme

2 large sprigs of tarragon

2 litres (8 cups) smoked Ham Hock Stock (see below) or vegetable stock

A few dashes of hot sauce

Sea salt and freshly ground black pepper

For the ham hock stock

1 small smoked ham hock

1 small onion

2 cloves

1 tsp allspice berries

3 bay leaves

To serve

Cooked long grain rice

Hot sauce

Filé (sassafras) powder

First, if using a smoked ham stock, cook the ham. Cover in cold water, bring to the boil and allow to boil for 5 minutes. This is the equivalent of desalinating and destarching the ham. Drain off the water, rinse the ham and the saucepan, then return the ham to the pan along with the onion, cloves, allspice and bay. Cover with water, bring to the boil, then turn down to simmer, partially covered, until the ham is tender – around 1½ hours. Remove the ham from the cooking liquid and strain – this will give you your stock. Any fat that collects at the top can be used either in the roux or to fry the vegetables. When the ham is cool enough to handle, remove the fat and bone and pull the meat apart into pieces. Set aside.

To make the gumbo, first prepare the greens. Wash everything thoroughly. Take any of the greens with thicker, fibrous stems and separate them from the leaves. Finely dice the stems and add to your Holy Trinity. Shred all the leaves.

Next, if using, cook the sausage. Heat 2 tablespoons of the oil or fat in a large casserole (Dutch oven) and add the sausage. Brown briefly on both sides over a medium heat, then remove. Add the onion, celery, green pepper and any stems and cook until they soften and very slightly brown – around 10 minutes, stirring every so often.

While the vegetables are softening, cook your roux. You might want to put the radio on – you are going to be here for a while. Melt the remaining oil or fat into a casserole dish or saucepan. When it has warmed through, add the flour and stir to combine. Cook over a very low heat, stirring constantly. This is important – if you leave it at any point, you run the risk of it burning. I would discard any roux that burns and has black flecks in as it will ruin the finished dish. Stir until the colour you end up with is a rich chestnut – think dark, glossy conkers. Cooking to this stage will take at least 20 minutes. You can take it further if you are brave, but I think this is the right colour for a gumbo z'herbes. Towards the end it may start crackling and spitting at you – use a deep pan and a long-handled spoon and you will keep out of harm's way.

When your vegetables are sufficiently soft, add them to the roux, along with all the aromatics – the garlic, allspice, bay leaves, thyme and tarragon. Cook together for a further 5 minutes – you will find that the roux will hiss softly as you add the vegetables and initially become thicker again. Add half the stock and season with salt and pepper. Start piling in the greens, in batches, letting them wilt down into the liquid before adding the next batch – the back of a wooden spoon will help press them down. When you have added them all, top up with enough stock so they are just covered, bring to the boil and turn down to a steady simmer. Partially cover and cook for at least 1 hour, preferably 2 hours. This sounds like a long time, and it is. It is the only time I would ever cook greens for this long, but it really is necessary for the finished texture. Add a little more stock if necessary – you want to be able to eat this as a soupy, swampy stew, with a texture that should be thin, but not watery. This is also the time to start adding a few dashes of hot sauce – don't go over the top at this point, just enough to warm the flavour. More can be added at the table.

To finish, add the shredded ham hock and/or the slices of smoked sausage. Ladle over rice and serve with hot sauce and filé powder.

Pork Escalopes with Fried Sage

Serves 4

4 pork escalopes, trimmed of fat

1 tbsp plain (all-purpose) flour

½ tsp rubbed sage

1 tbsp olive oil

1 tbsp butter

50ml (¼ cup) calvados or brandy

100ml (scant ½ cup) dry marsala

200ml (¾ cup) chicken stock

Sea salt and freshly ground black
pepper

For the fried sage leaves

1 tbsp olive oil

8 sage leaves

For the creamed cabbage

1 tbsp olive oil

1 tbsp butter

1 onion, finely chopped

2 garlic cloves, finely chopped

1 tsp juniper berries, lightly crushed

1 eating apple, grated

1 tbsp apple cider vinegar

500g (1lb 1½oz) Savoy cabbage,
shredded

100ml (scant ½ cup) double
(heavy) cream

Sea salt and freshly ground black
pepper

This is my favourite way to cook pork escalopes, but I have met with disagreement. In fact, years ago, I cooked it for my ex-husband, who incensed me so much with his moaning about not being given the breadcrumbed version that I saw red and put his dinner in the bin. He didn't speak to me for a week. My only regret is that I didn't keep his dinner for myself. Life as a food writer is full of instances of food not going down well. Not usually as dramatically as this, but when I am experimenting, there are often times when the children poke and prod at their dinner with suspicion or even dread.

First make the creamed cabbage. Heat the olive oil and butter in a large, lidded frying pan. When the butter foams, add the onion and cook over a gentle heat until it is soft and translucent, around 10 minutes. Add the garlic, juniper berries and apple and cook for a further 5 minutes. Pour over the cider vinegar then add the cabbage. Add enough water to the pan to cover the base by a couple of millimetres and season with salt and pepper. Bring to the boil, then cover, turn down the heat and leave to simmer until the cabbage is just tender. Pour in the cream and stir, making sure it doesn't boil again. Leave on a low heat.

To make the escalopes, place each slice of pork between 2 sheets of plastic wrap and bash with a mallet, a rolling pin, even a heavy frying pan. Aim to get the pork as thin as possible. Remove from the plastic wrap and set aside. Mix the flour and sage with a generous amount of salt and pepper. Use to dust the pork, patting off any excess.

Heat the oil and butter in a large frying pan. When foaming, add the escalopes and fry for 2–3 minutes on each side until crisp and brown. You may have to do this in batches – if so, keep them warm. Deglaze the pan with the calvados, followed by the marsala and stock. Bring to the boil and reduce by half, then stir in the sage.

For the garnish, heat the oil in a small frying pan and fry the sage until crisp – a few seconds. Drain on a kitchen towel. Spoon the sauce over the pork and serve with the cabbage and the sage leaves.

PARSLEY, SAGE, ROSEMARY AND THYME

A couple of years ago, I was driving through Scarborough with my family. It was raining, pouring in fact, a typical British summer day with dense, hoary sea frets rolling in from the coast. We all felt a bit miserable. Then my husband asked to listen to the Simon and Garfunkel version of 'Scarborough Fair'; when faced with horizontal rain and that intensely evocative sound of squeaky windscreen wipers, the tone felt even more melancholic, verging on dreary.

However, it did make me think. Here we were, on the north-east coast of England, listening to the lyrics of a traditional folk song that celebrates very Mediterranean herbs: 'Are you going to Scarborough Fair? Parsley, sage, rosemary and thyme.' Why?

In terms of why those particular herbs feature in the song, no one really knows and, in all likelihood, it was just because they flow nicely together. However, there are theories that the herbs brewed together as tea or carried as a nosegay would be effective at warding off the Black Death. Rosemary, in particular, was considered a protector, a sprig in your pocket warding off everything from the plague to evil spirits. Another theory is that the herbs reflect the song's theme of lost love – again, rosemary works especially well here, being the herb of love, fidelity and remembrance, frequently used in bridal posies and funeral bouquets alike. Greek scholars used to wear garlands of it when studying for and sitting exams and they were clever to do so, as it has since been proved to aid memory.

Thanks mainly to the Romans, our most-used herbs all stem from the Mediterranean and, as such, are chiefly associated with that region despite being part of the British culinary landscape for nigh on 2000 years. It is impossible to think of certain classic dishes without them; consider sage with onions to stuff a chicken, lamb with rosemary and garlic, or parsley in a classic sauce for fish.

The 'Scarborough Fair' herbs may well appear together in a bouquet garni – a term not used in the UK until the nineteenth century, but before that we did add bundles of herbs known as 'faggots' to our food. A classic combination is bay, thyme and parsley, but it might also include a strip of bacon, some chives, oregano, chervil, a few cloves studded into a slice of onion, all bound together, perhaps first wrapped in a piece of leek. The now ubiquitous use of a bouquet garni is about subtlety, though, rather than a fine chopping or pounding of herbs that might add bitterness or an abundance of flavour.

Garbure

Serves 4

1–2 Confit Duck Legs (see below)

100g (3½oz) smoked bacon, thickly sliced into lardons

2 onions, thickly sliced

3 carrots, thickly sliced

2 turnips, cut into wedges

4 celery sticks, thickly sliced

6 garlic cloves, finely chopped

250ml (1 cup) white wine

500ml (2 cups) chicken stock

500g (1lb 1½oz) Parsley and Cannellini Beans (see page 227) or 2 x 400g (14oz) tins

A bouquet garni of 1 tsp juniper berries, parsley, thyme and bay leaves

1 large floury potato, peeled and thickly sliced

1 large Savoy cabbage, cored and cut into thin wedges

1 small bunch of parsley, finely chopped

For the confit duck legs

4 duck legs

4 dried bay leaves

1 small bunch of thyme, leaves only

A few sprigs of rosemary (optional), roughly chopped

1 tsp juniper berries, crushed

1 tsp black peppercorns, crushed

3 tbsp sea salt

500g (1lb 1½oz) duck or goose fat

4 garlic cloves, thinly sliced, plus a head of garlic, broken into cloves

When you think about using leaves in cooking, a duck confit is probably not one of the first things that springs to mind, but the herbs are an integral part of the dish – not only do they flavour the meat, but the fat too, which means you can have bay/thyme/rosemary scented duck fat for frying for months on end. I can think of few things better for frying or roasting potatoes.

Garbure is a French classic that can be as luxurious or as frugal as you like. It is one of those dishes that traditionally relies on what is available at the tail end of winter; a few bits of preserved meat, root vegetables, and of course, that vegetable for all seasons, the cabbage. We have developed a national hatred of overcooked cabbage in the UK, and there is something to be said for keeping this quite fresh and green. But really, it can handle slow and tender cooking (in this respect, garbure has a commonality with gumbo, see page 188), so you can double the cooking time if you wish.

First, make the confit duck legs. Put the legs in a non-reactive dish. Crumble up the bay leaves and mix with the thyme leaves, rosemary, if using, juniper berries, black peppercorns and sea salt. Rub this mixture all over the duck – skin and flesh sides – then cover and leave in the fridge overnight.

The next day, preheat the oven to 150°C (300°F/Gas 2).

Remove the duck from the fridge. The surface of the duck should look wet because the salt will have drawn out some of the water inside the duck – pat dry, trying not to remove the marinade. Put into a casserole dish (Dutch oven) – it needs to be a snug fit – then cover with duck fat. Tuck in the whole garlic cloves. Cook in the oven for 2½ hours, or until you can see that the duck is starting to come away from the bone. Remove the duck from the casserole, transferring to a large, sterilised jar. Pour over the fat and leave to cool. As long as the legs are completely covered with the fat, they will keep for a very long time.

To start the garbure, scrape most of the preserving fat from 2 of the duck legs. Heat a large casserole then add the duck legs, skin-side down. Cook over a medium heat until the duck fat has rendered out, then turn over and fry on the other side. This process should take up to 15 minutes. Remove the duck from the casserole and place on a chopping board. Roughly cut the meat, discarding the bone.

Add the bacon to the casserole and fry until it is crisp and brown. Remove from the casserole with a slotted spoon, then add the onions, carrots, turnips, celery and sliced garlic. Cook until starting to take on a golden colour – around 10 minutes.

Add the wine, bring to the boil and then simmer until the wine has reduced by half, then add the stock, beans, bouquet garni and potato. Bring to the boil, then turn down the heat, cover, and simmer for half an hour, or until the vegetables are completely tender. Add the cabbage. You may have to push this down into the liquid with a back of a spoon, but don't worry if you can't submerge it all; it will collapse into the broth during the cooking process. Cover again and simmer for another 30 minutes.

When the cabbage is tender but still a bright green and yellow, add the reserved duck and bacon and stir through. Continue cooking for another 5 minutes to heat everything through. Remove the bouquet garni and garnish liberally with plenty of finely chopped parsley.

Beef Ragù

Serves 4

4 tbsp olive oil

1kg (2lb 3oz) beef (ox cheek or shin),
cut into 5cm (2in) pieces

750ml (3 cups) red wine

1 large sprig of thyme

1 large onion, finely diced

1 carrot, finely diced

2 celery sticks, finely diced

A bouquet garni of 2 bay leaves,
2 sprigs of rosemary, 2 sprigs of
thyme, 2 sprigs of parsley, tied up with
butcher's string or in a muslin bag

Zest from 1 Seville orange, zest cut to
matchsticks and boiled for 2 minutes
then drained 3 times (optional)

1 garlic bulb, cloves separated but
unpeeled

2 tsp dried oregano

2 anchovy fillets, finely chopped

2 tbsp tomato purée

300ml (1¼ cups) beef stock

Sea salt and freshly ground black
pepper

To serve

1 tbsp olive oil

1 large bunch of minestra nera
(spagiola kale), woody stems trimmed

1 x quantity Tarragon Vinegar Butter
Beans (see page 222)

I have included this dish to show off the humble *bouquet garni* – a varying collection of ingredients that are bundled together for ease of removal, which can have a transformative effect on the flavour of a dish. Serve this as a classic beef casserole, preferably with mashed potatoes and the Caramelised Endives (see page 160), or shred it into the sticky, oleaginous sauce and serve with the Tarragon Vinegar Butter Beans on page 222.

You need to use a fatty cut with plenty of connective tissue, as this will give it texture. Ox cheeks, or shin, either off the bone or cut crossways like osso buco (with the added benefit of bone marrow), are best.

Heat 1 tablespoon of the olive oil in a large casserole dish (Dutch oven). Sear the beef on all sides over a medium-high heat, allowing a dark crust to develop. Do this in 2–3 batches, adding more olive oil each time. Set aside.

Turn up the heat and pour in the wine along with the thyme. Bring to the boil, pushing the thyme around as you go. Reduce the wine by just over half, then pour off into a jug and discard the thyme. Wipe out the casserole dish.

Heat the remaining olive oil in the casserole and add the onion, carrot and celery. Cook until the onion and celery are translucent, then turn up the heat to caramelise slightly. Drop the bouquet garni into the casserole along with the orange zest, garlic, oregano, anchovies and tomato purée. Stir to combine, then return the meat to the pan. Pour over the wine and stock, then season. Bring to the boil, cover and reduce the heat. Leave over a very low heat for 2 hours, or until the meat is tender.

At this point you can serve the dish as a casserole. To turn it into a ragù, allow it to cool a little, then break up all the meat, removing any unforgiving pieces of connective tissue. Squeeze the garlic out of its skins and remove the bouquet garni. Stir well over a low heat to reduce to a thick sauce.

While the ragù reduces, heat 1 tablespoon olive oil in a large frying pan, add the minestra nera with 100ml (scant ½ cup) water and cover. Braise for 10 minutes, until the greens are just tender. Serve with the butter beans.

Stuffed Savoy Cabbage Leaves

Serves 4

12 large Savoy cabbage leaves

2 tbsp olive oil, plus extra for greasing

300g (10½oz) black pudding, skinned and sliced

1 large onion, sliced

3 garlic cloves, finely chopped or grated

150ml (⅔ cup) red wine

1 large sprig of thyme, leaves only

250g (1½ cups) cooked chickpeas (garbanzo beans), preferably black

2 large tomatoes, deseeded and chopped

100ml (scant ½ cup) chicken or vegetable stock

Sea salt and freshly ground black pepper

For the topping

30g (½ cup) breadcrumbs (optional)

A few sprigs of dried thyme (optional)

2 tbsp butter

To serve

200ml (¾ cup) sour cream

A sprinkling of onion powder

This is one of those dishes that came about because of what I had to hand on the day – I was about to embark on a traditional rice filling, when I remembered the bag of black chickpeas (garbanzo beans) I wanted to experiment with. The black pudding – especially the Spanish sort, morcilla, works really well with them. The texture of the black pudding is quite important; you need a crumbly one, nothing too dense, as this will make the sauce claggy.

Bring a large saucepan of salted water to the boil. Push the leaves down into the water and blanch for 3 minutes until soft but still bright. You need to make sure the stems are pliable enough to fold without snapping – if they aren't, trim down the thickness of the stem where it juts out from the back of the leaf. Refresh in iced water and drain.

To make the sauce, heat half the olive oil in a large frying pan over a medium heat and add the black pudding. Sear on all sides – it will blacken quickly – then remove. Add the rest of the oil with the onion. Cook over a medium heat until the onions have started to soften and brown, around 10 minutes – you want a little caramelisation. Add the garlic and fry for 1–2 minutes, then turn up the heat and pour in the wine. Let it bubble up and reduce, then add the thyme, chickpeas and tomatoes. Season, stir then cook for 2–3 minutes. Return the pudding to the pan, stir through and remove from the heat. Check for seasoning.

Preheat the oven to 180°C (350°F/Gas 4) and oil a rectangular dish large enough to fit the rolled leaves snugly.

To assemble, take each leaf and lay it with the base of the stem facing towards you. If you want to make sure you have exactly enough mixture for the rolls, weigh the stuffing mixture and divide by 12 – it should be approximately 2 heaped tablespoons of mixture. Put the mixture towards the base of the leaf, fold in the sides, then roll up, making sure the mixture doesn't escape. Place in the oven dish.

Pour over the stock, cover the dish with foil and bake for 20 minutes. Uncover and, if using, sprinkle over the breadcrumbs and thyme. Regardless, dot over plenty of butter. Return to the oven for another 10 minutes.

Sprinkle the onion powder on the sour cream and serve.

SIDES AND BASICS

Tomato Sauce

Serves 4

3 tbsp olive oil

3 garlic cloves, finely chopped

1kg (2lb 3oz) fresh plum tomatoes or
2 x 400g (14oz) tins chopped
tomatoes

A pinch of ground cinnamon

A pinch of caster (superfine) sugar
(optional)

2 tsp dried oregano or 1 tbsp rosemary
needles, finely chopped

Handful of tomato leaves

3–4 basil leaves

Sea salt and freshly ground black
pepper

This is a basic tomato sauce that you can use as the beginnings of a pasta sauce, or reduce down for pizza. I give options for tinned and fresh tomatoes. What I want to highlight with this recipe is that you can use tomato leaves in a sauce. I grow tomatoes, with varying degrees of success, but a few tomato leaves added to a sauce will enhance the flavour and aroma, especially if you are using tinned or sub-par tomatoes. I pick the leaves fresh from the garden or freeze them to use during winter, then remove at the end of the cooking time, just as I would a bay leaf.

If using fresh tomatoes, unless you have a very high-powered food processor that can blitz them smooth, skin and all, skin and deseed the tomatoes. You can do this by making a cross in the bottom, pouring over just-boiled water and leaving until you can see the skin starting to shrink – at this point, it should easily peel off. Deseed the tomatoes over a colander, collecting any juice.

Heat the olive oil in a large saucepan. Add the garlic and cook over a medium heat for a couple of minutes. You want to see bubbling around the garlic, but no colouration. Add the tinned or freshly prepared tomatoes along with a pinch of cinnamon (this helps add sweetness without really impacting on the flavour) and a pinch of sugar if you like. Sprinkle in the oregano or rosemary and season with salt and pepper. Bring to the boil, then turn down the heat and simmer for at least 45 minutes, until the sauce has reduced and thickened. Add a handful of tomato leaves for the last 10 minutes if you have them, along with the basil leaves, then remove them before serving.

Steamed Banana Leaf Rice

Serves 4

300g (1½ cups) basmati rice

200ml (¾ cup) coconut milk

250ml (1 cup) vegetable or chicken
  stock or water

A few sprigs of thyme

4 banana leaves

Sea salt

**Steaming rice this way isn't just for show. The flavour –
clearly related to banana but somehow greener and less
overwhelming – does delicately infuse the rice. This is a
really good side dish for any curry, especially something
quite hot and sour that might benefit from being paired
with something sweet and aromatic.**

Wash the rice in plenty of cold water until it runs
completely clear. Drain the rice thoroughly and put in a
saucepan with the coconut milk, stock and a few sprigs
of thyme. Add salt.

Bring to the boil, then turn down and cover. Cook for 12–
15 minutes, or until most of the liquid has been absorbed.

Cut your banana leaves into pieces 20–25cm (8–10in)
square and wash thoroughly – you will need 6 pieces of
this size. If they are very stiff (this varies enormously), run
the leaves over a low gas flame for a few seconds – this
will help to wilt them.

Divide the rice between the leaves, then fold in from the
sides. Seal either with cocktail sticks or by tying up each
parcel with twine. There are all kinds of shapes and sizes
for doing this, but I prefer to keep it simple.

Place in a steamer and steam for 10–15 minutes. The
colour of the banana leaf will dull in this time, but it will
gently flavour the rice. Open up the parcels and serve.

Stir Fried Lettuce with XO Sauce

Serves 4

1 tbsp vegetable oil

1 bunch of spring onions (scallions), whites and greens separated, cut into rounds

3cm (1¼in) piece ginger, peeled and grated

3 garlic cloves, grated

1 large lettuce or equivalent, roughly torn

2 tbsp light soy sauce

1 tbsp rice wine vinegar

1 tbsp XO sauce

A few drops of sesame oil

1 tsp sesame seeds

I always used to use Chinese (Napa) cabbage for this type of stir fry, until I realised that it works with anything with a similar structure. By that I mean any green with a thick stem that will retain a degree of crisp succulence and leaves that will soften and wilt. This applies to several types of lettuce – Cos, romaine, little gems, salad greens such as watercress, purslane, even puntarelle, and greens such as chard, morning glory (water spinach), bok choy and kai lan. I also like to make it with iceberg and other crisphead lettuces – the leaves don't wilt in the same way, but they do take on a very attractive, silky quality.

For most of the greens you would use in this dish, you don't need to separate stem from the leaf, but if you are using chard or kai lan, you may want to do so, so you can cook the stems for a minute or two longer than the leaves.

I have used XO for this, as I like the combination of juicy, thirst-quenching greens with seafood and chilli-infused oil. But this is entirely optional – you could use a plain chilli oil instead for a vegan dish.

Heat the vegetable oil in a wok. When the air above the oil is shimmering, add the whites of the spring onions along with any stems you might be using and cook for 2 minutes. Add the ginger and garlic and stir briefly to combine, then add the lettuce. Stir fry for another minute until the leaves have wilted into the wok slightly, then add the soy sauce, rice wine vinegar, the XO sauce and a dash of sesame oil. Continue to cook, stirring constantly so the lettuce is completely coated in the sauce and still looks glossy and green. Garnish with the greens of the spring onions and sesame seeds and serve immediately.

Deep Fried 'Seaweed'

Buttered Spinach

I do not love kale chips, but I really do love this shredded version, similar to the garnishes in Chinese restaurants (and, I'm whispering this, I always assumed this was seaweed, not cabbage, how embarrassing). The flavours are so moreish. I've put them here as a side dish, but really, I could just eat them in the same way I'd eat a bowl of popcorn – and with different flavours, too.

Take a bag of spring greens, spring cabbage or kale. Cut away the thick stems and shred the leaves as finely as you can. If you have a deep-fat fryer, heat vegetable oil to 180°C (375°F) – alternatively fill a wok or saucepan a third full with oil. Fry the cabbage a large handful at a time, for around a minute, until the cabbage is very crisp and brittle. Remove from the oil, drain on kitchen towels and continue until you have used all the cabbage. Dress with plenty of salt, some sugar and any spices you like – Chinese five spice is good, so is chilli, and any citrus-flavoured salt, but I often like just a sprinkling of sesame oil and seeds – or, just to make me feel better about the seaweed thing, some seaweed flakes.

This will work with any wilting greens. If you are using chard or kale, remove the stems and use them for something else.

Carefully wash 750g (1lb 10½oz) spinach and shake off some of the water. Heat a large saucepan, then add the spinach, large handfuls at a time, pushing it down with a spoon as you go, until it has all wilted into the saucepan. Drain immediately, pressing out as much water as you can, then carefully pull the spinach apart so it isn't one solid mass. Heat around 50g (1¾oz) butter in a large frying pan. When it has foamed, add one very finely chopped garlic clove. Fry for 2 minutes over a medium heat, then add 2 teaspoons sherry vinegar (optional). Add the spinach and toss it in the buttery sauce. Season with plenty of salt and pepper.

You can make a gratin of this if you like, in which case I would recommend the textured version. Top with breadcrumbs and dots of butter and perhaps a handful of grated Parmesan.

Sautéed Cabbage, Caribbean-style

Serves 4

1 tbsp olive oil

1½ tbsp butter

1 medium onion, finely chopped

2 seasoning peppers, deseeded and finely diced (optional)

½ Scotch bonnet, deseeded and finely chopped (optional)

½ white or green cabbage, finely shredded

½ tsp allspice berries, crushed

A pinch of ground cinnamon

1 garlic clove, crushed

1 tbsp finely chopped celery leaf

1 tbsp parsley, finely chopped

Sea salt and finely ground white pepper

This is a favourite from my Caribbean days. It is very hard to find seasoning peppers outside of the Caribbean, particularly those that are hybrids of a proper Scotch bonnet. Their aroma is hard to describe, but it has all the slightly smoky, floral and fruity scents of the Scotch bonnet without the heat. If you are unsure of what this is, take a Scotch bonnet and a habanero pepper, break each one open and smell – the habanero will have none of the complexity of aroma. It will be the same with a heatless habanero and a seasoning pepper. Don't be put off the dish if you can't get hold of them – it will not suffer from the lack.

Heat the olive oil and butter in a large frying pan until the butter has melted. Add the onion and peppers along with a pinch of salt and cook over a low heat until the onion has started to soften and go translucent, but hasn't taken on any colour, around 10 minutes. Add the cabbage and turn up the heat slightly. Fry, stirring regularly, until the cabbage has started to reduce in volume and is al dente. Stir in the remaining ingredients, including the seasoning and keep cooking over a low heat until the cabbage is tender.

Three Summer Sides

Buttered Cucumber with Borage

This is adapted from Sophie Grigson's *Herbs* book, and is just what I want to eat with some poached trout. The borage leaves are very similar in flavour to the cucumber, just slightly sweeter and greener.

Peel two cucumbers, then halve them lengthways, deseed, and cut into thick crescents. Heat a thick slice of butter in a pan and when it is foaming, add the cucumber along with plenty of seasoning. Cover and braise gently for 10 minutes, turning over at intervals, then add a handful of small, tender borage leaves. Allow to wilt down, then simmer until most of the liquid in the pan has evaporated. Add 100ml (scant ½ cup) double (heavy) cream and continue to simmer and reduce. Serve with a squeeze of lemon or lime juice, garnished with a few borage flowers.

Watercress and Petit Pois Purée

One of the simplest and most satisfying of summer side dishes, good with everything from some grilled trout or salmon to a piece of baked feta, or some lamb chops. There is the temptation to add herbs to this, which you can (maybe a little tarragon for balance), but it is one of the few cases when I don't think it is necessary.

Take 300g (10½oz) petit pois – I use frozen, as they are always the sweetest – and put in a saucepan. Cover with water and bring to the boil. Simmer gently until tender – it is up to you how far you take this. You can leave them a squeaky green or leave until very soft and starting to change from bright green to mustard

green – then add a large bunch of watercress – at least 500g (1lb 1½oz). Push the leaves down into the peas, then cover, and leave over a very low heat to wilt – another 5 minutes.

Drain, then transfer to a food processor. Season with salt and pepper and add a generous slice of butter. Blitz until smooth and serve hot or cold. It will even serve as a dip.

Early Broad Beans with Courgettes, Broad Bean Tops and Summer Savoury

Broad (fava) beans and summer savoury are a classic combination – one on which I was brought up, as it was one of my mother's favourite ways to cook them. If you are using very young, baby broad beans, you do not need to peel them, but if they are any larger than the nail on your little finger, blanching and peeling is the way to go. I like to add in a few leaves too. If you can't find savoury, other herbs that work beautifully with broad beans are dill, mint or most types of thyme.

Take 400g (14oz) broad (fava) beans. Blanch in boiling water for a couple of minutes if you are planning on peeling them, then strain and run under cold water to cool. Peel the larger beans. Heat 2 tablespoons olive oil in a large frying pan and add 2 slim courgettes (zucchini), sliced into rounds. Fry briskly, stirring regularly until the courgettes are browned on all sides and looking glossy and on the verge of floppiness. Add the broad beans along with a splash of water, then simmer gently for 2–3 minutes. Stir in finely chopped leaves from 2 sprigs of savoury or alternatives, then if you have any, wilt in the broad bean tops or leaves. Stir with a light grating of lemon zest.

Slow-Braised Greens

This is a method that will work with most kinds of robust greens. The cooking time will vary from green to green and will in part depend on the texture you want, but the aim is to think about the greens in terms of slow, tender cooking with a minimal amount of liquid so nothing becomes remotely soggy or sulphurous. My favourite green to do this with is cavolo nero, or its skinnier cousin, cavolo spigarello. Minestra nera, kalettes, and perhaps the darkest leaves of Savoy cabbage or a deep purple radicchio also work well. The texture after a long, slow braise is wonderful – rich, dark, very savoury. It is a very adaptable method. If I want to keep, for example, cime di rapa, fairly fresh and green, I will braise for less time, around 10–15 minutes, but cavolo nero benefits from 45 minutes–1 hour.

If you want to promote braised greens from side to main, use as the base for a pasta dish, stir cooked beans through them, or add to an earthy spelt risotto. Change the flavours to suit – I like ½ teaspoon each of sweet smoky and hot paprika, cut through with lemon zest. Add a small amount of meat – a few lardons of bacon, a few slices of a smoky sausage or chorizo, or perhaps a tin of mashed anchovies and a sprinkle of chilli flakes. You can also add a dash of cream towards the end.

Take a very large bunch of greens and discard any stems. Bring a large saucepan of water to the boil and salt generously. Blanch the greens for no more than 2 minutes, then plunge into iced water to help set their colour. Heat 2 tablespoons olive oil and 1 tablespoon butter in a large casserole dish (Dutch oven). Add a thinly sliced red onion and cook over a low heat until the onion is soft and just starting to change colour, then add a couple of cloves of finely chopped garlic. Cook for 2 minutes then add the greens. Season with salt and pepper and pour over 150ml (⅔ cup) stock. Cook slowly, partially covered, until the greens are tender and cooked through. You can take this as far as you like. I will cook cavolo nero for at least 45 minutes. Turn up the heat to boil off any remaining liquid and serve.

Quick-Sautéed Greens

There are a few greens that are robust and keep their shape when cooked, but still need very little cooking time. Agretti (monk's beard) is one, so is cavolo spigarello when it is very young with slender stems. In fact, many greens will work this way, it is just that the cooking time will vary a little depending on how thick the stems and leaves are. And very fine, wilting greens, such as spinach and nettles, will need no blanching, just a few moments in the pan. Incidentally, it is also the best way to prepare Greek *horta*.

If using anything remotely robust, bring a large saucepan of water to the boil and salt generously. Plunge in the greens – agretti, cavolo spigarello, curly kale or mustard greens etc., for 1 minute only, then drain and refresh under ice-cold water to help set the colour. Heat 2–3 tablespoons olive oil in a large frying pan and add a couple of chopped garlic cloves. Add the greens and cook over a high heat for 2–3 minutes. This is all they will need, regardless of whether they are the type that are usually blanching or not. Serve with some lemon zest and juice.

You can also quick-cook any Asian greens this way without blanching first, adding chopped ginger and dashes of soy and mirin. This will work with spinach, morning glory, young sweet potato or yam leaves and any of the mustardy greens such as spiky mizuna and mibuna.

Braised Little Gems with Kimchi

There is a soup recipe on page 90 that takes little gems and braises them with leeks and peas, which is also an excellent side dish if you take out most of the liquid. This is something entirely different. I use it as a side dish for fried chicken or mix it with some leftover roast pork and put over fried rice (perhaps with a cup of peas and/or a fried egg on top) or noodles. It is very simple and will also work with wedges of most sorts of cabbage.

Heat 1 tablespoon sesame oil in a frying pan. Take 3–4 little gems and halve them lengthways. Add to the pan, cut-side down, and cook for 3–4 minutes, until they've started to brown. Cook on the other side for 2 minutes and remove. Add the whites of 4 spring onions (scallions), 3 chopped garlic cloves, a piece of ginger and 3–4 tablespoons chopped kimchi to the pan and fry for 3–4 minutes. Return the little gems to the pan, add 200ml (¾ cup) stock (preferably chicken) along with 2–3 tablespoons kimchi juice from the jar and a dash of soy sauce. Simmer, partially covered, until the little gems are just tender and the sauce has reduced down. Serve garnished with a few sesame seeds, the greens from the spring onions and a few chilli flakes, if you like.

Braised Red Cabbage

There are plenty of ways to braise red cabbage – I was a devotee of Delia Smith's recipe for years – but, I've come to like this version more than any. It is a hot, sweet and sour affair and is a very useful side dish if you want to cut through anything rich or fatty.

Take a red cabbage and cut through the root into 8–12 thick wedges – you want to make sure that the leaves are still attached to the core. Heat 2 tablespoons olive oil and a generous slice of butter in a large frying pan and fry the wedges for a few minutes on each side until well seared. Remove from the pan and add 2 pears or apples, cored and cut into wedges (it is up to you whether you peel them). Brown these on all sides too, then remove. Finally, add a sliced red onion. When this too has softened, add 3 chopped garlic cloves and 2 finely chopped

pieces of stem ginger, along with 2 tablespoons of the ginger syrup or 1 tablespoon light soft brown sugar, ½ teaspoon cinnamon, ½ teaspoon allspice and ¼ teaspoon cloves. Add the leaves from a large sprig of thyme, too. Return the red cabbage to the pan. Pour over 100ml (scant ½ cup) ginger wine if you have it, otherwise wine, cider or apple juice, even water, and allow it to bubble up. At this point, if you want an al dente cabbage dish, add no more than 100ml (scant ½ cup) water, cover, and leave to braise for 5 minutes. Otherwise, add 500ml (2 cups) stock, bring to the boil then turn down the heat and partially cover. Cook until the liquid has reduced down into a syrupy consistency and the cabbage wedges are knife-point tender. Return the pear to the pan to heat through and serve immediately.

Grilled Chicory with Pangrattato

Serves 4

2 large heads of endive, cabbage or lettuce, such as chioggia

Lemon wedges

For the pangrattato

30g (½ cup) sourdough chunks

30g (1oz) walnuts

1 tbsp olive oil

2 garlic cloves, finely chopped

3 sprigs of rosemary, quite finely chopped

Zest of 1 lemon

One of the things I love about closed-leaf varieties of brassicas, chicories and endives is how beautiful they are when they are cut in half, or even into cross sections. This dish uses the central part of chicory to show this off – do not waste the rest of the chicory, it can be braised or shredded into a salad. You can use anything for this – including lettuces such as little gem, endives or wedges of cabbage. And they will lend themselves to all sorts of flavours. Try grilling and then melting over any of the butters on page 20.

First make the pangrattato. Crumble up the sourdough into fairly fine breadcrumbs and chop or process the walnuts to the same texture. Do not over-process the walnuts as they will start leaching oil. Heat the olive oil in a frying pan. Add the garlic and fry for a minute over a medium heat without colouring, then add the breadcrumbs and rosemary. Fry for a few more minutes until the breadcrumbs are golden brown. Stir in the lemon zest.

To cut 2 cross sections from each endive, cut around 2.5cm (1in) to the side of the core, then cut the centre piece you end up with down the middle. Heat a large frying pan and lightly coat with olive oil. When the pan is hot, add the pieces of endive and cook for 2–4 minutes on each side, until the flesh is lightly charred and the leaves are wilting.

Scatter over the pangrattato and serve with lemon wedges, for squeezing over.

Chickpea and Mint Pancakes

Serves 4

300g (2½ cups) chickpea (garbanzo
  bean) flour

1 tsp sea salt

1 tbsp dried mint

Olive oil, for frying

I made these specifically to serve with the Shakshouka on page 48, but they are great for scooping up any dips or anything with a sauce. I like them with Zhoug (see page 61), Borage Leaf Raita (see page 58) or any spicy curry.

Sift the chickpea flour into a large bowl – this is important as it does have a tendency to clump. Whisk in the salt and mint, then gradually add 500ml (scant 2½ cups) water until you have a smooth, runny batter. Leave to stand for 30 minutes just to allow the flour to soak up some of the liquid – after this time the consistency should be similar to single (light) cream.

Heat a small crêpe pan, or a frying pan around 20cm (8in) in diameter, over a medium-high heat. It is important to make sure it is really hot if you don't want to make a hash of your first pancake. Coat the base with a little olive oil. Add a ladleful of the batter and swirl it around the pan so the base is completely covered. When the underside is completely cooked, work a palette knife around the edges, carefully lift it away and flip to cook the top side. Remove to a plate and cover with a tea towel. Repeat, adding a little more olive oil each time, until you have used up all the batter.

Seaweed Blinis

Serves 4

100g (¾ cup) buckwheat flour

50g (scant ½ cup) plain (all-purpose) flour

½ tsp instant dried yeast

1 tbsp dried seaweed flakes

½ tsp salt

150ml (⅔ cup) whole (full-fat) milk

100g (½ cup) thick yogurt

2 eggs, separated

Butter, for frying

Try these with the cured fish recipe on page 53 – I love the combination of the fragrant sweet cicely along with the whiff of the sea from the caviar and these blinis.

Put the flours, yeast and seaweed flakes into a bowl with the salt and give a quick stir. Warm the milk to blood temperature, then whisk in the yogurt and egg yolks. Stir the wet ingredients into the dry so they are thoroughly combined, then cover the bowl with a damp cloth or plastic wrap and leave somewhere warm to stand for a couple of hours. You will find the mixture stays quite liquid, but that it will fill with bubbles.

Whisk the egg whites until they have formed stiff peaks, then fold a large spoonful into the blini batter to loosen it a little. Gently fold in the rest, mixing just enough to make sure there aren't any foamy white streaks in the batter, then cover again and leave to rest for 1 more hour.

When you are ready to cook the blinis, melt a small knob of butter in a frying pan. Drop spoonfuls of the batter into the pan and flatten slightly using a circular motion with the back of your spoon. As soon as bubbles appear on the top of the blinis and the underside has browned, flip over and cook for moments on the other side.

Serve warm from the pan, or cool and transfer to an airtight container or the freezer. They will reheat well, wrapped in foil in a warm oven.

CONIFERS

I have a bit of a thing for conifers in all their shapes and sizes. It isn't just the association with Christmas, although bringing those wonderful fir tree aromas into the house every December is something I look forward to. They are the epitome of winter, capable of stirring a feeling of danger (into the dark woods) and safety (the offer of shelter) that is so frequently juxtaposed in so many of the books of my childhood. They are best unadorned by anything other than sparkling, moonlit snow, though are beautiful lit up by candelight – the one coldly beautiful, the other warm and inviting. I love them in their natural habitat. Much of the woodland where I grew up was managed plantations of conifers, and my father had permission to go in and harvest trees for all the various family members and friends every December. Many of our childhood walks were within. The dank earthiness of the forest, combined with the crisp, resinous bite of the trees, aroma as sharp as their abundant needles, along with the sound of them – not just the crackle of fallen cones and bracken underfoot, but the whispering of the trees that followed me along endless, regimented rows – was magical to a child desperate to find herself in Enid Blyton's *Enchanted Wood*. I was fascinated by the trees, and I still am. I love the way the clumps of needles form and drop; steel-like bottle brushes, standing to attention, long, jaunty ponytails on the messier pines. And the way the branches grow – tightly packed, close to the trunk, creating a form as tall, slender and slightly crooked as an elongated witch's hat, or sparse, wide, squat and sometimes broadly magnificent. Then there is the magic of the way they throw out needles. Last year I watched how my blue spruce pushed out nut-like, russet-brown bumps at the end of its branches. I thought they were small cones, but no, the hard-brown crust eventually thinned to paper and split open. Brush these away or let them fall, and the soft, slightly sticky new growth underneath will be revealed – short, pale and green rather than the silver blue of the spruce, clumped together and as soft as the bristles on an old-fashioned shaving brush.

It is these new shoots that are the most valuable to the cook, not those available to use during the winter holiday season. Every Christmas the usual raft of features on how to eat your Christmas tree crop up. This is not a sensible thing to attempt. New shoots on pines, spruces and Douglas firs are tender and with distinct flavours, but by winter they are sharp and scratchy and far too tough to eat. There is also the issue of whether you want to eat something that has been commercially grown. We are used to being told, when using commercially grown flowers such as roses, to check whether they are suitable for consumption – the pesticides and herbicides that are okay for something designed to look at may not be suitable for those we want to eat and cook with. The same applies to your Christmas tree. If you have bought an organic one, or have cut it down yourself, you should be fine. But generally speaking, you won't be. So be careful! Having said that, if you can see your way to incorporating pine into your diet, please do. I grow a couple of dwarf varieties in my garden for this purpose.

As for the flavour – it is probably what you would expect. I generally avoid the pines, as they bring back memories of the ubiquitous pine disinfectant of my childhood, and – almost as bad – the resinous quality of Greek retsina. However, the flavour of spruces and firs is much more citrusy. Fresh and clean, very slightly resinous, they are lovely as a tea or in a syrup or vinegar, wonderful for adding freshness to a stock, and complex when charred in a pan and crushed to add to salt and butter.

Braised Mushrooms with Herb Vinegar

This is like a warm version of mushrooms à la Grecque – the name given to any vegetables that are cooked in flavoured oil and left to marinate and chill. I have never been fond of them chilled, but love them warm or at room temperature. The vinegar in the recipe replaces the lemon juice, which usually gives the dish a light acidity. You can use any herbs in this dish. I love the mushroom/tarragon/garlic combination, but will also use plenty of dill and dill vinegar – or, even better, Pine Needle Vinegar when I have some (see page 32). It is common to find edible mushrooms on the forest floor under conifers, so it makes perfect sense to bring them together on the plate.

Take around 400g (14oz) mushrooms – I favour a closed-cup variety for these, such as a large field white or a chestnut. Brush clean and halve if very large. Heat 3 tbsp olive oil in a large saucepan, then add the mushrooms. Cook over a high heat for a couple of minutes, just to get a little browning, then add 2 finely chopped garlic cloves, 2 large sprigs of tarragon and plenty of salt and pepper. Pour over 100ml (scant ½ cup) white wine and add 1 tablespoon tarragon vinegar. Allow to bubble up, then turn down the heat and simmer until the mushrooms are just tender. Taste and add a little more vinegar and seasoning, if you like. Serve with plenty of finely chopped tarragon and parsley.

Curry Leaf Fenugreek (Methi)

A quick side dish for curries. I will put it with marinated grilled meats or use as a topping for dal. It is pungent and smoky so will complement something sweet and coconutty, or perhaps a rich, meaty tomato sauce. You can use spinach in place of methi if you like, or go bitter with mustard greens, often labelled 'saag' in Indian grocers.

Heat 1 tablespoon ghee or oil in a large frying pan. Add 1 teaspoon mustard seeds and 20 curry leaves. The curry leaves will crackle – when the crackling has subsided, wait for the mustard seeds to pop, then add the leaves from a large bunch of fenugreek leaves (methi). Stir fry until just wilted down, then dress with a squeeze of lemon juice.

Curry Leaf and Coconut Quinoa

I often substitute rice for quinoa, which is how I came to apply to it some of the flavours I associate more with the Indian subcontinent than the Andes. This is a very simple recipe that you could adapt to use many different herbs. I will sometimes add coriander (cilantro) stems when cooking the quinoa, and the leaf just before serving.

Take 200g (1¼ cups) quinoa and rinse it thoroughly to remove any bitterness. Drain. Heat 1 tablespoon olive oil in a saucepan and add the quinoa. Toast until it is quite dry and has started to smell nutty, then season with salt and pour over 400ml (1¾ cups) water or stock, and 100ml (scant ½ cup) coconut cream. Bring to the boil, then turn down the heat and cover. Simmer for 15 minutes, then remove from the heat and leave to stand for 5 minutes. Meanwhile, make the temper. Heat 2 tablespoons oil in a frying pan and add a ½ teaspoon mustard seeds and 20 well washed curry leaves. The curry leaves will crackle – when they are looking crisp and glossy and the mustard seeds are popping, remove from the pan. Pour over the quinoa and garnish with a few coriander leaves or some fenugreek microleaves, if you have any.

Fig Leaf Pilaf

Serves 4

1 large fig leaf

2 tbsp olive oil

1 tbsp butter

1 onion, finely chopped

2 garlic cloves, finely chopped

1 tsp cumin seeds

1 tsp black peppercorns

1 tsp coriander seeds

1 tsp cardamom pods

3 cloves

A few shards from a cinnamon stick

1 piece pared lemon zest

300g (1½ cups) basmati rice, rinsed several times and drained thoroughly

450ml (scant 2 cups) hot vegetable or chicken stock or freshly boiled water

Green chillies and coriander (cilantro) leaves, to garnish

Borage Leaf Raita (see page 58)

Sea salt

This is a savoury pilaf, sweetened and fragranced by the earthy, milky-sweet fig leaf, which I think is closer to a floral tonka bean than coconut.

Set a pan over a medium heat. When it is reasonably hot, add the fig leaf and toast on each side for a few minutes until your nostrils are filled with an intense green tonka bean scent, and the stems have turned a very pleasing saffron yellow. Remove from the heat.

Set a heavy casserole dish (Dutch oven) or saucepan over a medium heat and add the olive oil and butter. When the butter has melted and started to foam, add the onion. Fry until the onion is soft and translucent, around 10 minutes. Turn up the heat and add the garlic, spices and lemon zest. Cook for a minute or two until you can smell the toasting spices, then stir in the rice.

When the rice is well coated with the oil and butter, pour in the stock or water and season with salt. Place the fig leaf on top. Bring to the boil, then turn down and cover, putting a tea towel or a few sheets of kitchen towel between the pot and lid. Simmer until the rice has absorbed all the liquid – it should look dry and slightly translucent, around 15 minutes. Turn off the heat and leave to steam for another 10 minutes. Serve scattered with sliced green chillies and coriander (cilantro) leaves and raita on the side.

Variation

To turn this into more of a main course than a side, you can add puy lentils that have been cooked to al dente, or perhaps a cup or two of peas or broad (fava) beans. Put on top of the fig leaf after you add it – it will act as a barrier between them and the water – then stir through and fluff up at the end.

Saag Aloo

Serves 4

1 tbsp olive oil

1 tsp mustard seeds

1 onion, thinly sliced

2 garlic cloves, finely chopped

5cm (2in) piece ginger, peeled and grated

1 Scotch bonnet, deseeded and finely diced

2 white sweet potatoes, peeled and diced

400g (14oz) fresh spinach, amaranth leaves or elephant ears, sliced

Sea salt

For the spice mix

1 bay leaf

3 cinnamon leaves, dried or 1cm (½in) piece cinnamon stick

1 tsp fenugreek seeds

1 tsp fennel seeds

1 tsp anise seeds

1 tsp ground coriander

1 tsp black pepper

¼ tsp cayenne pepper

½ tsp ground turmeric

This is another side dish I cooked a lot in the Caribbean. Sweet potatoes with a creamy white interior and pink skin are always my preferred choice here – they are nutty, rather than sweet, and are not prone to collapsing in quite the same way as their orange cousins.

Cinnamon leaves with any flavour at all are very hard to find in the UK, which is a great pity – they are subtler and more floral than the bark, and I loved using them to flavour everything from spice mixes, to rice dishes and sweet custards. I include them as an option in this recipe list in the hope that one day they will become available.

First, prepare the spice mix. Put the bay leaf and the whole spices into a dry frying pan and toast lightly until they smell very aromatic. Remove from the pan and allow to cool, then grind to a fine powder. Mix with the cayenne and turmeric.

Heat the olive oil in a large casserole dish (Dutch oven) and add the mustard seeds. When they start to pop, add the onion and cook over a gentle heat until very soft and translucent, around 10 minutes. Add the garlic cloves, ginger and chilli, along with the spice mix, and stir for a couple of minutes. Stir in the white potatoes and season with plenty of salt. Pour over just enough water to cover the potatoes and leave to gently cook for 5 minutes. Add the spinach and allow it to wilt down, then continue to cook until the potatoes are just tender and the liquid has evaporated. Try to avoid stirring too much at this stage, as you do not want the potatoes to break up. Serve immediately.

Broad Bean Purée with Cime di Rapa

Serves 4

500g (1lb 1½oz) dried, skinless broad
(fava) beans

1 tbsp olive oil

1 small onion, very finely chopped

½ garlic bulb, cloves peeled

1 large floury potato, diced

A few sprigs of winter savoury

For the greens

3 tbsp olive oil

2 garlic cloves, finely chopped

1kg (2lb 3oz) greens, cime di rapa
(broccoli rabe) or similar

100ml (scant ½ cup) stock or water

½ tsp chilli flakes

Sea salt and freshly ground black
pepper

Creamy dried broad (fava) beans, cooked down to a purée and served with something bitter is a classic Italian way, and there is much variation in what kind of greens are used. Here I use cime di rapa (broccoli rabe), but I might just as easily caramelise any type of endive to add a sweetness to the dish. Both summer and winter savoury are good companions to broad beans, and winter savoury is the one to use here. This is a hearty side dish to serve with roast lamb or turn it into the main event with a winter tomato salad on the side.

First, cover the broad beans with water and leave to soak overnight. When you are ready to cook the beans, put in a large saucepan with the olive oil, onion, garlic, potato and savoury sprigs. Cover with water and bring to the boil. Start skimming off any mushroom-coloured, starchy foam that collects on the surface until it has decreased considerably, then turn the heat down and simmer until the beans are just tender and close to collapse. This will take up to 1½ hours, depending on how fresh your beans are. Keep a close eye on them and top up the water as necessary. When they are cooked through, strain and remove the sprigs of savoury. Purée, then return to the saucepan to keep warm.

To cook the greens, heat the olive oil in a large frying pan. Add the garlic and cook over a gentle heat until fragrant, then roughly chop the cime di rapa and add this to the pan with plenty of salt and pepper. Cook for a few minutes, then add the stock or water, partially cover, and cook until the cime di rapa is just tender – this will take up to around 15 minutes. Sprinkle with chilli flakes and serve as a garnish for the beans.

Variation

Sometimes I will merge the Middle Eastern ful medames with the Italian flavour combinations. To cook whole dried fava beans (with their skins on), soak overnight, then strain, cover with fresh water and bring to the boil. Simmer until the beans are tender, then strain, and for texture, mash a few if you like. Toss with the greens as cooked above, with an extra drizzle of olive oil.

Pinto Beans

Serves 4

500g (1lb 1½oz) dried pinto beans

1 onion, sliced

3 bay leaves

1 large sprig of thyme or a few heads
of dried thyme flowers

2 sprigs of tarragon or Mexican tarragon

Stems from a small bunch of coriander
(cilantro), finely chopped (optional)

2 tsp dried epazote (optional)

Sea salt

To refry

1 tbsp oil or lard

1 onion, finely chopped

1 garlic clove, finely chopped

1 tsp ground cumin

500g (1lb 1½oz) cooked beans, plus
1 ladleful of the cooking liquid

Pinto beans – and most other beans in Mexico, you
can substitute black beans if you like – are traditionally
cooked with epazote, a spiky, pungent herb from Central
America, as it is reputed to lessen the flatulent effects of
the beans. It is available dried in the UK.

Mexican tarragon – also known as Mexican marigold,
among other things – is very similar in flavour to the
more commonly available French tarragon: aniseed, with
a hint of citrus and mint too. It is not something you will
commonly see in shops, but the seeds are easy to find
and it grows very well.

This makes a large pot of beans but they will keep in the
fridge for a week and in the freezer for months.

Cover the beans with water and leave to soak for at least
6 hours, or overnight. Drain the beans, then put in a large
saucepan. Cover with water and add the onion, bay leaves,
thyme and Mexican or regular tarragon. Add the coriander
(cilantro) stems and epazote, if you have it. Bring to the boil
and allow to bubble fiercely for 5 minutes, then reduce to a
simmer. Cook for at least 1 hour or until the beans are just
tender – you don't want them collapsing.

Alternatively, you can cook in a pressure cooker, with no
need to pre-soak. Put in the pressure cooker and cover with
water. Add 2 tablespoons oil, then bring to high pressure
and cook for 5 minutes. Release the pressure and drain.
Return to the cooker, add the aromatics, 1 teaspoon salt
and another 2 tablespoons olive oil. Bring up to pressure
again and this time cook for 18 minutes. Slow release.

To refry, heat the oil or lard in a large frying pan. Add
the onion and cook over a medium heat until soft and
translucent, around 10 minutes. Add the garlic and cumin
and cook for 2 minutes, then add the beans and the
cooking liquid. Bring to the boil, then turn down and
simmer for 2 minutes, then mash the beans in situ –
use a masher, or squash against the side of the pan with
a wooden spoon. Break up a third, then cook, stirring
regularly, so the broken beans thicken the liquid – around
5 minutes. Remove from the heat and leave to
stand briefly before serving.

Coriander and Blue Corn Tortillas

Serve 4

125g (1 cup) plain (all-purpose) flour

125g (1 cup) blue or yellow masa harina

½ tsp sea salt

50g (1¾oz) lard or vegetable shortening, melted and slightly cooled

4 tbsp finely chopped coriander (cilantro)

These have slightly more ingredients than a classic corn tortilla, but the plain (all-purpose) flour and the fat does make for a softer, more pliable wrap, which I make on occasion as my children prefer them. Use as you would any tortillas or for the brunch dish on page 54.

To make the coriander tortillas, put the flour, masa, and coriander in a bowl with the salt. Pour in the lard, then 150ml (⅔ cup) tepid water. Mix thoroughly – if the mixture is crumbly and not pulling in all the flour, add a little more water, a few drops at a time. Keep the mixing to a minimum – you don't want to work the gluten in the flour too much. You should end up with a soft, slightly tacky dough that will firm up more as the lard re-solidifies.

Divide the dough into 16 equal balls and either roll out as thinly as you can, or press in a tortilla press, making sure the dough is pressed between plastic wrap or non-stick baking paper. Heat a cast-iron frying pan or similar and when medium hot, cook the tortillas for a couple of minutes on each side until they are dappled brown. They may also puff up a bit – this will subside as they cool. Keep warm until ready to serve.

Tarragon Vinegar Butter Beans

Serves 4

500g (1lb 1½oz) butter (lima) beans, soaked overnight

1 tbsp olive oil

1 large onion, finely chopped

2 fat garlic cloves, finely chopped

1 bunch of tarragon, leaves and stems separated

1 small bunch of parsley, leaves and stems separated

2 tbsp tarragon vinegar

Sea salt

It might be unconventional, but I often cook beans with some kind of acidic element. I find that it helps to keep the beans from breaking up into a mush. Butter beans, or the similar *gigantes* beans from Greece, are a staple side dish in my house. I sometimes make them with tomatoes and lots of herbs, as is traditional, but they are more versatile without.

A note – if you grow your own parsley, this dish is improved beyond measure if you cook it when you have bolting parsley leaves that have elongated into slender fronds. The flavour turns into an intriguing cross between parsley and tarragon with another element that I can't quite put my finger on, but it is wonderful.

If you are a meat eater, please try them with the beef dish on page 194 – they are made for each other.

First soak the butter beans. You can do this the fast or slow way. Either cover with cold water and leave overnight, or for at least 8 hours, or put in a saucepan, cover with water and bring to the boil. Fast boil for 2 minutes, then remove from the heat and leave to stand for at least 1 hour. Drain.

Heat the olive oil in a large casserole (Dutch oven) or saucepan and add the onion. Cook over a medium-low heat until the onion is soft and translucent, around 10 minutes, then turn up the heat and allow the onions to brown a little. Add the garlic and cook for a further 2 minutes. Add the drained butter beans to the pan. Tie the tarragon and parsley stems into a bunch (for easy removal later) and drop the bundle on top of the beans. Cover with fresh cold water. Bring to the boil, then immediately turn down and leave to simmer for 30 minutes. By this time the beans will have started to soften. Add the tarragon vinegar and 1 teaspoon salt and cook until the beans are tender. This will take anything from upwards of 30 minutes – it all depends on the age of your beans, so just keep checking them at regular intervals.

When the beans are tender but still intact, fish out the bundle of herb stems. Check the liquid levels. Strain the beans if there is a lot of liquid, then add back a ladleful. Check for seasoning, then finely chop the tarragon and parsley and stir through.

Herb or Leaf Crackers

Makes around 40

300g (2½ cups) wholemeal rye flour

½ tsp baking powder

1 tbsp dried herbs or leaves

1 tsp honey

2 tbsp butter, softened

1 tsp sea salt

For brushing (optional)

1 egg white

Powdered dried leaves or crumbled
  dried herbs (see introduction)

I am not ashamed to admit that it was my son who
perfected these crackers for me. He often wants to
help in the kitchen and is shooed out when I am trying
to concentrate; however, this time I relented and let
him help me roll out these crackers. Well, he went at
these with the meat tenderiser (the closest I have to
a traditional *knackerbrod kruskavel*, a ridged rolling
pin, for dimpling your crackers) and made them much
thinner than I would – almost see-through – and while
this meant that they ended up being more irregular, the
texture was improved no end.

You can use any dried herbs or leaves. I particularly
like using kale, or seaweed, preferably dulse, or for a
sweeter cracker that goes well with goats' cheese – fig
leaves. For the topping, the texture is important. Try
dried herbs – za'atar, chopped rosemary, sage or thyme,
but for leaves, a powder is better.

Preheat the oven to 180ºC (350ºF/Gas 4).

Put the flour in a bowl with the baking powder, dried
herbs or leaves, honey and butter. Add the salt, then work
in 175ml (¾ cup) warm water, adding it a little at a time
until you have a soft dough. It may be sticky at this point.

Turn the dough out onto a floured surface and knead until
smooth, around 5 minutes. You now have various options
regarding how you shape the crackers. You can roll out
large pieces of dough and cut out with a cookie cutter –
you will get around 40 crackers with a 7cm (3in) cutter.
But I prefer to make larger, irregular crackers, which will
break up pleasingly. To do this, divide the dough into
12 pieces and roll out the dough as thinly as you can.
Next either prick the dough all over with a fork, or lightly
press the ridged side of a meat tenderiser all over – or, of
course, if you have one, roll over a *kruskavel*.

Transfer to several baking (cookie) sheets. Brush with egg
white if you want a glossy cracker – you can also sprinkle
over more dried leaves here, but be careful – herbs will be
fine, but the texture of some leaves will not work so well.

Bake for 8–12 minutes, until crisp and browned. Transfer
to a wire rack to cool, then store in an airtight container.

Ways with Brussels Sprouts and Their Tops

A friend used to write to me every year about Brussels sprouts. 'Catherine, it's 11th November and I haven't put the Brussels sprouts on for Christmas dinner yet, whatever am I going to do?!' Long-standing jokes about their cooking times aside, sprouts do have a reputation for being badly cooked – either hard, indigestible bullets or cooked into a waterlogged, sulphurous oblivion. They are clearly considered hard to get right. It is true, it is hard to get the centres just al dente without making the outer layers soggy, and the tradition of scoring a cross in the base doesn't do much to help this. I usually solve this by cutting them in half. They will not shed leaves as they will all be connected to the stem, and they cook much more evenly that way.

Here are some of my favourite ways to eat them.

Steamed Sprout Tops

This is the seasonal vegetable I look forward to more than any other. It is the top of the dense, woody stalk of Brussels sprouts, where the stem, still dotted with tiny nuggets of nutty-flavoured sprouts, broadens into a perfect head of tightly furled leaves surrounded by a loose crown of floppy green leaves. I cook all these elements together. To prepare, I nick off the sprouts with a sharp knife and pull off all of the looser leaves. I will discard the woodiest part of the stem, then cut the head into wedges. I love the first cut to a cross section – the way the leaves stretch around the head are perfect for the time of year. Look at the shapes and you will see what I mean.

To cook, put a large slice of butter in a pan with a splash of water. When the butter has melted, add everything together and season with salt. Toss gently, then tightly cover and leave for around 10–12 minutes over a gentle heat, checking regularly. When you can easily pierce the sprouts with a knife tip, they are done.

Serve immediately with the buttery juices.

A wonderful sauce to serve with these tops is the anchovy dressing on page 130. Or make a buttery version – put 100g (3½oz) butter into a pan with a tin of anchovies and 3 crushed garlic cloves and mash together once the butter has melted. Add the juice of a lemon and a few chilli flakes, if you like.

Sautéed Brussels Sprouts with Cranberries and Chestnuts

For a Christmas side dish, this takes some beating, but if you don't want to add cranberries or chestnuts *et al.*, just pare down the recipe as it's the best way to cook them. And of course it will work with olive oil as well as goose fat. Take 500g (1lb 1½oz) Brussels sprouts (or use wedges of cabbage if you prefer), and blanch them in water for 2 minutes. Strain and pat dry. Heat 1 tablespoon duck or goose fat in a frying pan that will hold the sprouts in a single layer. Add 150g (5¼oz) bacon lardons and fry until crisp, then remove. Add the sprouts, arranging them cut-side down. Leave to brown for a few minutes then flip over and cook on the reverse side. Sprinkle over 1 teaspoon thyme leaves and continue cooking until the sprouts are tender. Meanwhile, put 100g (3½oz) dried cranberries in a saucepan with 150ml (⅔ cup) marsala. Bring to the boil, then turn down to a very low simmer for 5 minutes. Add the Brussels sprouts along with 150g (5¼oz) cooked chestnuts and the reserved bacon. Shake everything together and serve immediately.

Puréed Brussels Sprouts

This is a wonderful purée – I have started serving it at Christmas instead of bread sauce, as it has similar flavours, without the texture, which to me is too close to porridge to love. It means I can sometimes serve the Brussels sprouts three ways – the tops buttered, as per the previous recipe, and this way. You can do this with virtually any brassica – don't limit yourself to sprouts.

Take 500g (1lb 1½oz) Brussels sprouts, trim and halve them. Steam for 4–5 minutes, or until just tender. It is important to steam, not boil, as they need to be as dry as possible. Meanwhile, take 100ml (scant ½ cup) double (heavy) cream and add to it 1 slice of onion, 2 bay leaves, 6 cloves and 1 mace blade. Bring almost to the boil, then remove from the heat and leave to infuse. Put the Brussels sprouts into a food processor and strain over the cream. Season with plenty of salt and pepper, then add a thick slice of butter. Blitz until you have a purée. If you want more texture, just purée two thirds of the sprouts, then add the rest and pulse so they are broken up but not smooth – or shred finely with a sharp knife before adding. Taste and adjust the seasoning, then stir through plenty of grated nutmeg.

Parsley and Garlic Cannellini Beans

Serves 4

500g (1lb 1½oz) dried cannellini beans

1 large bunch of parsley, leaves and
    stems separated

1 garlic bulb, left whole

Olive oil, for drizzling

I very rarely cook beans completely plain – there is always stock or a few herbs or spices or even just a slice of onion with a clove to be added. This pot of beans makes a useful base for all sorts of things, including the Garbure on page 192.

Cover the beans with water and leave to soak for at least 6 hours, or overnight. Alternatively, bring to the boil for 10 minutes and leave for 2 hours. Drain the beans and put in a large saucepan. Tie the parsley stems together and add these to the pan, then cover with water. Bring to the boil and allow to bubble fiercely for 5 minutes, then reduce to a simmer. Add 1 teaspoon salt and cook for 45 minutes, then add the garlic. Continue to cook until the beans are just tender, probably at least another 30 minutes.

Remove the garlic from the pan and squeeze the flesh out of the cloves. Finely chop the parsley leaves and add to the pan with the garlic flesh. Stir everything through and drizzle with olive oil.

Variation

You can add more liquid and turn this into a soup. I prefer the soup to be textured, so I purée half the beans and lightly crush the rest. You can also replace the water with any kind of stock.

Squash Leaves Braised with Tomatoes and Peanut Butter

Serves 4

1 large bunch of squash leaves

2 tbsp olive oil

1 onion, thinly sliced

2 celery sticks, sliced

2 garlic cloves, finely chopped

3 medium tomatoes, peeled and chopped

1 sprig of thyme

1 tsp hot sauce

2 tbsp peanut butter, smooth or crunchy

Sea salt and freshly ground black pepper

When I talk about squash leaves here, I include pumpkin and courgette (zucchini) leaves too, all of which can be used interchangeably. These leaves are generally large, covered in a fine down, with prickles down their spines and stems; I can hand on heart say one of the most satisfying jobs in kitchen prep involves their de-prickling. If you have young, tender leaves, this process is not strictly necessary, but I recommend it with late-season, sun-toughened ones. Flavour-wise, they are surprising – they do not have a trace of bitterness, but are nutty, almost sweet, with a hint of smokiness to add depth. Well worth the effort.

If you remove the peanut butter from this recipe, this makes an excellent sauce for pasta – the ever-thrifty Italians would do so, perhaps substituting the hot pepper sauce for a pinch of chilli flakes.

First the fun bit – prepare your squash leaves. Take each leaf and starting at the tip of the stem, break through a half to a third of it at the back with your thumbnail, so the flesh snaps and the fibres are left attached (this is similar to deveining celery). Pull the fibres down the length of the leaf – you will see that all the thorns along the veins will cleanly come away. Repeat this around the whole stem. When you have finished, shred the leaves and stems finely.

Bring a large saucepan of water to the boil. Add salt and then drop in the shredded leaves. Cook for 3–4 minutes, then strain, pushing out as much of the water as you can.

Heat the olive oil in a large, lidded frying pan. Add the onion and celery and fry over a medium heat until they have softened and turned translucent Add the garlic, tomatoes and thyme and season with salt and pepper. Pour in 200ml (¾ cup) water and simmer for 5 minutes.

Add the squash leaves and continue to cook for 2–3 minutes. Stir in the hot sauce and the peanut butter, making sure it completely breaks down into the sauce and coat the greens evenly. Serve as a side dish with grilled meat or fish, or stirred through some cannellini beans.

DESSERTS
AND BAKING

Blackcurrant Leaf Ice

Serves 4

Around 50g (2–3 large handfuls)
  blackcurrant leaves

300g (1⅓ cups) caster (superfine) sugar

Zest of 1 lemon

Juice of 3 lemons

1 egg white (optional)

I do not love blackcurrants – I find the taste of them overwhelming. However, the leaves are something else – the flavour and aroma is still there, but softened into something subtler and to me, more palatable. They are best picked early on in the season before the fruit has set. This is adapted from Mark Diacono's book *A Year at Otter Farm*.

Wash the leaves then shake off any excess water and give them a good scrunch in your hands to bruise them a bit – this will help release the flavour.

Put the sugar and 700ml (scant 3 cups) water into a saucepan and heat very gently, stirring, until the sugar has dissolved. Add the leaves and lemon zest and bring to the boil. Simmer for 5 minutes, then remove from the heat and leave to cool down completely – at this stage you can even put it in the fridge and leave to chill and infuse overnight.

Strain the liquid and add the lemon juice. If you have an ice-cream maker, churn the liquid until it has frozen to a soft and scoopable texture following the manufacturer's instructions, then decant to a freezerproof container and freeze. If using the egg white, whisk it thoroughly until completely broken up and add for the last 5 minutes of churning. If you don't have an ice-cream maker, pour the eggless liquid into a shallow freezerproof container. Freeze for an hour or so, then check – it should have frozen round the edges. Transfer to a bowl and whisk with a fork, handheld whisk or an electric whisk until you have a homogeneous slush, then return to the freezer. Repeat this another 3–4 times, adding the egg white when you whisk it for the last time.

When you want to serve the sorbet, remove it from the freezer and transfer to the fridge to soften if it is very hard. I find that this is not always necessary – the sugar content is high enough that it stays scoopable.

Fig Leaf Panna Cotta with Fig Leaf and Black Pepper Biscuits

Makes 4

Neutral-tasting oil, for brushing

300ml (1¼ cups) double (heavy) cream

4 small/medium fig leaves

200ml (¾ cup) buttermilk

75g (2¾oz) honey

3 gelatine leaves

For the fig leaf and black pepper biscuits

1 large dried fig leaf

¼ tsp black peppercorns

50g (¼ cup) granulated sugar

125g (1 cup) plain (all-purpose) flour

100g (3½oz) butter

1 egg yolk

Sea salt

Fig leaf panna cotta is quintessentially Italian, but for me, the flavour is so redolent of coconut and tonka bean that I also like to pair it with something a little more tropical. I will therefore serve this with slices of very ripe, slippery mango, with these biscuits on the side.

First, prepare 4 ramekins by brushing with oil and wiping over with kitchen towel. Put the fig leaves in a dry frying pan and toast lightly – the veins on the leaves will turn the colour of saffron, and it will be very aromatic.

Put the cream into a small saucepan. Cut or tear up the fig leaves and scrunch them to release flavour, then add to the pan. Heat gently until the cream is close to simmering, then remove from the heat and leave to infuse and cool.

Add the buttermilk and honey and return to the heat. Again, keeping the heat very gentle, stir to melt the honey. Soak the gelatine leaves in a little cold water. When they have softened, wring them out and stir into the cream mixture while still on the heat. When the gelatine has completely dissolved, strain through a sieve, then divide between the moulds. Leave to cool to room temperature, then chill for several hours until set.

To make the biscuits, first toast the dried fig leaf as above. Remove from the heat and cool. Put in a spice grinder or powerful food processor with the black peppercorns and sugar and blitz until you have a texture similar to icing (confectioners') sugar.

Rub the flour and butter together. Add the flavoured sugar and a generous pinch of salt and stir to combine. Add the egg yolk and combine until you have a soft dough. All of this can be done in a stand mixer if you prefer. Wrap in plastic wrap and chill until firm – at least 45 minutes.

Preheat the oven to 180°C (350°F/Gas 4).

Roll out the dough to a thickness of 5mm (¼in), and cut out 5–6cm (2–2½in) rounds. Re-roll until you have used up all the dough – you should have around 16 biscuits. Arrange over a baking (cookie) sheet and bake for 12–14 minutes, until dappled brown. Transfer to a wire rack to cool. Serve the biscuits on the side of the panna cotta.

Pineapple Carpaccio with Tequila and Coriander Syrup

Serves 4

1 pineapple

Sea salt

4 tsp tequila

Squeeze of lime juice

Microherbs, such as basil, coriander (cilantro), mint or borage, to decorate

For the syrup

125g (⅔ cup) caster (superfine) sugar

1 small bunch of coriander (cilantro)

½ tsp black peppercorns

½ tsp allspice berries

I have a feeling people will be very 'Marmite' about this. Coriander (cilantro) is a divisive flavour at the best of times, and it isn't often used in sweet dishes. You could substitute a combination of mint and basil in its place if you like – try cinnamon basil.

First, prepare the syrup. Put the sugar into a saucepan and cover with 125ml (½ cup) water. Roughly chop the coriander and add this to the saucepan along with the peppercorns and allspice berries. Set over a gentle heat and stir until the sugar has dissolved, then bring to the boil. Turn down the heat and simmer for 5 minutes. Remove from the heat and leave to stand for 10 minutes, then strain. This will keep for weeks in the fridge.

Next prepare the pineapple. Cut off the skin, then cut out the pocks of seeds – the best way to do this is to follow their lines diagonally from top to bottom of the pineapple and cut them out in long strips. Core the pineapple, then slice as thinly as you can – use a mandolin if you have one.

Arrange the pineapple over 4 plates. Sprinkle with a small amount of very finely crumbled sea salt, then drizzle with the syrup, followed by the tequila and a squeeze of lime. Decorate with a mixture of herb sprigs or microherbs if you can get them. I like micro basil and coriander, tiny mint leaves, and – if it is the right time of year – the tiniest of borage leaves from the garden.

Variations

The flavours in this salad also make a wonderful sorbet. Make double the amount of syrup, blitz it with the pineapple and a double measure of tequila, and freeze into a sorbet. The flavour is warm, spicy, tart and quite complex.

I found out quite by accident (leftovers!) that this syrup works surprisingly well with strawberries. Try in place of the pineapple.

Yogurt Cake with Lemon Verbena and Lemon Thyme

Serves 8

15g (½oz) fresh lemon verbena leaves

5g (¼oz) fresh lemon thyme leaves

160g (5½oz) granulated sugar

250g (2 cups) plain (all-purpose) flour

½ tsp baking powder

½ tsp bicarbonate of soda (baking soda)

250g (8¾oz) Greek yogurt

5 tbsp butter, melted

Juice of ½ lemon

2 eggs

For the cream

250ml (1 cup) double (heavy) cream

2 tbsp lemon verbena leaves

1 tbsp icing (confectioners') sugar

To serve

Fresh strawberries, hulled

Crystallised leaves of lemon verbena, basil, mint or fennel (see page 272)

This is one to make at the height of summer when your pot of lemon verbena is throwing out leaves. There are also a few weeks when greengrocers might sell bundles of them. Keep your eyes peeled – the stuff that comes in from Italy is sublime and intense and sherbety.

Preheat the oven to 180°C (375°F/Gas 4). Butter a 23cm (9in) loose-bottomed cake tin, then line the base with baking paper.

Put the lemon verbena and lemon thyme leaves into a food processor with the sugar and blitz until the leaves have broken down. The sugar will have turned the colour of mint ice cream and will have a texture like powder.

Mix the flour and raising agents together thoroughly.

Beat the sugar with the yogurt, butter, lemon juice and eggs, then fold in the flour, keeping the mixing to the bare minimum. Scrape into the prepared tin and bake for around 30 minutes, until the cake is well risen, springy to touch and slightly shrunken away from the sides of the tin. Leave in the tin for 10 minutes then turn out onto a wire rack to finish cooling.

To make the cream, put the cream in a saucepan with the lemon verbena leaves. Heat gently, until almost on the point of boiling, then remove from the heat and leave to infuse until cooled to room temperature. Transfer to the fridge to chill. Just before you want to whip it, remove the leaves. Add the sugar to the cream then beat until it reaches the soft peak stage. Pile into the centre of the cake then tumble the strawberries and crystallised leaves together over the top of the cream.

Shiso and Raspberry Jelly

Serves 4–6

2 shiso leaves (preferably red, but whichever you prefer, taste-wise), shredded

3 lemongrass stalks or some green lemongrass tips, chopped

100g (3½oz) caster (superfine) sugar

500g (1lb 1½oz) raspberries

Juice of 1 lime

5 gelatine leaves

The method for this jelly is relatively involved, but will give you a beautiful, crystal-clear result, so it is definitely worth it. I feel the need to reiterate – do not press/squeeze/bash the raspberries about in any way. The shiso adds a not-quite-menthol, cool spiciness to it.

First infuse the shiso leaves and lemongrass. Put half the sugar into a mortar with the shiso leaves and chopped lemongrass and muddle a little until the shiso leaves have broken up. Transfer to a small saucepan and pour over 150ml (⅔ cup) water. Heat gently, stirring until the sugar has dissolved, then remove from the heat and leave to infuse for at least a couple of hours. Strain and set aside.

Put the raspberries in a heatproof bowl and sprinkle the remaining sugar. Cover with plastic wrap to prevent any steam escaping, then place on top of a saucepan of simmering water. Leave this over a gentle heat for around 30 minutes, in which case the raspberries will have given up most of their juice and the sugar will have dissolved.

Line a sieve with muslin or kitchen towel and strain the raspberries into a bowl. Leave to stand.

Put the gelatine into a bowl and cover with water. Mix the shiso syrup with the raspberry juice and lime juice. Add enough water to bring it up to 500ml (scant 2½ cups). Put half of this into a saucepan and again, heat gently.

When the gelatine leaves have softened, add to the heated liquid. Stir until the gelatine has completely dissolved, then remove from the heat. Add the remaining liquid and strain everything once more through a sieve into a jug. Divide between 4 or 6 glasses.

Leave to cool, then transfer to the fridge to set and chill for at least 3–4 hours.

Tarragon Milk Ice Lollies

Makes 6

450ml (1¾ cups) whole (full-fat) milk

250ml (1 cup) double (heavy) cream

125g (⅔ cup) caster (superfine) sugar

1 bunch of tarragon, leaves only, lightly bruised with the back of a knife

100g (3½oz) dark or milk chocolate, for drizzling (optional)

1 tbsp vegetable or coconut oil (optional)

Tarragon sugar, see page 271 (optional)

This is such a gentle flavour – like a grown-up version of the Mini Milk ice lollies I ate as a child. The recipe is one based on the minted milk recipe in the *Ice Kitchen* cookbook, and the method will work with other soft herbs including mint and basil.

My family goes a bit ice lolly crazy in the summer.; it is a daily after-school ritual, but I also think they are particularly good when you have decamped to the garden to eat and you have them ready to whip out of the freezer for a quick dessert.

Put the milk, double (heavy) cream and caster sugar (superfine) into a saucepan and slowly heat, stirring until the sugar has dissolved. When the milk is close to boiling, remove from the heat and add the tarragon. Leave to infuse for as long as you can – at least until the cream has completely cooled.

Strain the liquid into a jug, then pour into ice lolly moulds. Add the sticks and freeze until solid. At this point, you have a choice – at the height of summer when an ice lolly mould is in demand, I will decant from the moulds, wrap each lolly in waxed paper and put into an airtight container. You may have to dip the moulds briefly in just-boiled water to remove them.

To serve, you can of course serve as is, but to dress them up, drizzle with melted chocolate. To melt the chocolate, break it into a bowl with the oil (the oil stops the chocolate from cracking when it is frozen) and melt. Either dip the lollies in the chocolate, or drizzle it over them with a spoon. Sprinkle with the sugar if you like, but you will have to move very quickly in order to do it before the surface of the chocolate has completely set. You can refreeze or eat immediately.

Melon, Cucumber, Borage and Mint Sorbet

Serves 4

½ large, green-fleshed melon, cut into chunks

1 cucumber, peeled and deseeded

Juice of 1 lime

100g (½ cup) caster (superfine) sugar

A handful of borage leaves

A handful of mint leaves

This sorbet is made by a cold infusion/no-cook method, which I am giving as an alternative to the usual sugar syrup method. I've left it non-alcoholic, but it lends itself very well to the addition of a shot or two of vodka or gin. Alternatively, pour these over on serving.

Put the melon, cucumber, lime juice and sugar in a food processor and blitz to a purée. Transfer to a fridge-friendly container. Bruise the borage and mint leaves lightly, then add to the purée. Transfer to the fridge and leave to infuse overnight.

Strain the purée, discarding the leaves, then either churn in an ice-cream maker following the manufacturer's instructions until thick before transferring to the freezer. Alternatively, pour a fairly shallow layer into a freezerproof container and freeze for 1 hour, or until it has started to form crystals around the edge. Whisk the crystals into the rest of the sorbet and refreeze. Repeat at several intervals until the sorbet is only just soft enough to whisk, then leave to freeze solid. At this stage you can also remove and whisk with an electric whisk for a minute just to increase the volume.

Instant Mango Sorbet
with Ginger Rosemary

Serves 4

3 mangoes, peeled and cut into chunks

100ml (scant ½ cup) Ginger Rosemary Syrup (see page 271)

Juice of ½ lime

4 tbsp glucose syrup (optional)

This is a recipe which shows how quickly a sorbet can be made without an ice-cream maker, with the freezing done at the beginning instead of the end. I use Ginger Rosemary Syrup (see page 271) in this recipe, not just because both ginger and rosemary are wonderful with mango, but because I hope that if I include it enough in recipes, and I say this seriously, everyone might be encouraged to go and get themselves a plant. The fruit can be anything frozen – I also like these flavours with crisp, green apples. I often buy bags of frozen fruit from the supermarket (they're good as a standby) and would use these here too.

Line a couple of baking (cookie) sheets with baking paper and arrange the mango chunks over them. Freeze until solid – this will take a few hours. Transfer to a food processor or blender with the Ginger Rosemary Syrup, the lime juice and – if you want to freeze the sorbet and want to keep the texture manageable and stop it from freezing solid and forming too many crystals – the glucose syrup.

Blitz until you have a creamy, sorbet-like texture. You can eat immediately, or freeze until firmer.

Pandan Leaf Rice Pudding

Serves 4

70g (⅓ cup) short grain rice

7 pandan leaves, 1 tied in a knot, 6 chopped

600ml (2½ cups) whole (full-fat) milk

400ml (1¾ cups) coconut milk

4 tbsp caster (superfine) sugar

Butter, for greasing

Sea salt

This recipe comes from my friend and food writer Jenny Linford, who is part Singaporean and who spent some of her formative years there. It is a recipe she developed to showcase the flavour of pandan – and it really does. It's hard to describe the flavour of pandan. It is sweetly and subtly green, slightly smoky with a hint of forest-floor earthiness about it. Very distinctive but still hard to pin down – I really love it.

Preheat the oven to 150°C (300°F/Gas 2).

Put the rice, the knotted pandan leaf and the milk into a saucepan. Bring to the boil, then turn down the heat and leave to simmer for 5 minutes. Remove from the heat and allow to cool and infuse.

While the milk is simmering, make the pandan extract. Blitz the pandan leaves with 50ml (¼ cup) water until it is a deep green sludge. Strain through a fine-meshed sieve, pushing down to extract as much juice and flavour as possible.

Add the pandan extract, coconut milk and caster (superfine) sugar to the simmered milk and rice along with a generous pinch of salt. Butter an ovenproof dish and pour in the rice mixture. Bake in the oven for 3 hours, then serve.

Bay Leaf Rice Pudding Gelato with Blackberry Swirl

Serves 4

100g (½ cup) Italian risotto rice or short grain rice

750ml (3 cups) whole (full-fat) milk

150g (5¼oz) caster (superfine) sugar

4 bay leaves

2 strips of pared lemon zest

5 egg yolks

250ml (1 cup) single (light) cream

Sea salt

For the blackberries

200g (7oz) blackberries

2 tbsp caster (superfine) sugar

1 tsp lemon juice

1 tbsp crème de mûre

This brings together two of my favourite desserts – bay-infused rice pudding and gelato. The flavours, for me, are late summer, after I've had my fill of pairing blackberries with bright summery herbs such as lemon verbena or lime leaves and want something that moves me gently towards autumn.

I love making this gelato with fig leaves, too, but in this instance I would probably forget the swirl and just serve it with some figs instead.

First make the rice pudding. Preheat the oven to 170°C (340°F/Gas 3).

Put the rice, milk and a third of the sugar into an ovenproof dish with the bay leaves, lemon zest and a pinch of salt. Cover with foil and bake for 1 hour.

Remove from the oven, stir in the remaining sugar and return to the oven, this time uncovered, for another 30 minutes.

Whisk in the egg yolks, followed by the cream. Remove the bay leaves and lemon zest, then process very briefly with a stick blender, so some of the rice pudding is broken up, then leave to cool. Transfer to the fridge to chill. You can return the bay leaves to the dish while it is chilling, if you like.

Meanwhile, make the blackberry swirl. Put the blackberries in a saucepan with the sugar, and stir over a low heat until the sugar has melted and the fruit has completely broken down. Bring to the boil, then immediately remove from the heat. Push through a sieve to remove the pips (there is texture enough in this gelato with the rice), then stir in the lemon juice and crème de mûre. Transfer to the fridge to chill.

Churn the rice pudding gelato in your ice-cream maker, following the manufacturer's instructions, until it is thick, then transfer to a freezerproof container. Spread it evenly, then pour over the blackberry sauce. Stir it through, creating ripples, then freeze until solid.

Remove from the freezer 20 minutes before you want to serve it to allow it to return to a scoopable consistency.

Bay Custard Tart

Serves 8

3–4 tbsp mulberry or wild myrtle jam
(optional)

300ml (1¼ cups) goat's milk

2 bay leaves

A piece of pared lemon zest

150ml (⅔ cup) double (heavy) cream

40g (¼ cup) caster (superfine) sugar

2 whole eggs, plus 2 yolks

For the pastry

250g (2 cups) plain (all-purpose) flour

150g (5¼oz) butter, chilled and diced

50g (½ cup) icing (confectioners') sugar

2 egg yolks

Sea salt

To serve

Seasonal berries, or fresh mulberries,
to serve

Single (light) cream

I had to include at least one custard tart in this book. Custard is the ideal receptacle for leaf infusions, and there are many options; this is a hybrid, as it takes the method of the classic English custard tart and marries it with the flavours I associate with *galaktoboureko* – the Greek filo custard pie. A friend of my parents, a hunter, beekeeper and goat farmer swears by goat's milk for the custard. Here, it is definitely the best way to go.

In the Greek village where my parents live, I was often confused by the pavements, covered as they were in blue-black inkblots. It took me a while to realise that this was from mulberries left to ripen and drop. I found this heartbreaking as they are so hard to come by in the UK. I make do with jam or jelly most of the time, but if you ever find fresh mulberries, serve them with this.

First, make the pastry. Put the flour in a bowl or stand mixer along with the butter and add a large pinch of salt. Process or rub in until it resembles fine breadcrumbs, then stir in the icing sugar. Add the egg yolks with 1 tablespoon chilled water and bring it all together into a dough. Knead very lightly to make sure it is smooth, then chill for 1 hour.

Preheat the oven to 180°C (350°F/Gas 4).

Roll the pastry out on a floured surface and line a deep 20cm (8in) tart tin, allowing it to overhang slightly. Prick the base with a fork, then freeze for 20 minutes.

Line the pastry with baking paper and fill with baking beans. Bake for 20 minutes, then remove the beans and cook for another 10 minutes until golden brown. Remove from the oven and cool. Spread with the jam, if using.

To make the custard, heat the milk with the bay and lemon zest in a saucepan. Bring almost to the boil, then remove from the heat and leave to infuse and cool. Add the cream to the milk and heat. Beat the sugar and eggs to combine then pour the liquid from a height over the eggs, whisking as you go. Strain, removing the bay and lemon.

Put the tin on a baking (cookie) sheet, pour in the filling and bake for 35–40 minutes, until set but still wobbling in the centre. Serve with berries and cream.

White Tea and Lychee Jelly

Serves 6

400ml (1¾ cups) cold-brewed white or jasmine tea

1 tbsp neutral honey or sugar (or to taste)

4 gelatine leaves

16 lychees, peeled and stoned, left whole

To serve

1 tbsp granulated sugar

Zest from 1 mandarin, very finely grated

I like to make this with a cold brew infusion (see page 281), as the flavour is more delicate and not taken over by tannins, but it can be made with regularly brewed tea as well, as long as it isn't too stewed. The sweet element is necessary here. An unsweetened tea is perfectly palatable as a hot or cold drink (cold if cold-brewed), but not as a jelly. And the honey or sugar really does bring out the flavour of the jasmine and the lychees.

Put the tea into a saucepan with the honey or sugar. Heat very gently, stirring until the honey or sugar has dissolved. Taste. Bearing in mind that it will taste less sweet when it is chilled, add more honey or sugar, if you like. I prefer mine with the minimum.

Meanwhile, soak the gelatine leaves in cold water. When they have softened, wring them out and add to the liquid. Stir until they have completely dissolved, then strain through a fine sieve into a jug.

Divide the lychees between 6 glasses, preferably wedged in so they will not be lifted up by the liquid. Pour over the liquid jelly, then leave to set and chill in the fridge, at least 3–4 hours.

For the garnish, mix the sugar with the mandarin zest and sprinkle over the top of the jellies.

Trifle

Serves 8

400g (14oz) Yogurt Cake (see page 234), left out overnight to stale, or any other Madeira-style cake

1–2 tbsp peach jam

150ml (²/₃ cup) dessert wine

300ml (1¼ cups) double (heavy) cream

50g (½ cup) flaked almonds, toasted (optional)

Edible flowers such as borage, jasmine and rose petals

For the peaches

A handful of rose geranium leaves, bruised

75g (²/₃ cup) caster (superfine) sugar

3 peaches, cut into wedges

For the lemon verbena custard

300ml (1¼ cups) whole (full-fat) milk

A large handful of lemon verbena leaves

75g (²/₃ cup) caster (superfine) sugar

4 egg yolks

2 tbsp cornflour (cornstarch)

300ml (1¼ cups) double (heavy) cream

When I think of the classic combination of lemon and rose, winter and the Christmas box of Turkish Delight are foremost in my mind. However, swap them out for these leafy alternatives and you have summer epitomised. This is a glorious way to end a meal.

First infuse the peaches. Bruise the rose geranium leaves and put in a saucepan with the sugar and 75ml (generous ¼ cup) water. Heat gently until all the sugar has dissolved, then simmer for 5 minutes. Remove from the heat and cool for a few minutes, then pour over the peach wedges. Leave to cool completely then transfer to the fridge to chill.

Next, make the custard. Put the milk in a saucepan with half the lemon verbena leaves. Bring to the boil, then immediately remove from the heat and leave to cool and infuse. Strain. Take the remaining lemon verbena and blitz it with the sugar until you have a pale green powder.

Whisk the egg yolks, sugar and cornflour together until mousse-like, then gradually add the milk, followed by the cream. Strain into a saucepan, then cook over a very low heat until the mixture has thickened to a spoonable custard. Transfer to a bowl and cover with plastic wrap, making sure the plastic wrap is resting on top of the custard to prevent a skin from forming. Leave to cool.

To assemble, cut the cake into slices and spread with peach jam. Sandwich together and cut into fingers. Arrange over the bottom of a trifle bowl, then pour over the dessert wine. Next spoon in the peach slices, discarding the rose geranium leaves as you go. Spoon over the custard and chill.

Whisk the double cream until it is soft and billowy – don't let it get too firm, you want to be able to slowly pour it over the trifle, not have to smooth it over with a palette knife. Cover and leave to chill in the fridge for at least 2 hours.

If you want a bit of crunch, top with toasted flaked almonds, but at the height of summer I would be more likely to decorate with edible flowers, in particular borage, jasmine and rose petals from the garden.

LEAVES I LOVE

What attracts us to the ingredients we love? There is of course
the physical reaction – our olfactory senses working with
taste buds to tell us they find them particularly appealing.
But there's a romantic element to it too. I find I value those
ingredients I have to work harder at getting to know, or have
previously cordially disliked. I learned to love all the bitter
leaves, despite initially recoiling, because I came to appreciate
how well bitter works with and enhances other flavours or
ingredients – think of the flavour of buttery, caramelised
endives, the sharp hit of vinegar with dandelion leaves or
chicory. Then there are those leaves that you learn, through
experience need careful handling, as everything you value
in them is so fleeting. Wild garlic can behave like this, but
the most vexing of all for me is the curry leaf. Those smoky
undertones and citrus top notes can vanish in a moment,
before you have even grasped that first tantalising whiff,
leaving behind only pungency and bitterness. Capturing it
in vinegar (see page 32) was a revelation, but even here, the
whole, rounded flavour thins with age.

One of the flavours with which I have a slight obsession, no
doubt in part because of the number of years I spent trying
to hunt it down, quest-like, was that of laksa leaf. For a long
time, I didn't know that it was this I wanted. All I knew was
that certain dishes I was cooking, lacked an ingredient. This
'secret' ingredient was, I knew, widely used in restaurants,
but was hidden from ingredients lists. If I asked, I was told
coriander (cilantro) or mint, or even basil. It was immensely
frustrating. I can't remember when I bought my first
Vietnamese coriander plant, on a whim in the garden centre,
but realising that it was the same thing as laksa leaf (it is also
called Vietnamese or Cambodian mint, rau ram – and, right
under my nose all along in Chinatown – praew leaf) and that
it had exactly the aroma and flavour that had been eluding me
for years was a relief. That aroma and flavour is hard to pin
down. It is slightly soapy, and I don't quite understand it, but
this is a good thing. It has peppery heat and spice and a hint
of bitter, but at the same time possesses a cooling, sweet,
mouth-filling succulence that lingers well after the heat has

faded. I add it to all kinds of things in the most inauthentic of ways, and when I don't, I notice its absence.

There are, of course, some plants you just love immediately, which induce laugh-out-loud delight. Enlivening, sherbety lemon verbena was one such for me, but top of this particular list has to be ginger rosemary. I am usually a bit dismissive of all these endless hybrids, as you can get lost in them – think of how many mints, sages, basils and thymes there are, for example – and I am sometimes left feeling that the combination of two flavours can diminish both. But ginger rosemary is special. Its hint of menthol (only apparent when you inhale deeply) softens into an aroma that still has that herbal, rosemary astringency, but is mellowed by the warmth of ginger as well as sweet caramel notes – think of a dark, well matured, rosemary-spiked ginger cake and you will almost be there. Also – and this is the elusive bit and something I find quite bizarre – there is something close to a musky tuber rose in the mix too. I now use it more than regular rosemary, and always add it to any sweet bake or dessert I make with ground ginger – it rounds out the spicier notes beautifully.

The herbs in a bouquet garni (see page 194) along with coriander, basil, tarragon and perhaps dill, are the most popular herbs used today. If I could, there are three others that I would make universally available so cooks start using them regularly: first, summer and winter savoury. Both are peppery in flavour, so were once used as a replacement for the much more expensive peppercorn; summer savoury has thyme notes – this is the one to eat with broad (fava) beans) – while the winter version is reminiscent of pine. They are used in Italy (not least for flavouring salamis) and work magically against the effects of beans. The other – and this one really confounds me – is chervil. It is such a beautiful herb: delicate and lacy, but surprisingly hardy and robust, and the flavour – take a subtle anise hit of tarragon and combine it with the greenness of parsley and you might be somewhere close to imagining the taste. The French value it – it features in *fines herbes* along with parsley, chives and tarragon, but sadly here it is rarely used and highly underrated.

Russian Caravan Gypsy Tart

Serves 6

410g (14½oz) tin evaporated milk

1 tsp smoked tea, ideally Russian
Caravan

1 piece of pared lemon zest

300g (1½ cups) muscovado sugar

A squeeze of lemon juice

Double (heavy) cream, to serve

Sea salt

For the pastry

200g (1¼ cups) plain (all-purpose) flour

2 tbsp icing (confectioners') sugar

100g (3½oz) butter, chilled and diced

1 egg yolk

Sea salt

**For the red wine-poached pears
(optional)**

Squeeze of lemon juice

8 slender pears, such as conference

750ml (3 cups) red wine

250g (1¼ cups) caster (superfine) sugar

1 large sprig of thyme

1 piece of pared orange zest

The idea for this came to me purely because I was thinking about smoky tea, Russian caravan specifically, and what I could infuse it in, and I made a word association with 'caravan' and 'gypsy'. As you can imagine, I desperately wanted it to work, and I was so happy that it did. If you like any of the smokier teas, you should like this.

Gypsy tart is a Kentish classic that seems deceptively easy to make. However – and I give you fair warning here – it can be tricky to get right. Please do not under-whisk your filling, make sure your oven temperature is accurate, and do not leave it in too long – if it is too hot for too long the filling can liquidise.

Russian caravan has a relatively mild smokiness so if you are using a stronger smoked tea, such as lapsang souchong, you can reduce the quantity a little.

Put the evaporated milk in a small saucepan and add the tea and lemon zest. Quickly heat until just too hot to hold a finger in, then put a lid on and leave to cool. This should be done quickly as you want minimal evaporation to take place. When the milk is completely cool, transfer to the fridge and leave to infuse overnight.

On the following day, make the pastry. Put the flour and sugar in a bowl with a pinch of salt and add the butter. Rub in the butter until the mixture resembles fine breadcrumbs, then add the egg yolk and just enough chilled water to make a clump-forming dough. Bring the dough together into a ball then wrap in plastic wrap and chill for 30 minutes.

Preheat the oven to 190°C (380°F/Gas 5).

Lightly flour a work surface and roll the dough out to fill a deep 23cm (9cm) flan tin, preferably loose-bottomed. Line the tin with the pastry, then line the pastry with baking paper and add baking beans. Bake in the oven for 15 minutes, then remove the beans and paper and bake for a further 5 minutes until the base is a light golden brown. Trim the edges of the pastry case and set the tin onto a baking (cookie) sheet.

continued overleaf

Russian Caravan Gypsy Tart (cont.)

Reduce the oven temperature to 170ºC (330ºF/Gas 3).

Make the filling. Strain the infused milk into a bowl and add the sugar, a pinch of salt and lemon juice. Using electric beaters or a stand mixer, gradually work up to full speed and whisk until the mixture is very well aerated, the colour of café au lait, and has a loose texture of lightly whipped double (heavy) cream. This will take at least 10 minutes, probably closer to 15.

Pour the mixture into the tin and bake for 10–12 minutes. The filling should have set on top – it will be smooth without a hint of tackiness – but be wobbly underneath. Leave to cool, then transfer to the fridge to set overnight.

To make the pears, half-fill a bowl with water and add a generous squeeze of lemon juice. Peel the pears, leaving the stalks on, and trim out the bottom of the core. Drop into the acidulated water as you go.

Put the wine, sugar, thyme and orange zest into a large saucepan. Heat gently, stirring until the sugar has dissolved, then add the pears. If you find they float, make a cartouche by cutting a round of baking paper the size of your saucepan, crumpling it up, then straightening it out and lying it on the surface of the wine. Poach the pears for anything between 20 minutes–1 hour – the cooking time will depend on how ripe the pears are, but they should be fork tender. Remove the pears from the wine and bring the wine to the boil. Simmer until it has reduced a little to a syrupy consistency. Store the pears in the syrup – they will keep for several days in the fridge.

To serve, cut the tart into wedges and serve with cream and poached pears to cut through the richness.

Leaf-Wrapped Baked Ricotta

Serves 4

2–3 fig leaves (or similar, see above)

400g (14oz) ricotta, drained

100g (3½oz) mascarpone

2 tbsp caster (superfine) sugar
  (plain or herb-infused, see page 271)

2 eggs, separated

A few basil leaves, to serve

For the fruit

2 tbsp honey

Juice of 1 orange

A few sprigs of lemon or orange thyme
  or rosemary

1 tbsp olive oil

6 figs, halved

Knob of butter

This is a recipe that shows how easy it is to perfume a dish simply by wrapping. It uses fig leaves, which I really like to use with their fruits.

You can use all kinds of leaves for this – and indeed, use leaves on the base of any baking you might do to impart subtle flavour and fragrance. If you have any citrus trees or have access to a market that sells citrus fruit loose, with their leaves, try those – I love sour orange leaves, lemon leaves and mandarin leaves. You can criss-cross the tin with pandan leaves, so they come over the sides, sprinkle over any number of herbs (bay, lemon verbena, geranium, fennel, cinnamon basil). The possibilities are endless.

I have limited the amount of sugar in this as it is served with syrup. You could increase it substantially – up to 100g (3½oz) – if you liked.

Preheat the oven to 180°C (350°F/Gas 4). Line a 20cm (8in) cake tin with baking paper and cover with either a large leaf or two, or a number of smaller leaves. Push them up the sides if possible. Set aside.

Whisk the ricotta with the mascarpone, sugar and egg yolks in a large mixing bowl, until smooth. Whisk the egg whites to the stiff peak stage, then fold this gently into the creamy mixture. Pour into the prepared tin and smooth down. Bake in the preheated oven for 25–30 minutes. You will find that it will have souffléed up and will probably have cracked – don't worry, it will collapse back down again. Allow to cool, then leave to chill, preferably overnight – the texture will become denser and smoother.

To make figs, put the honey and orange juice in a small saucepan with the lemon or orange thyme or rosemary and heat gently until the honey has melted. Leave to infuse for a little while. Heat the olive oil in a frying pan and add the figs. Fry cut-side down, then flip over for another minute. Flip back again, then add the knob of butter to foam around the edges of the figs. Reheat the honey and orange juice and pour it around the figs. Allow it to bubble up – when it subsides you should find you have a syrupy consistency. Serve with the ricotta cream, garnished with a few basil leaves if you like.

Basil and Kaffir Lime Leaf Cheesecakes

Serves 12

125g (4½oz) ginger biscuits (make the Gingernuts on page 268 with or without the ginger rosemary or use a shop-bought biscuit)

3½ tbsp butter, melted

6 kaffir lime leaves

115g (½ cup) caster (superfine) sugar

8 basil leaves

300g (10½oz) cream cheese

125g (4½oz) sour cream

Juice of ½ lime

2 eggs

Icing (confectioners') sugar and basil leaves, to decorate

This is not the first time I have paired basil and lime together like this – they make a first-class ice cream flavour too, which you can find in my *Citrus* book. These are a favourite with my children – I first made them for an 'enchanted woodland' picnic Adam was having at school. They were decorated with edible flowers (borage, jasmine, basil) and I sat them on a bed of edible leaves – lots of sweet, frondy herbs, such as fennel. The idea was to get the children to try different things, as not very many of them had eaten flowers or fresh herbs before.

Preheat the oven to 160ºC (320ºF/Gas 3). Line a 12-hole muffin tin with paper cases.

First make the base. Blitz the biscuits to a fine crumb – you can do this in a food processor or put them in a bag and bash with a rolling pin or kitchen mallet. Add the biscuits to the butter and mix to combine, then divide between the paper cases. Spread evenly across the base and press down.

Bake the bases in the oven for 5 minutes, then remove from the oven to cool down.

Remove and discard the stems from the kaffir lime leaves and finely chop the leaves. Put in a spice grinder or a small food processor with half the sugar and blitz to a powder. You can sieve out any larger bits of leaf if you prefer. It isn't strictly necessary, but the overall flavour will be better without them. Finely chop the basil leaves and stir into the remaining sugar.

Put the cream cheese, kaffir sugar, sour cream, lime juice and eggs in a bowl and beat together until smooth. Spoon the mixture over the biscuit bases. Bake in the oven for around 25 minutes, until the cheesecakes are slightly puffed up and starting to crack.

Remove from the oven and leave to cool – you will find that they will deflate a little at this point. If possible, chill overnight – this will improve the texture, which will become denser and fudgier, as well as giving the flavours time to develop. Serve dusted with icing (confectioners') sugar and decorated with basil leaves.

Baklava

Makes around 20

130g (4½oz) butter, melted, plus extra for greasing

150g (5¼oz) blanched almonds, see method

150g (1½ cups) ground almonds

1 tbsp granulated sugar

1 tsp ground cardamom

12 sheets of filo pastry, cut to fit your tin

100g (3½oz) pistachios, roughly chopped

For the syrup

250g (1¼ cups) granulated sugar

50g (1¾oz) honey

A big handful of rose geranium leaves

It is possible to make as many versions of this baklava as there are types of herb and leaf-infused syrups. This basic recipe uses rose geranium, but if you like baklava, please consider the variations at the end. The reason why the quantities of this recipe are relatively small compared to most Greek recipes is that I do like to make more than one sort at a time. However, the recipe will double up easily, too.

I always find getting the first couple of squares of baklava out of the tin very tricky, so I line the baking tin with foil, allowing the whole thing to be lifted out. This also means it is easier to cut through the pastries again once they have cooked.

First make the syrup. If you can, make this in advance. It isn't so important with rose geranium as it gives its flavour out readily, but for some of the woodier herbs – rosemary or pine leaves for example – the syrup will need longer to infuse. Put the sugar, honey, 150ml (⅔ cup) water and rose geranium leaves into a saucepan. Stir over a low heat until the sugar has dissolved, then turn up the heat slightly and leave to simmer for 10 minutes, until it looks syrupy. Leave to cool and infuse. Taste. If you think it needs longer to infuse, please do – the flavour should be clear and distinctive. When you are satisfied, strain.

To make the baklava, preheat the oven to 180°C (350°F/Gas 4). For easy removal of the baklava later, line a 20cm (8in) square baking tin with a double layer of foil, leaving enough foil on opposite sides to serve as handles. Line the foil with a piece of baking paper and generously butter.

Prepare the filling. Chop the blanched almonds – you want a mixture of textures from quite fine to coarse. Mix with the ground almonds, sugar, cardamom and 3 tablespoons of the melted butter.

Carefully drape the first sheet of filo over the baking paper. Brush with butter, then add another layer of filo. Continue until you have used 6 sheets of filo in total. Sprinkle over the nuts, making sure they are evenly spread but not pressed down too much, then add the remaining 6 sheets of filo, making sure you brush thoroughly with butter between each addition.

Cut the pastry into portions – the usual way to do this is making a diamond shape, but regular squares work just as well. Put in the oven and bake for 25 minutes, then remove from the oven, sprinkle over the pistachios and return to the oven for another 10 minutes, or until the nuts and pastry are lightly browned.

Leave the baklava to cool, then gently reheat the syrup. Pour this over the baklava, concentrating on the lines in between the pastry rather than pouring it over the pastry itself. Doing it this way instead of pouring the cooled syrup over the hot baklava helps prevent the bottom layers of filo from becoming sodden.

Leave to cool for several hours to help it all glue together, then lift out of the tin. Cut down the lines again – I find using a metal dough scraper works really well as you can push straight down right through the bottom layers of pastry – then transfer the squares to an airtight container.

Variations

Rosemary, or ginger rosemary
Blitz 1 tablespoon needles with the granulated sugar for the filling. Grind 150g (5¼oz) walnuts and mix with 150g (5¼oz) chopped walnuts, reserving 2 tablespoons for the topping. Bruise several sprigs of rosemary to add to the syrup in place of the rose geranium.

Pine needles
This one is best made in spring when you can use new shoots, or use pine sugar. Blitz 1 tablespoon pine needles with the granulated sugar for the filling and add 1 teaspoon of lemon zest. Replace the blanched almonds with pine nuts, reserving 2 tablespoons for the topping. Roughly chop a large handful of pine needles and add to the syrup in place of the rose geranium. This syrup is best made the day before for a long infusion.

Anise hyssop
Use walnuts as for ginger rosemary. Blitz a large handful of anise hyssop flowers and leaves with the granulated sugar and mix with the nuts. Make a syrup with a large handful of leaves – again, this will benefit from a long infusion.

Pear and Rosemary Upside Down Cake

Serves 8

200g (7oz) butter, softened

200g (1 cup) golden caster (superfine) sugar

1 tsp rosemary needles, very finely chopped

100g (¾ cup) plain (all-purpose) flour

100g (¾ cup) dark rye flour

3 tsp baking powder

4 eggs

Sea salt

For the topping

5 tbsp butter

100g (½ cup) light soft brown sugar

Needles from 2 sprigs of ginger rosemary or normal rosemary

2–3 pears, peeled, cored and sliced into wedges

Another outing for my favourite ginger rosemary (see page 249), but if you don't have it, regular rosemary will be just as good. This is probably my favourite autumnal dessert.

Preheat the oven to 170°C (340°F/Gas 3).

To make the topping, smear the butter over the base of a 21cm (8½in) cake tin or ovenproof frying pan. Sprinkle on the sugar and the rosemary, then arrange the pears on top.

Next, make the sponge. Beat the butter, sugar and finely chopped rosemary together until very soft, pale and well aerated. Mix the flours and baking powder together with a generous pinch of salt. Add the eggs one at a time to the sugar and butter, adding 1 tablespoon of the dry ingredients with each addition, then gently fold in the remainder – be careful not to overwork the mixture. Spoon this over the pears and spread evenly.

Bake in the preheated oven for around 50 minutes, until the sponge is well risen and springy to touch. It should be a deep, rich brown. Run a knife around the sides just to make sure the cake will come away, then upturn it onto a large plate. Serve hot or warm with cream.

Mint Chocolate Fondants

Makes 8

200g (7oz) butter, cubed, plus melted
  butter for brushing

200g (7oz) dark chocolate

2 tbsp vodka

110g (½ cup) caster (superfine) sugar

4 eggs, plus 4 egg yolks

4 tbsp plain (all-purpose) flour

Sea salt

For the ganache
100ml (scant ½ cup) double (heavy)
  cream

5g (a packed ⅓ cup) fresh mint leaves

100g (3½oz) white chocolate, chopped

I've been making the non-minty version of these puddings ever since I saw them in Delia Smith's *How to Cook*. Like all of her recipes, they have never failed me. For this version, I've inserted a white chocolate and fresh mint ganache, so you end up with two lots of molten-ness. My children are the judge of all things mint chocolate in our house, and they love it.

I use a combination of a variety of mint called After Eight and a regular peppermint, but you could use just peppermint.

First make the ganache. Put the cream into a small saucepan. Scrunch up the mint and add that too, then gently heat until it is almost at boiling point. Remove from the heat and leave to cool down completely. Push through a sieve, scraping it vigorously to extract as much flavour as possible, then return to the saucepan. Add the white chocolate and heat gently again, stirring constantly, until the chocolate has melted into the cream and has formed a thick sauce. Scrape into a bowl and cover. Leave to chill and firm up in the fridge.

To make the puddings, first brush 8 small pudding moulds with melted butter. Set aside. Preheat the oven to 200°C (400°F/Gas 6) if you are going to cook the puddings straight away.

Break up the chocolate and put it in a heatproof bowl with the butter. Set over a simmering saucepan of water – making sure the base of the bowl does not touch the water – and melt together. If you are very, very careful, you can do this directly in a saucepan instead, but if you do not watch it constantly, it can split. When the butter and chocolate have melted together, add the vodka.

Put the sugar, eggs and egg yolks in a large bowl or stand mixer and whisk until the mixture has increased in volume and has the consistency of a light mousse. It should also hold its shape for a few seconds if you drizzle a trail over it.

Pour the chocolate and butter mixture around the sides of the sugar and egg mousse. Add a pinch of salt to the flour, then sift this over the top. Then fold everything together – you need to be as gentle as possible when you do this as you don't want to knock all the air out of it, but please be thorough – the batter will eventually be a rich burnt umber.

To assemble, remove the ganache from the fridge and roll into eight balls. Divide half of the chocolate batter between the eight pudding moulds, then place a ganache ball in the centre of each. Top with the remaining batter.

Place the moulds on a baking (cookie) sheet and bake in the preheated oven for 12 minutes. If you want to prepare these ahead, you can cover them and keep in the fridge until needed. If you cook them straight from the fridge, they will need a little longer – 14 minutes. You can also cook them from frozen, which will take longer still – 15 minutes with a couple of minutes to stand at the end.

The puddings are done when well risen and shrinking away from the sides. If in doubt, they are probably done and should be taken out – overcooking will set the centres. Lever them out with the help of a palette knife around the edges and turn out onto serving plates. Serve immediately – if you don't, the chocolate and the ganache filling will start to set.

Rosemary and Orange Cake

Serves 8–10

375g (3 cups) plain (all-purpose) flour

2 tsp baking powder

½ tsp bicarbonate of soda (baking soda)

175g (6¼oz) butter, softened

225g (generous 1 cup) caster (superfine) sugar

2 tsp rosemary, very finely chopped

Zest of 1 orange

4 eggs

300ml (1¼ cups) buttermilk

2 tsp orange blossom water

For the buttercream

50g (¼ cup) granulated sugar

A few rosemary needles

350g (1⅔ cups) icing (confectioners') sugar

225g (8oz) butter

2 tsp orange blossom water

For the filling

Orange and Rosemary Curd (see page 276) or shop-bought orange curd

For the praline (optional)

150g (¾ cup) granulated sugar

100g (3½oz) blanched hazelnuts, lightly chopped or crushed chunkily

2 tsp rosemary needles, very finely chopped

I wanted to make a celebratory/special occasion cake with many elements to it, but don't feel you have to go down that route. For a superb everyday cake, you don't have to make your own curd, you could buy one instead, and you certainly don't have to make praline. I recommend you at least try them at some point though.

Preheat the oven to 180°C (375°F/Gas 4). Butter and line 3 x 20cm (8in) sandwich cake tins and set aside.

Put the flour, baking powder and bicarbonate of soda (baking soda) in a bowl with a generous pinch of salt and mix well. Beat the butter and sugar together with the rosemary and zest until very pale. Add the eggs one at a time with 1 tablespoon of the flour mixture, then work in the rest of the flour, keeping the mixing to a minimum. Fold in the buttermilk and orange blossom water.

Divide the cake mixture between the 3 tins. Bake in the preheated oven for 25–30 minutes, until well risen and springy to touch. Leave in the tins for a few minutes before turning out to cool on a wire rack.

Next make the buttercream. Put the sugar and rosemary into a food processor and blitz until fine. Mix with the icing (confectioners') sugar. Beat the butter until it is very soft, then gradually start adding the icing sugar. I do this in a stand mixer with a tea towel draped over to stop sugar clouds coating everything in the vicinity. When it is all incorporated, add the orange blossom water.

For the praline, line a baking (cookie) sheet with baking paper. Put the sugar in a small saucepan. Give it a shake to make sure it is evenly covering the base of the pan, then add 50ml (1¾fl oz) water. Simmer until the sugar has dissolved, then turn up the heat and allow to bubble until a light golden brown. Immediately remove from the heat and stir in the nuts and rosemary. Pour onto the baking sheet then leave it to cool. Break into shards or blitz to a coarse powder, depending on how you want to use it.

To assemble, spread a thin layer of the buttercream over one of the cakes then pipe a border of buttercream around the edge. Fill the inside of the border with the curd. Top with the second cake and repeat. Cover the sides and top with buttercream. Decorate with the praline.

Swiss Chard Tart

Serves 8

1 large bunch of chard, around 900g (1lb 15oz), leaves only

50g (⅓ cup) raisins or sultanas

50ml (¼ cup) brandy or eau de vie

1 tsp orange blossom water

50g (⅓ cup) pine nuts, lightly toasted and chopped

½ tsp ground cinnamon

¼ tsp ground mace

¼ ground cloves

50g (1¾oz) Parmesan cheese or similar, finely grated

2 eggs

75g (¼ cup) light soft brown sugar

2 crisp eating apples, peeled, cored and sliced

1 tbsp demerara sugar

Icing (confectioners') sugar, for dusting

For the pastry

300g (2½ cups) plain (all-purpose) flour

1 tsp baking powder

100g (3½oz) butter, softened

75g (⅓ cup) caster (superfine) sugar

2 eggs

Sea salt

There is a tradition across the Mediterranean for making tarts that are designed to confuse the taste buds. Sweet or savoury? Main course or dessert? Last time I was in Greece and trying every kind of *spanakopita*, I tried a sweet one with raisins and a honey-sesame crust. I could not work it out. This is based on a French tart, *tourtes de blettes*, but it occurred to me when I was cooking it for the first time that it was in the same mould as the original English version of the mince pie, just vegetarian.

The leaf/stem ratio on chard varies enormously. I have worked out that the average is just over half leaf to stem. From a 900g (1lb 15oz) bunch of chard, you should expect around 500g (1lb 1½oz) leaf, so if you want to use any other leaf, work on this basis.

First make the pastry. Mix the flour with the baking powder and a pinch of salt. Rub in the softened butter, then mix in the sugar and eggs. Bring everything together and knead very gently, keeping your touch light, until you have a smooth ball of dough. Leave to rest for 1 hour.

Meanwhile, make the filling. Shred the chard very finely then blanch in a saucepan of boiling water for 3–4 minutes. Drain and when cool, squeeze out as much water as possible. Put the raisins in a small saucepan and pour over the brandy. Bring to the boil, then remove from the heat and leave to stand for 30 minutes, until most of the liquid is absorbed. Add the orange blossom water.

Stir the raisins into the chard, along with the pine nuts, spices and cheese. Whisk the eggs and sugar together and combine this with the chard.

Preheat the oven to 180°C (375°F/Gas 4).

Roll out two thirds of the pastry to line a 23cm (9in) preferably non-fluted, tart case. Arrange the chard mixture over the case, then arrange the apple slices on top and sprinkle over the demerara sugar. Roll out the remaining pastry, place on top and crimp the edges together. Bake for 35–45 minutes, until a light golden brown. Dust with icing (confectioners') sugar before serving.

Banana, Thyme and Chocolate Bread

Serves 8

175g (1½ cups) plain (all-purpose) flour

2 tsp baking powder

¼ tsp bicarbonate of soda (baking soda)

125g (4½oz) butter, melted

100g (½ cup) light soft brown sugar

2 eggs, beaten

3 large bananas, mashed

75g (2½oz) chocolate, chopped
  (optional)

Fine sea salt

The first time I made this, the controversial element was not the thyme, but the chocolate. I had braced myself for the children not to like the thyme, so I was relieved. I now make it with or without the chocolate – if you make it with, I recommend using dark chocolate or a milk chocolate with a high percentage of cocoa solids that will stand up to the thyme. And cutting it up into shards and adding, crumbs and all, is much better than using chocolate chips.

This cake is a great keeper – and one of the things I like to do with it is turn it into French toast. To make it, whisk a couple of eggs with a splash of milk, dip the cake into it, fry in butter, sprinkle with demerara sugar and cinnamon and serve with banana and cream.

Preheat the oven to 170°C (340°F/Gas 3) and line a large loaf tin with baking paper or resuable cake liner.

Measure the flour, baking powder and bicarbonate of soda into a bowl and either sift or whisk to remove any lumps. Add a large pinch of fine salt.

Let the butter cool slightly, then mix in the sugar, followed by the eggs and bananas. Whisk thoroughly to combine. Fold in the flour, as gently as possible, then stir through the chocolate.

Scrape into the loaf tin, then bake in the preheated oven for between 1–1¼ hours. The loaf will probably form a peak and crack along the centre – it will subside a little once it has cooled.

Leave to cool in the tin for 10 minutes then transfer to a wire rack. This will keep very well in an airtight tin for at least a week.

Tea Bread

Serves 8

150g (1 cup) sultanas or raisins

150g (1 cup) currants

100g (⅔ cup) glacé cherries, chopped

400ml (1¾ cups) strong tea – flavour up to you, but Earl Grey is distinctive

50g (¼ cup) light soft brown sugar

2 eggs

300g (2½ cups) self-raising flour

Sea salt

This is such a useful recipe. I make it regularly as it satisfies the children's desire for cake, but is slightly better for them. I made it my mission to cut down on the added sugar. The first recipe I tried contained a massive 250g (1¼ cups), and I worked all the way down to none at all, before settling on the 50g (¼ cup) you see in this recipe. No sugar works perfectly well – the texture is slightly firmer for the first day or so, and you don't get the same glossy sheen on the crust – but then it softens up a bit. However, I preferred it with just a little.

You can use any variation on the dried fruit, and any variation on tea. I always seem to have lots of different-flavoured loose teas that I don't get around to drinking, so I see this recipe as an opportunity to use them up. Combinations I like are chopped dried figs with anything smoky; jasmine tea with dried mulberries; pretty much anything with Earl Grey or regular black tea.

Put the dried fruit in a bowl and pour over the strong tea – you should find it is just enough to cover the fruit – then put a plate on top and leave to steep overnight. The next morning, you will find the fruit is plump and the tea will have thickened to a syrup.

Preheat the oven to 160°C (320°F/Gas 3). Line a large loaf tin with baking paper or reusable cake liner.

Whisk the sugar and eggs together to combine, then stir in the flour along with a generous pinch of salt. Drain the fruit, reserving the liquid, and mix into the cake batter. Gradually work in just enough of the soaking liquid to form a reluctant dropping consistency.

Scrape into the prepared tin, then bake in the oven for up to 1½ hours, checking every 10 minutes after an hour. When the sponge has shrunk away from the sides and is springy to touch, it will be done. Remove from the oven and leave to cool in the tin. Store in an airtight container – it should be okay for at least 2 weeks.

Rosemary Gingernuts

Makes 25 biscuits

150g (1¼ cups) plain (all-purpose) flour

½ tsp bicarbonate of soda (baking soda)

1 tbsp ground ginger

50g (1¾oz) golden syrup

3½ tbsp butter

1 generous tbsp ginger rosemary
  needles, very finely chopped

100g (½ cup) light soft brown sugar

1 egg yolk

Sea salt

Until a couple of years ago, I never would have thought that ginger and rosemary were flavours that obviously belonged together. Then I discovered ginger rosemary, thanks to Mark Diacono and his Otter Farm nursery, and I realised that actually, they have a great affinity.

I had a bit of a eureka moment with this recipe, as I was thinking about where to use ginger rosemary when I was baking a regular batch of gingernuts – a biscuit I love to make at least every other week as they are so quick and easy. Now I only make them with the ginger rosemary. But if you don't have it, you can use regular rosemary instead and add an extra teaspoon of ground ginger to the mixture.

Preheat the oven to 190°C (380°F/Gas 5).

Sift the flour into a bowl with the bicarbonate of soda (baking soda) and the ground ginger. Add a generous pinch of salt and mix together thoroughly. Set aside.

Put the golden syrup and butter into a saucepan and set over a low heat until they have melted. Stir in the ginger rosemary and leave for a minute, then remove from the heat. Beat in the sugar and egg yolk.

Add the dry ingredients and stir everything together until you have a firm, slightly oily-looking dough. It will feel to start with as though the mixture is much too dry, but keep going and it will all come together beautifully.

Pinch off walnut-sized pieces of dough and space out over 2 baking (cookie) sheets. Bake in the preheated oven for 12–15 minutes, until the biscuits have turned a rich ochre and have a cracked surface. They will still be very soft, but do not worry about this – they will firm up as they cool.

Remove from the oven. Leave for a few minutes to firm, then transfer to a wire rack. Store in an airtight container.

SWEET PRESERVING, PRESERVES AND DRINKS

How to Make Sugars and Syrups

How to make herb sugars

There are two ways to make herb sugars. If you have time, take a handful of any fresh herb – or if you have just dried it yourself, dried herb – and mix with granulated or caster (superfine) sugar. Use a sprig or 3–4 leaves per 100g (½ cup) sugar and lightly crush/muddle them. Put in a jar, making sure it isn't quite full so you can give it regular shakes and leave to infuse. Check regularly – if you have used fresh, soft herbs, they will have some moisture in them, which will make the sugar clump together, but this doesn't matter; it will break down again very easily. Leave somewhere dark for a week or two before using.

For an instant herb sugar, again, using either fresh or dried herbs, you can simply blitz a handful of herbs with granulated sugar – it will turn green and it will also grind to a fine powder – it will also take on more of the taste of the herb, as well as the flavour, so you might end up with a hint of bitter in your sugar.

How to make herb syrups

It is very difficult to give precise amounts for herb syrups, because the strength of the herbs varies enormously – not just between the types of herbs, but with the herbs themselves – when you pick them, how they have been grown, at what stage of growth they are … there are endless variables. Some leaves are really generous and throw out their flavours and aromas readily – I would include fig leaves, geranium leaves, verbena and the woodier herbs in this category. Others take more persuasion. So really, all I can do is say taste, taste, taste, and to start with, keep the quantities quite small. Herb syrups will keep in the fridge for a few weeks – if you want to prolong the shelf life, add a couple of shots of a spirit such as vodka, or you can add citric acid.

Mix one part sugar with one part water – I usually do around 150g (5¼oz) of each. You can vary the sugar. I usually stick to a caster (superfine) sugar, but will occasionally mix it up – for example, I really love ginger rosemary syrup with golden rum and ginger ale, so I might make the syrup with a light muscovado sugar to complement it.

Put the sugar and water in a saucepan and heat gently, stirring until the sugar has dissolved. Bring to the boil and add a handful of herbs, then simmer for a few minutes, adding a teaspoon of citric acid for the last minute, if using, and stirring until it has dissolved. At this point start tasting to see if the flavour is strong enough. The syrup will continue to take on flavour as it cools. If you are happy with the flavour when it is cool, you can strain into a bottle, or you can leave it for longer – it will continue to infuse until you strain it. To preserve the shelf life, strain through muslin or kitchen paper you have just poured boiling water over, and decant into a sterilised bottle.

Crystallised Leaves

Leaves – especially mint, lemon verbena, lemon balm, lemon thyme, fennel, basil or rosemary

1 egg white, well beaten

Caster (superfine) sugar

This is an incredibly easy and effective way of creating leaf decorations, and as the leaves do dry out, they can also be crumbled up to use as toppings or as a flavoured sugar. You can use pretty much any leaf you would want to use in a dessert, as long as it's not too tough. If you are worried about salmonella, you can use carton or dried egg whites instead of fresh.

Make sure your leaves are completely clean and dry. Brush each one with egg white – for larger sprigs (for example, rosemary) dipping is more effective than brushing. Sprinkle sugar over a plate and dip each leaf into it, coating both sides, then shake off the excess. Arrange on baking paper and leave for a few hours to dry. Once they are completely dry, store them in an airtight tin – they should be okay for at least a week.

Peach and Lemon Verbena Jam

Makes 3–4 x 225g (8oz) jars

1kg (2lb 3oz) peaches
juice of 1 lemon
A handful of lemon verbena leaves
750g (3¾ cups) jam sugar

If you have made any lemon verbena sugar, you can substitute some of the sugar below, but just poking a leaf or two into the jam when it sets will be enough to give plenty of flavour. This method works really well with other combinations, too. Try a pear jam, made in exactly the same way, with ginger rosemary or rosemary, or plum with tarragon, or blackberries with bay leaf.

I should note here that I have reduced the quantity of sugar a little in these recipes, as I like a slightly softer, French-style set. For a much firmer jam, you can use equal quantities. Conversely you can also reduce the amount of sugar by around a third. The reduced-sugar jams will not keep so well – a few months, unopened, and then they must be stored in the fridge.

Score a cross at the base of each peach, then dip into just-boiled water for 30 seconds. This will help loosen the skin – it should peel off easily. Cut the peaches in half, remove the stones and dice.

Put the peaches in a large saucepan or preserving pan with 50ml (generous ¼ cup) water, lemon juice and most of the lemon verbena leaves. Cook very gently until the peaches have softened, then add the sugar. Stir until the sugar has dissolved, then turn up the heat and boil, stirring regularly to prevent catching, until setting point is reached. To test for this, chill a saucer in the freezer and drop a little jam onto it – let it cool, then push it with your finger – if it wrinkles, it is ready. Remove the lemon verbena leaves from the jam and ladle into sterilised jars. Dip the remaining lemon verbena leaves in just-boiled water and dry thoroughly. Put a couple of leaves in each jar, then seal down.

Quince and Rose Geranium Jelly

Makes 1 large jar

1kg (2lb 3oz) quince, roughly chopped

2 handfuls of geranium leaves, lightly bruised

Caster (superfine) sugar (see method)

2 tbsp lemon juice (if the quince are very ripe)

This is made in exactly the same way as the more savoury jellies on page 37, but I have put this one here as I use it mainly as a sweet jelly. It is one of my favourite things to eat on buttered brioche or with a croissant.

Put the quince – skin, seeds and all – into a large saucepan or preserving pan. Add a handful of the geranium leaves and 1 litre (4 cups) water and bring to the boil. Turn down the heat and leave to simmer until the quince has broken down into a pulp – any piece should collapse against the pressure from the back of a wooden spoon.

Sterilise a jelly bag or a sieve lined with muslin by pouring boiling water over it and suspend or set over a large bowl. Add the quince pulp, cover and leave to strain for several hours, or until the pulp looks very dry.

Measure the quince liquid back into your saucepan or preserving pan and add 450g (2¼ cups) sugar for every 600ml (2½ cups) liquid. Add the lemon juice and the second handful of geranium leaves and heat gently until the sugar has dissolved. Bring to the boil and keep boiling, stirring regularly, until setting point is reached (see opposite). Ladle into sterilised jars, then seal down.

Orange and Rosemary Curd

Makes 1 large jar

150ml (⅔ cup) freshly squeezed
orange juice

3½ tbsp lemon juice

Zest from 2 oranges

A few sprigs of rosemary, roughly
chopped

125g (⅔ cup) caster (superfine) sugar

125g (4½oz) butter

2 eggs, plus 3 egg yolks

The rosemary flavour is quite subtle in this curd – the orange seems to bring out its sherbety side. I love to use it to sandwich an orange-scented cake or the rosemary cake on page 262.

Sterilise a large jar, by washing it in hot water and putting it in a warm oven to dry out.

Put all the ingredients in a saucepan and set over a low heat. Break up the eggs, then start stirring. The butter will melt, the sugar will dissolve, and you will end up with a smooth, runny liquid. Keep stirring over a low heat until the mixture starts thickening – it will be almost imperceptible to start with, then it will suddenly speed up. Keep stirring, making sure you scrape all over the base of the pan (you don't want any egg to scramble), until the curd has thickened enough so that when you coat the back of a spoon, you can trace a thick line down it with your finger.

Remove from the heat and strain into a jug, then pour into the sterilised jar. Leave to cool then transfer to the fridge.

Kaya

Makes 1 large jar

7 pandan leaves, roughly chopped

5 eggs

75g (⅓ cup) caster (superfine) sugar

75g (⅓ cup) palm sugar (or light soft brown sugar or jaggery)

250ml (1 cup) coconut milk

I had almost given up on the idea of kaya – I had bought many, but never found one that tasted sufficiently of pandan – or, for that matter, coconut. Then my friend Jenny Linford told me that a good homemade one is a completely different beast, with the flavours singing out, so I decided to try for myself and was very happy with the results.

It is usually referred to as a jam, but really, it is more like a curd.

Put the pandan leaves in a food processor with 50ml (¼ cup) water and blitz until they are very broken down. Strain through a fine sieve.

Put all the other ingredients into a bowl and set over a pan of simmering water, making sure the bowl with the ingredients isn't touching the water. Add half the pandan extract. Start stirring the mixture until everything is well combined and the sugar has dissolved, then keep stirring until the mixture has thickened to a custard-like consistency. Taste and add more pandan extract, if you like, and cook for a little longer. The whole process will take at least 20 minutes. Strain through a sieve just to make sure there are no egg solids in the curd, then pour into a sterilised jar (see opposite). It will thicken as it cools to a spreadable consistency.

Variation

For a much milder flavour, infuse the pandan leaves instead of making an extract. Bruise a couple of pandan leaves and tie them into knots. Put in a saucepan with the coconut milk and heat gently to almost boiling point. Remove from the heat and leave to cool and infuse, then strain and use as above.

Rhubarb and Sweet Cicely Cordial

Makes 2.2 litres (9 cups)

1.5kg (3lb 5oz) red rhubarb, trimmed and roughly chopped

Pared zest of 1 orange

Pared zest of 1 lime

2 handfuls of sweet cicely tips, around 8, each 15cm (6in) long, stalk and leaves

Up to 600g (3 cups) caster (superfine) sugar, to taste

1 heaped tsp citric acid (optional)

This recipe comes from my friend, author Fiona Bird, who is a well-known foraging expert and who not only sent me this recipe, but a bottle of the finished cordial, too. Unsurprisingly, the sweet cicely is a natural sweetener, so you might not need all of the sugar. I would start with 400g (2 cups) and add more to taste. The citric acid is optional, but it does prolong the shelf life of the cordial.

This recipe can be adapted to other fruits and herbs. I tend to make half-amounts when using strongly flavoured herbs, as I don't want to tire of them. My favourite is to keep the rhubarb in the recipe, use the maximum amount of sugar and replace the sweet cicely with ginger rosemary.

Put the rhubarb, zest and sweet cicely into a saucepan and cover with 750ml (3 cups) water. Bring to the boil then lower to a simmer, cover, and leave until the rhubarb has collapsed down and is tender.

Remove from the heat and leave to stand overnight to infuse.

The next day, ladle the contents of the pan into a scalded jelly bag or muslin-lined sieve and leave to drip through – this will take several hours. Do not be tempted to push it through to speed things up, as you will end up with a cloudy cordial.

Taste the juice for acidity (it will be quite tart) and transfer to a saucepan. Heat gently and start adding the sugar, stirring until it has dissolved. Add around 400g (2 cups) then taste and add more if you like.

When you are satisfied with the flavour (remember that it will taste less sweet when chilled) add the citric acid, if using, and stir to dissolve.

Decant the cordial into sterilised bottles and keep in the fridge.

Stevia-Sweetened Drinks

It is possible to make really good drinks without any sugar at all if you use stevia leaf. The downside to these is that they don't have sugar's natural preservative, so will not keep. I have a couple of stevia plants that do very well outside and are then cut back in the winter and brought in to sit on the windowsill. They continue to throw out leaves and as each leaf is so incredibly potent, this will probably be enough for you. You can dry the leaves too – do this before the plants flower because the flavour will become less sweet/more bitter at this stage. I have tried to buy good-quality dried leaves or unadulterated powder (as opposed to all the sweeteners made with stevia but full of other artificial ingredients) and I haven't been satisfied with the flavour – they have become muddy with an unpleasant aftertaste. Make your own, and it will be clean-tasting.

To get an even distribution of sweetness throughout the drink you are making, it is better to infuse the leaves in water first. Remember that if you are using dried leaves, they will be much stronger than a fresh leaf, so amend accordingly. They will also vary in strength according to growing conditions/time of year. This seems like not much leaf to water, but it just shows you how sweet the leaves are.

Take a handful of fresh (bruised) leaves or dried (crumbled) leaves and pour over 200ml (¾ cup) spring water or – if you want this to keep for any length of time – vodka. Cover and leave to stand somewhere dark or in the fridge for 1–2 days until you have a sweet flavour. You can make a more instant version by using freshly boiled water instead – it will take minutes as opposed to days.

You will find that 1 tablespoon of the extract is the equivalent to around 100g (¾ cup) sugar, so you can adjust your recipes accordingly. Here is one to get you started.

Limeade with Mint and Tarragon

This is how I like limeade – really sour, but tempered by the sweeter herbs and the stevia.

Take 10 limes. Roughly chop them, then put in a blender with a few sprigs of mint and tarragon (no stems) and 200ml (¾ cup) water. Blitz until the limes are broken down – you should end up with a green-flecked liquid. Strain into a jug. You can leave the liquid now until you are ready to serve.

Put the lime juice into a jug and pour over a bottle of soda water. Start adding stevia to taste, 1 teaspoon at a time, stirring thoroughly between each addition so the stevia extract is evenly distributed, until you are happy with the sweetness. This will vary drastically from person to person. Add more sprigs of herbs and lime slices to the jug and serve.

Variations
Make with any other type of citrus in place of limes and try different herbs – bush basil, sweet cicely (which will also help the overall sweetness), rosemary or lemon verbena. An interesting combination is to add half a cucumber to the limes – sounds strange, but it does work.

Shrubs

A shrub is a drink that has been gaining popularity in recent years, possibly because more of us are looking for grown-up alternatives to alcohol – and because we want to reap the health benefits of vinegar. I won't say it is decidedly grown-up (my children like them), but it is a more rounded and satisfying drink for evening drinking than sweeter alternatives.

There are numerous methods for shrub making, but I prefer this one as I find the uncooked flavours are cleaner. It does require some tasting of the syrup as you go, just to make sure the flavour of the herbs isn't overwhelming the fruit. It's all about balance.

The quantity of the fruit isn't important, but make a note of how much sugar you use and use the same amount of vinegar when you come to mix it. The flavour will initially seem unpleasantly tart, but leave it for a week or so – it will mellow over time.

In terms of fruit, pretty much anything goes as long as it isn't a fruit that needs cooking first. I like orchard fruits, especially pears, plums and peaches, as well as soft fruits such as blackberries and strawberries. If you want to add citrus notes, use pared zest as one of the aromatics. The best vinegar to use for this is cider vinegar, but if you decide you want to ramp up the herb flavour, you could substitute a tablespoon or two for a herb vinegar (see page 31).

Here is a basic method for one small bottle. Take around 250g (9oz) of your chosen fruit and either chop it up or crush it very lightly. Put into a non-reactive bowl (one that will fit into your freezer) and add herbs, just a few sprigs, lightly bruised, and any other aromatics. Sprinkle with around 125g (⅔ cup) sugar (or honey, if you prefer), and stir. Cover with plastic wrap and put in the fridge. Leave for 2–3 days, checking and stirring fairly regularly. The fruit will give out liquid, the sugar will dissolve and take on the flavour of the fruit and herbs. Taste for flavour at regular intervals. If you are satisfied the herb flavour is strong enough, remove from the bowl – I usually leave in for the duration. Strain through a sieve – this is one time when it is okay to press down on the fruit to extract more juice – then mix with the same quantity of vinegar to sugar. If any sugar hasn't dissolved, add it to the strained liquid as it will dissolve in the vinegar. Decant into jars or bottles and leave for at least a week before using.

To drink, dilute with anything sparkling, or add to cocktails.

Some Flavours to Try

Melon and cucumber with mint or tarragon

Strawberry with Thai basil

Pineapple or mango with ginger rosemary

Blackberry with bay, cinnamon and cardamom

Tomatoes with coriander (cilantro), laksa and smoked chilli, which is a good one to mix with vodka and tomato juice, and it's also good drizzled over a chilled soup; in which case, add a pinch of salt to it.

You can also make these without the fruit. Simply use herb sugar, pour over the vinegar and stir until the sugar has dissolved. Decant to a jar or bottle and leave for a week before drinking. I do, however, prefer the flavour of a fruit and herb combination.

Cold Brew Teas

Alcoholic Infusions

In the summer months (or weeks, if I'm realistic, living in the UK as I do), I will frequently have bottles of teas brewing in the fridge. This is a very simple thing to do with everything from regular tea, to various herbs and even pine needles, and the benefits are that you get a very clean, fresh flavour without the bitterness you expect from hot-brewed tea.

The method is very straightforward. You can vary the strength as you like, but I will usually use around a teaspoon of any type of tea for every cup of water. I will use spring or filtered water (I don't like the taste of chlorine). Put the tea in a glass bottle or jar, cover with the water, and leave to steep in the fridge. Leave for several hours or overnight. The beauty of cold-brewed tea is that while the flavour might continue to develop, it will never taste too strong, and certainly won't become bitter. Strain the tea, and if you like, replace the water – you can reinfuse the same tea a couple of times.

My favourite teas to do this with are white and jasmine, but it is also the way I like to drink green tea – usually with a few sprigs of mint added to the bottle. Others that work really well are pine needle tea (use spruce, pine or fir in spring when the tips are green and giving), rosemary with lemon zest, thyme with orange zest or any of the fruitier sages. In fact, any of the fruit teas made with leaves – blackcurrant, blackberry, peach or raspberry – are much more pleasant made this way than with hot water. There isn't any astringency.

If you want to sweeten cold brew tea, this is best done after infusion. I usually stir in honey, dissolved in a tiny amount of hot water, rather than sugar – but really, the flavours are so good you don't particularly need it.

Most cultures have a tradition of infusing herbs with alcohol – many of them have evolved into the bitter digestifs, but some are much simpler affairs, such as the classic zubrowka vodka, which has a single bison grass leaf in each bottle. I have been into bars when the local spirit (rum or vodka) have been infused with just about every aromatic you can imagine. This is a very simple process. Scald your chosen sprig of herb, dry it thoroughly, and add it to the alcohol. Leave indefinitely to steep, drinking at will. I'm not going to give any recipes, but please try ginger rosemary in rum and make a Dark and Stormy with it. (Yes, I know I talk about ginger rosemary a lot. Sorry.)

Teas and Tisanes

The process of infusing leaves into liquid feels as old as time. Virtually every culture has its favourite leaves to steep, often with a host of traditions, rites and accoutrements to go alongside. Drinking tea is something done frequently with other people – it is a drink that is totally acceptable to consume endlessly, on one's own, but also lends itself to highly formal settings – think of the intricate Japanese, Chinese and Korean tea ceremonies, and the tradition of afternoon tea in the UK. Or look at the ceremony surrounding Argentinan *yerba mate* – still very ritualistic, with the refilling and passing round of the gourd – a shared drink, with everyone having their own *bombilla*, which is a clever straw with a filter at the end.

It is impossible to list all the types of teas and leaves used to make *tisanes*. I think most of us know enough that mint makes a good digestive, as does lemongrass; that chamomile, lime leaf and lemon balm and verbena are all calming and good to drink at night; or that nettles can be diuretic (amongst numerous other claims). I don't think too much about medicinal properties of the herbs; I go solely on what I feel like drinking. Herbal tea drinking for me is either postprandial or, especially from late spring onwards, preceded by a crepuscular stroll around the garden, collecting leaves as I go – the lemon verbena from the pot by the back door, the chamomile patch in the corner of the lawn, a pinch of rosemary or low-lying sprawling lemon thyme, the perpetually spreading peppermint, nettle (only if I've remembered to grab the gardening gloves), lemon balm (don't drink this when in flower, it turns from lemon to goaty overnight). I also have large bags of dried leaves – olive leaves, gentle-tasting and mild, but strangely satisfying, mountain tea from Greece – dusty smelling, with the flavour of hay and a hint of sage –and also those fragile indoor leaves – the lemongrass shoots – citronella, used as a bush tea in tropical parts.

I'm not going to insult anyone's intelligence by putting in any recipes here. If you can pick fresh herbs or take a few dried ones and have a recently boiled kettle of water (the best temperature for herbal infusions is around 80°C/175°F) you can make an infusion. You can probably reinfuse the herbs at least once and sweeten if you like. I rarely do unless I have a cold and I want a strong infusion of thyme, rosemary or sage with a twist of lemon and some honey. The other exception is the Moroccan way with mint tea; this I like to make in a warmed pot with sugar to taste, but as everyone has a different idea on how sweet it should be, I like to pour it (from a height of course) over a sugar cube. Very refreshing in the heat of summer.

Index

Acknowledgements

First of all, thanks to everyone at Quadrille, especially Sarah Lavelle and the dream team that is food stylist Marina Filippelli (aided brilliantly by Becks Wilkinson and Shambala Fisher), photographer Mowie Kay, designer Nicola Ellis and prop stylist Louie Waller – what a beautiful thing you have created between you! Thank you also to Eve Marleau for such helpful and sensitive editing. Thanks also to Clare Hulton, my ever-supportive agent who has become a real friend over the years.

I feel lucky that so many kind and talented people have been interested in this book, and helped me with advice, recipes and ideas as well as being just generally inspirational. They include Fiona Bird, Jeni Hewlett, Annie Levy, Clare McQuillan, Thane Prince, Angela Clutton, Mike Warner, Nicola Miller, Tim Hayward, Diana Henry, Genevieve Taylor, Sue Quinn, Jane Baxter and Christie Dietz. Jenny Linford gave me much help and advice in her usual warm and generous way as well as a cracking recipe. Jinny Johnson, as always, let me think aloud whenever I needed it. Mark Diacono was his usual good-humoured self when dealing with a (possibly constant) barrage of stupid questions and thoughts, as well as conjuring up and sending impossible to find out-of-season plants at a moment's notice. He is also responsible for introducing me to ginger rosemary.

Lots of people around and about helped me to source various leaves and told me about secret foraging spots, but a special mention to Lisa Martin, who let me collect all sorts of goodies from her allotment.

Thank you to the late Patrick O'Brian for creating my beloved Stephen Maturin and Jack Aubrey books, and for Ric Jerrom for his brilliant reading of them. These audiobooks have accompanied me through long hours of prep for recipe testing as well as reminding me at regular intervals about the importance of cabbage.

Finally, much gratitude goes to my family, who embrace each book project with me. Going right back to the beginning, my mother was particularly keen for me to tackle leaves. She and my father have made it their business to keep me constantly supplied with packages of Mediterranean leaves from their Greek garden and the mountainsides round about. Shariq, Adam and Lilly ate and critiqued their way through months of recipe testing, while Shariq was patient and constructive when regularly having to listen to chunks of prose, often moments after stepping through the door after a long day's commute. Thank you all.